ESSAYS AND REVIEWS.

VOL. II.

ESSAYS AND REVIEWS.

BY

EDWIN P. WHIPPLE.

IN TWO VOLUMES.

VOL. II.

SECOND EDITION.

BOSTON:
TICKNOR, REED, AND FIELDS.
M DCCC LI.

Stereotyped by
HOBART & ROBBINS,
BOSTON.

CONTENTS.

ESSAYS AND REVIEWS.

OLD ENGLISH DRAMATISTS.*

Among the English critics of the present century, none was entitled to speak with more authority of the Old English Dramatists than Charles Lamb. His letters and essays show that his choicest hours were spent in their company. Their scenes and characters did not merely pass before his mind for review, but seemed to run into his blood and imagination, and blend with his life. He was the representative of the Elizabethan age to the nineteenth century, and enforced the claims of his stalwart veterans to attention with a nicety of criticism which had the sureness of a fine instinct. The notes to his Specimens, quaint, keen, and short, are good examples of penetrating and interpretative criticism. The fine fusion in Lamb's mind of humor and imagination gives to these meagre notices a peculiar raciness and

* Specimens of English Dramatic Poets who lived about the time of Shakspeare. With Notes. By Charles Lamb. New York: Wiley & Putnam. 1845. 16mo. pp. 448.

Lectures on the Dramatic Literature of the Age of Elizabeth. By William Hazlitt. New York: Wiley & Putnam. 16mo. pp. 216. — *North American Review, July*, 1846.

sweetness, unlike most retrospective criticism. Marlowe, Decker, Webster, Massinger, Ben Jonson, Beaumont and Fletcher, were not to him mere names of persons who once existed, but he had a genial sense of their presence, as he bent lovingly over their time-stained pages. Their hearts and imaginations spoke directly to his own; theirs were the old familiar faces, known from his youth upwards. We conceive of him, at times, as being present at the wit contests at the Mermaid, and as feeling the "words of subtile flame" which flashed from the lips of Shakspeare, Jonson, and Fletcher. From his realization of them as persons, he was less likely to exaggerate their merits as authors. He saw them as they were in their lives, and judged them as a kindly contemporary spirit. Consequently, his volume of Specimens is infused with the very soul of the time; and it may be set down as one of the most fascinating of compilations.

The Lectures of Hazlitt on the same period are a good counterpart to Lamb's book. They display more than his usual strength, acuteness, and animation, with less than the usual acerbities of his temper. His stern, sharp analysis pierces and probes the subject down through the surface to the centre; and it is exercised in a more kindly spirit than is common with him. His volume is enriched with delicious quotations. Hazlitt had a profound appreciation of the elder dramatists, though a less social feeling for them than Lamb; and their characteristic excellences drew from him some of his heartiest bursts of eloquent panegyric. From his Lectures and Lamb's Specimens, the general reader would be likely to gain a more vivid notion of the intellectual era they commemorate, than from any other sources, except the originals themselves.

The period of time in which those whom we call the Old English Dramatists flourished runs from the middle of the reign of Elizabeth to the Great Rebellion, — about sixty years. The most brilliant portion of this period was the reign of James the First. The drama commenced with Buckhurst, and died out in Shirley. In the intervening time, we have the names of Marlowe, Shakspeare, Webster, Decker, Tourneur, Heywood, Middleton, Chapman, Ben Jonson, Marston, Massinger, Ford, and Beaumont and Fletcher, — a constellation of genius, which, in power and variety, in imagination, passion, fancy, wit, sense, philosophy, character, nature, is unexampled in the intellectual annals of the world. Bacon, Hooker, Hobbes, Browne, Cudworth, Barrow, Taylor, Napier, Spenser, Sidney, Raleigh, and, we may add, Milton, may be classed in the same generation. These sixty years were most emphatically "rammed" with intellectual life. Great men, men of originating minds in different departments of literature and science, men eminent in action and speculation, men whose names ring now as sweet music in the ears of all who speak the English tongue, seemed to have been crowded and crammed into this era, "infinite riches in a little room." Yet the age was what we would call rude and coarse in its manners, the language had not been trained into a facile instrument of thought, few people were "educated," in our sense of the term, and civilization had but imperfectly done its work on the old barbarism; and yet, we doubt if external circumstances were ever more propitious to the development in a people of the greatest energies of intellect and passion.

The age to which we refer was one of vast intellectual and moral activity. That great movement of the European mind at the revival of letters, whose splendid results were seen in the invention of gunpowder and printing, in the Reformation, the discovery of the American continent, the overthrow of feudalism, the new importance given to the middle class, the circulation of the classics, the creation of national literatures, the assertion of individual rights, and the general tendency to transfer the sceptre of influence from the soldier to the thinker, was most deeply felt in England during this period, and, as regards literature, it achieved there its mightiest triumphs. When we contrast the age with that which immediately preceded it, we seem almost to realize the vision of Milton, of a "mighty and puissant nation rousing itself, like a strong man after sleep, and shaking his invincible locks." Everything was in motion. Great events stimulated great passions. An old order of life, with its institutions, its manners, its superstitions, was shaken to its foundations. New ideas and images were rushing into the national life from a thousand sources. Greece, Rome, Italy, Spain, poured into the one great channel their blended streams. In the vast background of the national history, in the manners and passions of the feudal age, were exhaustless materials of heroic romance. What was passing away in actual life was transferred to the imagination, to reäppear idealized in poetry. The old times were sufficiently recent to be ideally apprehended. They lingered in knightly feelings and accomplishments, and shaped the highest minds of the age in a mould of heroism. An artificial civilization had neither tamed nor refined the energies of the heart. There were great diversities of culture, character, manners, ranging from extreme coarseness to high delicacy, and a corresponding external costume, which afforded the poet a wide variety of subjects, from which to select striking individualities and picturesque images. The intellect of the country was prying, inquisitive, bold, disposed to innovation, and yet creative. The understanding and the imagination were both alive and active. There was a certain fulness, roundness, and harmony of mental development, in the great men of the time, which gives a character of majestic ease to their sturdiest exertions of power. None of their faculties acquired a diseased activity at the expense of the rest. It was not a time to produce Humes or Schellings in philosophy, Crabbes or Wordsworths in poetry. Taken altogether, it would be difficult to find a class of minds more comprehensive, profound, practical, and available. The philosophers were poets, and the poets philosophers. There was a strong development and happy equipoise of those powers which relate to actual life, and those which refer to the world of imagination. The literature of the period has body as well as soul. Things were grasped in the concrete, and so stated that their substance and vital spirit could not be separated. Great minds nursed Utopias in their capacious and far-darting imaginations, without being troubled with a diseased self-consciousness, and without whining about their circumstances. The noblest spirit of them all was an actor and manager of a theatre, who excelled all his contemporaries as much in prudence as in genius, and is one of the three professional authors of Great Britain who obtained a competence by literature.* The age was not troubled with "gifted spirits," "earnest minds," or "poet-souls."

The intellectual and moral activity of which we have spoken, though it was felt in nearly all departments of

* Shakspeare, Pope, and Scott.

philosophy, literature, and action, and produced in all magnificent results, left perhaps its most wonderful traces on the dramatic literature of the period. The originality and power of this as a mirror of life cannot be contested, however much may be said against the rudeness and inartistical shape of the majority of its products. Were a man to exhaust the literatures of all other times and nations, he could not be introduced to the English drama without being startled from the complacency of his settled tastes, and compelled to acknowledge the existence of a new province of imagination, not implied or foretold in any canons of criticism. The reading of the Old Dramatists to such a person would be like gazing at the earth's central fires through cracks in the ground made by an earthquake. He would see the nature of man revealed in its most terrible aspects of crime and suffering, — all the restraints both on depravity and virtue torn violently away, — and the heart in its naked reality laid open to view. All the conventional proprieties and linen decencies of language, he would find continually violated. The bad and the good, the great and the mean, wisdom and folly, mirth and grief, he would see jostling each other in seemingly inextricable confusion. He would hear not only the natural language of passion, even to the lowest tone that the heart half whispers to itself, but that language as modified by the thousand diversities of character. Oaths and vulgarities would ring through his brain, just as some exquisite strain of poetry had died away on his ear. He would stand amazed to find so much genius and impassioned action associated with so much flutter and rant, and perhaps would seek, in the phrase "irregular genius," a convenient passage out of astonishment into contented ignorance.

The fine audacity that distinguishes these writers has, we believe, no parallel in literature. It led often to monstrous violations of taste and probability, but it still enabled them to reach heights and sound depths, which equal powers, wielded by a less daring will, could never have achieved. We shall see, also, that, though plain to coarseness in speech, when they undertook to represent coarse characters, they rarely, with the exception perhaps of Fletcher, tampered with moral laws. A good, wholesome, English integrity generally underlies their vulgarities. Their works would not be so likely to corrupt the mind as some of Byron's and Moore's; for, though they represent immorality, they do not inculcate it. Their robust strength of nature preserved them from sentimentality, if not from bombast and buffoonery. Their minds breathed the bracing air of their time, — a time which would tolerate what would now be considered breaches of decorum, but would not tolerate the smaller vices of intellect and sentiment. Of course, in these remarks, as far as they touch upon gross faults, we do not mean to include Shakspeare among his brother dramatists. He excelled them all as much in judgment as in genius.

The first playhouse built in England was erected in Blackfriars, in the year 1569 or 1570, about twenty years before Shakspeare commenced writing for the stage. Previously to this establishment of the "regular drama," there had been three different species of theatrical representations, — miracles or mysteries, written by priests on religious subjects, and performed by them on holydays, in which, as Campbell phrases it, "Adam and Eve appeared naked, the devil displayed his horns and tail, and Noah's wife boxed the patriarch's ears before entering the ark;" — moralities, which sprang from the mysteries, and approached nearer to regular plays, their characters being composed of allegorical personifications of virtues and vices; — and free translations from the classics, performed at the inns of court, the public seminaries, and the universities.

In 1574, the queen licensed a company of actors, called the Earl of Leicester's Servants, to play throughout England, "for the recreation of her loving subjects, as for her own solace and pleasure when she should think good to see them." Theatres rapidly increased. In 1606, there were seven in London; in 1629, we believe there were seventeen. They were opposed, in an early stage of their career, by the Puritans and the graver counsellors of the sovereign. In 1583, at the time that Sir Philip Sidney published his Defence of Poesy, he could find little in their performances to approve. Though forbidden, after the year 1574, to be open on the Sabbath, the prohibition does not appear to have been effective during the reign of Elizabeth. Secretary Walsingham laments over the whole matter in this wise: — "The daily abuse of stage plays is such an offence to the godly, and so great a hindrance to the Gospel, as the Papists do exceedingly rejoice at the blemish thereof; for every day in the week the players' bills are set up in sundry places in the city, — some in the name of her Majesty's men, some of the Earl of Leicester's, some the Earl of Oxford's, the Lord Admiral's, and divers others, so that, when the bell tolls to the lecture, the trumpet sounds to the stage. The playhouses are filled, when the churches are naked. It is a woful sight to see two hundred proud players jet in their silks, when five hundred poor people starve in the streets."

As the taste for theatrical exhibitions increased, the task of providing the theatres with plays became a profession. Most of the precursors, contemporaries, and successors of Shakspeare, were young men of education, who came down to the city from the universities, to provide themselves with a living by whatever cunning there was in their brain and ten fingers. Some became actors as well as writers. The remuneration of the dramatist was small. Poverty and dissoluteness seem to have characterized the pioneers of the drama. As the theatre was popular as well as fashionable, the "groundlings," who paid their sixpences for admission, had their tastes consulted. This accounts, in some degree, for the rant and vulgarity which strangely disfigure so many of the plays. The usual miseries and vices which characterize men of letters in an unlettered age, when authors are numerous and readers are few, distinguish the lives of many of the elder dramatists. Ben Jonson, in the Poetaster, makes Tucca exclaim, with a side reference to the poets of his own day, that "they are a sort of poor, starved rascals, that are ever wrapt up in foul linen; and can boast of nothing but a lean visage peering out of a seam-rent suit, the very emblem of beggary." We suppose this was too true a picture of many, whose minds deserved a better environment of flesh and raiment.

Of those who preceded Shakspeare, the best known names (leaving Buckhurst and Still out of the list) are Lyly, Kyd, Nash, Greene, Lodge, and Marlowe. Much cannot be said in praise of these, if we except the latter. Lyly is full of daintiness and conceit, with sweet fancy and sentiment occasionally thrown in. He translates everything into quaint expression. Thus, his Endymion professes that "his thoughts are *stitched* to the stars." Another of his characters looks forward to the time when "it shall please the fertility of his chin to be delivered of a beard." Peele has melody of versification, and a sort of Della-Cruscan fancy. His David and Bethsabe contains striking passages, as when Zephyr is addressed: —

> "Then deck thee with thy loose, delightsome robes,
> And on thy wings bring delicate perfumes;" —

or the resolution of David: —

> "To joy her love I 'll build a kingly bower,
> *Seated in hearing of a hundred streams.*"

Kyd wrote The Spanish Tragedy, a play bad enough in itself, but celebrated from the additions made to it by "eminent hands." Its bombast was probably popular. Ben Jonson was one of those engaged to write additional scenes; but he has ridiculed the whole play in Every Man in his Humor, in the scene between Bobadil and Master Mathew, the town gull. Bobadil says, "I would fain see all the poets of these times pen such another play as that was!" Greene's death was more tragic than anything he wrote or conceived. He is now principally remembered for having called Shakspeare "an upstart crow."

But a more potent spirit than any of these, and beyond all question the first in rank among the precursors of Shakspeare, was Christopher Marlowe. His "mighty line" has been celebrated by Ben Jonson; Drayton finely ascribes to him "those brave sublunary things that the first poets had;" and according to old George Chapman, —

> "He stood
> Up to the chin in the Pierian flood."

Marlowe, indeed, towers up among his contemporaries, huge, lawless, untamable, the old Adam burning fiercely within him, his frame of mind

> "Betokening valor and excess of strength,"

and in his strange compound of sublimity and rant, giving an impression half-way between a thunder-scarred Titan and an Alsatian bully. From the impress of perverse and turbulent power that his dramas bear, and the evident heartiness with which he deifies self-will, we may well suppose that his life diverged considerably from the strait line of the commandments. The two prominent features of his biography are exceedingly characteristic. In his life, he labored under the imputation of infidelity, and is said to have blasphemed the Holy Trinity; and he died in a tavern brawl, in 1593, or 1594, about the time that Shakspeare was writing Richard the Second. Campbell suggests, that, had Marlowe lived, Shakspeare might have had something like a competitor. This we think is too high praise; for Marlowe, with all his fire and fancy, is limited in his range of character, and stamps the image of himself on all his striking delineations. He is intense, but narrow. The central principle of his mind was self-will, and this is the bond which binds together his strangely huddled faculties. Of all English poets, he most reminds us of Byron; ruder, it may be, but at the same time more colossal in his proportions. He is a glorious old heathen, "large in heart and brain," — a fiery and fickle Goth, on whose rough and savage energies a classical culture has been piled, tossed among the taverns, and theatres, and swelling spirits of London, to gratify the demands of his senses in some other way than by acts of brilliant pillage. In his lustiness, his absence of all weak emotions, his fierce delight in the mere feeling of self, in the heedlessness with which he heaps together rubbish and diamonds, and in the frequent "starts and strange far-flights of his imagination," he is the model of irregular genius. His mind, in its imperiousness, disregarded by instinct the natural relations of things, forced objects into the form of his individual passions, and lifted his vices into a kind of Satanic dignity, by exaggerating them into shapes colossal. His imagination, hot, swift, impatient of control, pervaded by the fiery essence of his blood, and giving wings to the most reckless desires, riots in the maddest visions of strength and pride. Of all writers, he seems to feel the heartiest joy in the mere exercise of power, regardless of all the restraints which make power beneficent. His most truculent characters, Tamburlaine, Eleazar, Barabbas, Faustus, all have blazoned on their brows, "Kit Marlowe, his mark." There is no mistaking his heaven-defying energy, nor his Ishmaelitish strut and swagger. His soul tears its way through his verse, "tameless, and swift, and proud," scorning all impediments, and ever ambitious to go

> "Right forward, like the lightning
> And the cannon-ball, opening, with murderous crash,
> Its way to blast and ruin."

From this headlong haste come his bombast and extravagance, "his lust of power, his hunger and thirst after unrighteousness, his glow of imagination, unhallowed save by its own energies." Whether his muse cleave the upper air, or draggle in the dirt, it ever gives unity of impression. In Lust's Dominion, or the Lascivious Queen, the rapid movement of the man's mind is very characteristic,— rattling recklessly on through scenes of murder, cruelty, and lust, — now striking off "burning atoms" of thought, and now merely infusing fire into fustian, — his faculties at times stretched on the rack, writhing in fearful contortions, and smiting the ear with the wild screams of a tortured brain, — but still marching furiously forward, daring everything, and playing out the game of tragedy freely and fearlessly. In this play he somewhat reminds us of the actor who blacked himself all over when he performed Othello, and called that "going thoroughly into the part." Marlowe scatters lust and crime about in such careless profusion, that they cease to excite horror. His Muse must too often have appeared to him in some such form as the hideous phantom in Clarence's dream, —

> "A shadow like an angel, with bright hair
> Dabbled in blood."

But amidst all his spasmodic and braggart lines in the vein of King Cambyses, his mind continually gives evidence of possessing pathos, sweetness, and true power. Imaginations of the greatest beauty and majesty will sometimes rush up, like rockets, from the level extravagance of his most ranting plays, "streaking the darkness radiantly;" — as in that celebrated passage in Tamburlaine, which Shakspeare condescended to ridicule through the lips of Ancient Pistol: —

"*Enter Tamburlaine, drawn in his chariot by Trebizon and Soria, with bits in their mouths, reins in his left hand, in his right hand a whip, with which he scourgeth them.*

"*Tamb.* Holla, ye pampered jades of Asia!
What, can ye draw but twenty miles a day,
And have so proud a chariot at your heels,
And such a coachman as great Tamburlaine?
But from Asphaltis, where I conquered you,
To Byron here, where thus I honor you?
The horse that guide the golden eye of heaven,
And blow the morning from their nostrils,
Making their fiery gate above the glades,
Are not so honored in their governor
As you, ye slaves, in mighty Tamburlaine."

From the same play, which has passed into a synonyme of bombast and "midsummer madness," but which contains lines that Beaumont and Milton have not hesitated to appropriate, Leigh Hunt extracts the following exquisite passage: —

"If all the pens that ever poet held
Had fed the feeling of their master's thoughts,
And every sweetness that inspired their hearts,
And minds, and muses, on admired themes;
If all the heavenly quintessence they still
From their immortal flowers of poesy,
Wherein, as in a mirror, we perceive
The highest reaches of a human wit;
If these had made one poem's period,
And all combined in beauty's worthiness;
Yet should there hover in their restless heads
One thought, one grace, one wonder, at the best,
Which into words no virtue can digest."

The description of Tamburlaine's person has a rude, Titanic grandeur, which still tells on the ear and brain, as in the lines, —

> "Of stature tall, and straightly fashioned;
> Like his desire, lift upwards and divine,
> So large of limb, his joints so strongly knit,
> Such breadth of shoulders as might mainly bear
> Old Atlas' burthen."

In the whole description, Marlowe's predominating desire to accumulate round his characters images of strength and majesty, and to dwarf all other men in comparison, is finely exemplified. Tamburlaine is

> "Pale of complexion, wrought in him with passion;"

his eyes are "piercing instruments of sight,"

> "Whose fiery circles bear encompassed
> A heaven of heavenly bodies in their spheres."

The breath of heaven "delights" to play with his curls of "amber hair;" his bent brows "figure death," their smoothness, "amity and life;" his "kindled wrath can only be quenched in blood;" and he is "in every part proportioned like a man" who has the right divine to subdue the world. We are astonished that Carlyle has not yet puffed Tamburlaine as made after Marlowe's image. The Scythian shepherd deserves a proud place among his heroes.

Most of Marlowe's powerful scenes are well known. His best plays are The Rich Jew of Malta; Edward the Second, the "reluctant pangs of whose abdicating royalty," says Lamb, "furnished hints which Shakspeare scarce improved in Richard the Second;" and the Tragical History of the Life and Death of Dr. Faustus, which is his greatest and most characteristic performance, sadly disfigured, however, by bathos and buffoonery, and inspired in part by the very imp of mischief. Barabbas, the Jew, has been mentioned as suggesting Shylock. The character, however, has little resemblance to Shakspeare's Jew. It is Marlowe all over. In the celebrated scene where Barabbas gloats over his vast wealth, his imagination glows like his own "fiery opals." The death-scene in Edward the Second, according to Lamb, "moves pity and terror beyond any scene, ancient or modern," with which he is acquainted. We think this praise altogether too extravagant, affecting as the scene undoubtedly is.

We take leave of Marlowe with an extract from the last scene in Faustus. The verse has the sinewy vigor and sonorous chime which generally distinguish his style. It is, however, intensified by the agony one might feel on viewing his own name traced in flaming characters on the black rolls of the damned.

"FAUSTUS *alone.—The clock strikes eleven.*

"*Faust.* O Faustus,
Now hast thou but one bare hour to live,
And then thou must be damned perpetually.
Stand still, you ever-moving spheres of heaven,
That time may cease, and midnight never come.
Fair Nature's eye, rise, rise again, and make
Perpetual day: or let this hour be but
A year, a month, a week, a natural day,
That Faustus may repent and save his soul.
O lente, lente currite, noctis equi!
The stars move still, time runs, the clock will strike,
The devil will come, and Faustus must be damned.
O, I will leap to heaven! Who pulls me down?
See where Christ's blood streams in the firmament:
One drop of blood will save me; O, my Christ,
Rend not my heart for naming of my Christ!
Yet will I call on him. O spare me, Lucifer!

Where is it now? 't is gone!
And see, a threatening arm, and angry brow!
Mountains and hills, come, come, and fall on me,
And hide me from the heavy wrath of heaven.
No? then I will headlong run into the earth:
Gape, earth. O no, it will not harbor me.
You stars that reigned at my nativity,
Whose influence have allotted death and hell,
Now draw up Faustus like a foggy mist
Into the entrails of yon laboring cloud;
That when you vomit forth into the air,
My limbs may issue from your smoky mouths,
But let my soul mount, and ascend to heaven.
[*The watch strikes.*]
O half the hour is past! 't will all be past anon.
O if my soul must suffer for my sin,
Impose some end to my incessant pain!
Let Faustus live in hell a thousand years,
A hundred thousand, and at the last be saved:
No end is limited to damned souls.
Why wert thou not a creature wanting soul?
Or why is this immortal that thou hast?
O Pythagoras, Metempsychosis, were that true,
This soul should fly from me, and I be changed
Into some brutish beast.
All beasts are happy, for when they die,
Their souls are soon dissolved in elements;
But mine must live still to be plagued in hell.
Curst be the parents that engendered me:
No, Faustus, curse thyself, curse Lucifer,
That hath deprived thee of the joys of heaven.
[*The clock strikes twelve.*]
It strikes, it strikes; now, body, turn to air,
Or Lucifer will bear thee quick to hell.
O soul, be changed into small water-drops,
And fall into the ocean; ne'er be found.
[*Thunder, and enter the Devils.*]
O mercy, Heaven, look not so fierce on me!
Adders and serpents, let me breathe a while:
Ugly hell, gape not, come not, Lucifer:
I'll burn my books: O Mephistophilis!"

It is supposed that Marlowe wrote the principal portion of the old plays which Shakspeare altered into the Second and Third Parts of Henry the Sixth. Malone, on comparing the latter with their originals, found that 1771 lines had been taken without alteration, 2373 altered, and only 1899 had been added. Greene, in his Groat'sworth of Wit, published in 1592, addressing, it is conjectured, Marlowe, exclaims, — "Yes, trust them not [the players], for there is an upstart crow, beautified with our feathers, that, with a tiger's heart wrapped in a player's hide, supposes he is as well able to bombast out a blank verse as any of you, and, being an absolute Johannes factotum, is, in his conceit, the only *Shake-scene* in a country."

Next to Shakspeare, there is no dramatist of the period whose name is so familiar to English ears as that of BEN JONSON, though he is probably less read than either Massinger or Fletcher. The associations connected with his name have contributed towards keeping it alive, for he is, in most points of his character, the very embodiment of England, a veritable, indubitable John Bull. The base of his character is sound, strong, weighty sense, with that infusion of insular prejudice which keeps every true Englishman from being a cosmopolite, either in literature, arts, government, or manners. He has also that ingrained coarseness, which, in the Anglo-Saxon mind, often coëxists with the sturdiest morality, and, though it disconnects virtue from delicacy, prevents vice from allying itself with refinement. In reading Jonson we continually fall upon expressions which "no young lady ought to read;" but there is nothing which tends to corrupt the morals, as well as to vulgarize the speech. Virtue and vice, honesty and baseness, indulge in no coquetry in his representations. We are acquainted with no dramatist whose characters, bad and good, are better adapted to excite in us the same feelings that we should experience, if we met them in actual life.

With this basis of sound English sense, Jonson has fancy, humor, satire, learning, a large knowledge of men and motives, and a remarkable command of language, sportive, scornful, fanciful, and impassioned. One of the fixed facts in English literature, he is too strongly rooted ever to be upset. He stands out from all his contemporaries, original, peculiar, leaning on none for aid, and to be tried by his own merits alone. Had his imagination been as sensitive as that of many of his contemporaries, or his self-love less, he would probably have fallen into their conscious or unconscious imitation of Shakspeare; but, as it was, he remained satisfied with himself to the last, delving in his own mine. His "mountain belly and his rocky face" are good symbols of his hard, sharp, decided, substantial, and arrogant mind. His life and writings both give evidence of great vitality and force of character. Composition must have been with him a manual labor, for he writes with all his might. The weaknesses of his nature, his perversity, his bluff way of bragging of his own achievements, his vanity, his domineering egotism, his love of strong food, his deep potations, and the heartiness, good-will, and latent sense of justice, which underlie all, are thoroughly English, and make him as familiar to the imagination as a present existence. We speak of Shakspeare's mind, but Jonson starts up always in bodily proportions. He seems some boon companion, whom we have seen in a preëxistent state. Shakspeare's creations, from Hamlet to Falstaff, are more real to us than Shakspeare himself; but we have a more intense conception of Jonson than we have of any of his characters, not even excepting Bobadil and Sir Epicure Mammon. His life was commensurate with the whole generation of great poets to which he belonged. He survived Shakspeare twenty-one years. His biography is better known than that of any of his contemporaries.

Jonson's life was checkered by many vicissitudes. He was born in the city of Westminster, in the year 1574. His father went out of the world about a month after our poet came into it; and his worthy mother shortly after married a master-bricklayer. By the aid of some friend, whose name is unknown, he was sent to Westminster school, and transferred thence to Cambridge university. After staying there a short time, his resources failed him, and he returned home to work at the trade of his father-in-law. This occupation, however, he could not long endure, and he went as a volunteer in the army serving in Flanders. He distinguished himself by his valor, and prided himself no little on having conquered and killed an enemy, in the view of both armies, in single combat. The trade of arms, however, does not appear to have been attended in his case with any lucrative results, and he returned home at the end of one or two campaigns. Shortly after, at about the age of nineteen, he went upon the stage, as actor and journeyman writer; but for four years seems to have done little more than make additions to old plays, or furnish scenes to other dramatists. In 1596, however, when he was only twenty-two years old, his Every Man in his Humor, the most generally popular of his plays, was produced. Previously to this, he had killed a brother-player in a duel, and came near being hanged for it; had turned Roman Catholic, and been suspected of a share in a Popish conspiracy; and had got married; three incidents in the life of a young man just at maturity, which show quite an extraordinary aptitude for affairs.

The scene of Every Man in his Humor, as originally written, was laid in Italy. It was popular from the first. In 1598, Jonson became acquainted with Shakspeare, and through his influence was enabled to bring out his play, as now remodelled with English names, at the Blackfriars theatre. Shakspeare is supposed to have acted the part of the elder Knowell in this comedy. In 1599, Jonson brought out Every Man out of his Humor, the first representation of which was attended by Queen Elizabeth. In the epilogue to the play, hyperbole is racked to find terms of adoring admiration for the queen. Jonson, in his conversations with Drummond, did not hesitate to give his real opinion about the haughty Tudor's susceptibility to flattery. In this play the author shows that contempt for public opinion which breaks out in so many of his prefaces. He calls the public "that many-mouthed, vulgar dog." Cynthia's Revels was acted in 1600, and excited much opposition. Decker and Marston were prominent among those it offended; and in consequence, Jonson's next play, The Poetaster, was especially devoted to satirizing them and exalting himself. To any one who desires to know Jonson's sway over the vocabulary of scorn, contempt, hatred, and invective, we would commend this comedy. Decker and Marston are introduced under the names of Crispinus and Demetrius, and remorselessly ridiculed. The opinions they are made to express of Jonson himself are exceedingly racy, and enable us to judge what were the feelings experienced towards him by some of his contemporaries. Thus, Demetrius (Marston) says, —"Horace! he is a mere sponge; nothing but humors and observation; he goes up and down sucking from every society, and when he comes home squeezes himself dry again." Another calls him "a sharp, thorny-toothed, satirical rascal;" one that would "sooner lose his best friend than his least jest;" a thing "all dog and scorpion, that carries poison in his teeth, and a sting in his tail." In the arraignment, Decker is called poetaster and plagiary; Marston, play-dresser and plagiary; and they are accused of taxing Jonson falsely of "self-love, arrogance, impudence, railing, filching by translation," &c., for a base and envious purpose. In their sentence we are favored with a view of the "local habitations" of the poets of the day; for they are forbidden to defame our poet "at booksellers' stalls, in taverns, two-penny rooms, tyring-houses, noblemens' buttresses, and puisné's chambers." The enemies of Jonson are summed up as "fools or jerking pedants," "buffoon, barking wits," tickling "base, vulgar ears," with "beggarly and barren trash." In the "Apologetical Dialogue," at the end of the play, all phrases of scorn and contempt are exhausted to cover his opponents with infamy. He speaks of his own works as

> "Things that were born when none but the still night
> And his *dumb* candle saw his pinching throes;"

and he closes with a lofty expression of his own studious habits and devotion to letters: —

> "I that spend *half my nights and all my days*
> Here in a cell, to *get a dark, pale face*
> To come forth with the ivy or the bays,
> And in this age can hope no other grace, —
> Leave me! there 's something come into my thought

That must and shall be *sung high and aloof,*
Safe from the wolf's black jaw and the dull ass's hoof."

There is in this play a good representation given of the different feelings with which different classes at that day regarded poetry. Thus, one of the characters calls Homer "a poor blind rhyming rascal, that lived obscurely up and down in booths and tap-houses, and scarce ever made a good meal in his sleep, the *** hungry beggar;" while Jonson, speaking through the lips of another, exclaims,

"Would men but learn to distinguish spirits,
And set true difference 'twixt those jaded wits
That run a broken pace for common hire,
And the high raptures of a happy Muse,
Borne on the wings of her immortal thought,
That kicks at earth with a disdainful heel,
And beats at heaven's gates with her bright hoofs,
They would not then, with such distorted faces
And desperate censures, stab at Poesy;
They would admire bright knowledge, and their minds
Should ne'er *descend on so unworthy objects*
As gold, or titles."

The character of Virgil, in this play, has been conjectured to refer to Shakspeare, and Horace's (Jonson's) encomium on him is characteristic and true.

"*Hor.* His learning savors not the school-like gloss,
That most consists in echoing words and terms,
And soonest wins a man an empty name;
Nor any long, or far-fetched circumstance,
Wrapt in the curious general'ties of arts;
But a direct and analytic sum
Of all the worth and first effects of arts.
And for his poesy, 't is so rammed with life,
That it shall gather strength of life, with being,
And shall live hereafter more admired than now."

Lamb, Vol. II., p. 68.

The Poetaster made Jonson many enemies, as well it might. Decker replied in The Satiromastrix, or the Untrussing of a Humorous Poet. It contains some beautiful poetry, and some capital hits. One of the females in the play says, " That same Jonson has a most ungodly face, by my fan; it looks for all the world like a rotten russet apple, when 't is bruised. It 's better than a spoonful of cinnamon-water next my heart, for me to hear him speak; he sounds it so i' th' nose; — and oh, to see his face make faces, when he reads songs and sonnets!" Again, — "Look at his par-boiled face, look, — his face puncht full of eyelet holes, like the cover of a warming-pan." This is characteristic, and gives probably as true a representation of the personal appearance of Jonson, as the "dark, pale face" he has himself celebrated.

In 1603, Jonson produced his weighty tragedy of Sejanus, a noble piece of work, full of learning, ingenuity, and force of mind in wielding bulky materials. It was brought out at the Globe theatre, with the greatest poet the world ever saw acting in one of the inferior characters. It is difficult to conceive that a man who had at this time produced A Midsummer Night's Dream, As You Like it, Hamlet, and Henry Fourth, should play in one of Ben Jonson's tragedies. Jonson and Shakspeare seem at this period to have been at the height of their friendship. The "wit-contests" at the Mermaid Tavern date from the appearance of Sejanus. Fuller, speaking of these, compares Shakspeare to an English man-of-war, and Jonson to a Spanish great galleon. "Master Jonson was built far higher in learning; solid, but slow in his performance: Shakspeare, lesser in bulk, but lighter in sailing, could turn with all tides, and take advantage of all winds, by the quickness of his wit and invention." Fuller speaks further of Ben, as a man whose parts "were not so ready to run of themselves as able to answer the spur; so that it may be truly said of him, that he had an elaborate wit, wrought out by his own industry." Those must have been great meetings where Shakspeare, Jonson, Beaumont, Fletcher, Raleigh, Selden, Camden, and Donne, were among the party. Beaumont, in a letter to Ben, gives his testimony to the brilliancy of the conversation, when he exclaims, —

> "What things have we seen
> Done at the Mermaid! heard words that have been
> So nimble, and so full of subtle flame,
> As if that every one, from whom they came,
> Had put his whole wit in a jest."

Jonson seems to have held anger but a short time, and was far from being malignant. On the accession of James, he chose his old opponent Decker to be his associate in designing an entertainment for the reception of the king, — a metrical job given to him by the court and city; and was connected, also, shortly after, with Marston and Chapman, in writing Eastward Hoe, a comedy which came near subjecting all three to the grossest indignities, on account of some satire it contained against the Scotch. They were all imprisoned for a short time, and it was rumored that their ears and noses were to be slit. Jonson's mother, who appears to have been a strong-minded woman, told her son, after he had been liberated, that she intended to have mixed some "strong and lusty poison in his *drink*," sooner than have him thus disgraced. This little event in his life does not appear to have injured him with King James, who was his patron through life. Between the years 1605 and

1611, he wrote his three comedies, Volpone, Epicœne, and The Alchemist, and also his tragedy of Catiline, together with a number of masques represented at court. These last contain much of his most delicate and fanciful poetry, and many of his most bewitching lyrics. About the year 1616, he succeeded Daniel as poet laureate, and probably wrote his noble poetical tribute to Shakspeare soon afterwards. In the summer of 1618, he set out on his celebrated pedestrian journey to Scotland. After some hospitable delays, he arrived at the house of Drummond of Hawthornden, in April, 1619. He talked rather recklessly to his brother-poet, and probably swaggered considerably on his reputation. The record left by his host of this free and easy conversation is honorable to neither, and has irretrievably damned Drummond. His name, which might have been preserved as an agreeable bewailer of imaginary love miseries, has become associated with treachery and inhospitality.

In 1625, King James died. From this period, Jonson's life assumes its darker aspects. Poverty, sickness, and palsy, came upon him. In 1629, he had sufficiently recovered to produce his play of The New Inn. This was unsuccessful, though it contains some of his best scenes, and the character of Lovel has sweet and noble traits, not common to Jonson's heroes. Lovel's definition of true love in this play is Platonic in its fineness and purity. The following lines, in which he speaks of the power of the passion on himself, have a winning beauty of expression which is exquisite.

> "*Lov.* There is no life on earth, but being in love!
> There are no studies, no delights, no business,
> No intercourse, or trade of sense, or soul,
> But what is love! I was the laziest creature,

The most unprofitable sign of nothing,
The veriest drone, and slept away my life
Beyond the dormouse, till I was in love!
And now I can out-wake the nightingale,
Out-watch an usurer, and out-walk him too,
Stalk like a ghost that haunted 'bout a treasure;
And all that fancied treasure, it is love!"

Lamb, Vol. II., pp. 78, 79.

In this comedy, also, the author's tough diction melts, at one moment, into this melodious imagination: —

"Then showered his bounties on me, *like the Hours,*
That open-handed sit upon the clouds,
And press the liberality of heaven
Down to the laps of thankful men."

The last eight years of Jonson's life vacillated between comfort and want. He seems to have had friends, who came to his assistance in his extreme need. His habits of expensive living must have kept him poor. To support a man of his "unbounded stomach" required more than the ordinary remunerations of literature. He seems, however, to have had intervals of prosperity in his later years. Howell, writing in 1636 to Sir Thomas Hawk, has a most vivid picture of him, as he appeared in all the glory of conviviality. "I was invited yesternight to a solemn supper, by B. J., where you were deeply remembered. There was good company, excellent cheer, choice wines, and jovial welcome. One thing intervened which spoiled the relish of the rest, — that B. began to engross all the discourse, to vapor extremely of himself, and by vilifying others to magnify his own Muse. . . . . . But, for my own part, I am content to dispense with the Roman infirmity of Ben, now that time has snowed upon his pericranium." In Sir John Suckling's Session of the Poets, we have another most characteristic portrait of Jonson, as he appeared in his old age.

> "The first that broke silence was good old Ben,
> Prepared before with Canary wine,
> And he told them plainly he deserved the bays,
> For his were called works where others' were but plays.
> * * * * *
> "Apollo stopped him there, and bade him not go on;
> 'T was merit, he said, and not presumption,
> Must carry 't; *at which Ben turned about,*
> *And in great choler offered to go out.*"

Jonson died on the sixth day of August, 1637, at the age of sixty-three. He survived both his wife and his children. He was buried in Westminster Abbey. A common pavement-stone, laid over his grave, bears the inscription, "O Rare Ben Jo*h*nson!" (not Jonson, as it is always printed,) — a phrase which has passed into the current speech of England.

Jonson drenched his large and heavy brain freely with stimulants. It was said that every line of his poetry cost him a cup of sack. "He would," according to Aubrey, "many times exceed in drink; Canary was his beloved liquor; then he would tumble home to bed, and when he had thoroughly perspired, he would then to study." In the bacchanalian phraseology of that day, he was called a Canary bird. He is said to have weighed twenty stone. Barry Cornwall has the courageous gracelessness to commend Ben's festivities, saying that "the Muses should be fed generously, — that good meats and sound wines nourish and invigorate the brain, and enable the imagination to send forth spirited and sounding strains." In Jonson's case, we imagine wine was necessary to set the huge substance of his brain in motion. Charles the First probably understood the poet's wants, when he added the tierce of Canary wine to his yearly stipend of £100, as poet laureate. Habits of hard drinking were common in those days.

With the exception of this too potent conviviality, and bating some inherent faults of character, Jonson seems to have been one of the best men of his time. He was honest and honorable. He had a hearty hatred of meanness and baseness, and shot his sharp invective at the crimes and follies of his day with commendable courage. More than most of his contemporaries, he estimated the dignity of the poet's vocation. In the dedication of Volpone he feelingly alludes to the bad reputation into which his order had fallen; and in the midst of much pedantry and arrogance, we discern a true love for his art. He anticipates Milton in asserting "the impossibility of any man's being the good poet, without first being a good man." With terrible force he lashes those of his craft who have betrayed the good cause by ribaldry and profaneness, and also declaims against the depravity of the age which supports them in their sins. But that all the dramatic poets are "embarked on this bold adventure to hell," he calls a malicious slander; and to show his own innocence, pounces on those "miscelline interludes," where, he says, "nothing but the filth of the time is uttered, and with such impropriety of phrase, such plenty of solecisms, such dearth of sense, so bold prolepses, so racked metaphors, with brothelry able to violate the ear of a pagan, and blasphemy to turn the blood of a Christian to water." He laments, that, through the insolence of these writers, the name of poet, once so honorable, has become "the lowest scorn of the age;" and in a sentence worthy of Milton, asserts, that, if the Muses be true to him, he will "raise the despised head of poetry again, and, stripping her out of those rotten and base rags wherewith the times have adulterated her form, restore her to her primitive habit, feature, and majesty, and render her worthy to be embraced and kissed of all the great and master spirits of our world." These are brave and bright words, and show deep feeling. His works display, in a hundred places, a similar spirit. He rails at the age continually for its degeneracy and wickedness; and takes the strong ground, that the "principal end of poesie is to inform men in the best reason of living." Jonson really scorned the office of pander to depraved tastes. We do not think that he ever consciously surrendered principle to profit. The exaggerated notion he entertained of his own powers made him more disposed to lead than to follow; and the worst that can be said of him is, that, if he failed in an honest effort, he went growling back into his den, savage but unconquered. Fletcher's lighter brain and looser principles allowed him to slide more easily into the debasing habit of meeting a demand for brilliant profligacy with ample supplies.

The dramas of Jonson are formed of solid materials, bound and welded rather than fused together. Most of his comic characters are local, and representative of particular traits or humors, — dramatic satires on contemporary follies and faults. His greatest delineation we conceive to be Sir Epicure Mammon, in The Alchemist, though Volpone and Bobadil might contest the palm. The "riches fineless" of learning and imagery lavished upon this character perfectly astound the imagination. Nothing can be more masterly than the manner in which it is sustained; — the towering sensuality of the man, the visions of luxury and wealth in which his mind roams and revels, his intense realization of the amazing fictions he himself creates, the complete despotism established by his imagination over his senses, and the resolute credulity with which he accommodates the most obstinate facts to his desires, make up a character which, in originality, force, and truth of delineation, seems to us only second to Falstaff, or, at least, to have, out of Shakspeare, no peer among the comic creations of the English drama.

Volpone, Bobadil, Sejanus, and Catiline are strong delineations, which we cannot pause to consider. As a specimen, however, of Jonson's ponderous style, we cannot refrain quoting a few lines in the tragedy of Catiline, from the scene in the first act, on the morning of the conspiracy. Lentulus says: —

> "*Lent.* It is methinks a morning full of fate.
> It riseth slowly, as her sullen car
> Had all the weights of sleep and death hung at it.
> She is not rosy-fingered, but swoln black.
> Her face is like a water turned to blood,
> And her sick head is bound about with clouds,
> As if she threatened night ere noon of day.
> It does not look as it would have a hail
> Or health wished in it, as on other morns."

Catiline, in allusion to the massacres of Sylla, gives a stern and terrible image of death: —

> "*Slaughter bestrid the streets, and stretched himself*
> *To seem more huge;*"

and he exclaims afterwards: —

> "Cinna and Sylla
> Are set and gone; and we must turn our eyes
> On him that is and shines. Noble Cethegus,
> But view him with me here! He looks already
> As if he shook a sceptre o'er the senate,

And the awed purple dropt their rods and axes.
The statues melt again, and household gods
In groans confess the travails of the city;
The very walls sweat blood before the change;
And stones start out to ruin, ere it comes."

It would be easy to extract largely from Jonson's plays to illustrate his powers of satire, fancy, observation, and wit; and to quote numberless biting sentences, that seem steeped "in the very brine of conceit, and sparkle like salt in fire." His masks are replete with beautiful poetry, as delicate as it is rich. We have only space, however, to introduce from The Sad Shepherd one specimen of his sweetness, which seems to have been overlooked by others.

"Here she was wont to go! and here! and here!
Just where those daisies, pinks, and violets grow:
The world may find the spring by following her,
For other print her airy steps ne'er left.
Her treading would not bend a blade of grass,
Or shake the downy blow-ball from his stalk!
But like the soft west wind she shot along,
And where she went, the flowers took thickest root,
As she had sowed them with her odorous foot."

Tennyson has a similar idea in The Talking Oak, but has added a subtle imagination, which our old bard's mind would not have been likely to grasp:—

"And light as any wind that blows,
So fleetly did she stir,
The flowers, she touched on, *dipt and rose,*
And turned to look on her."

The plays of Thomas Decker, honest old Decker, are the records of one of the finest and most lovable spirits in English literature. His name has suffered much from Jonson's cutting scorn, and, indeed, with many readers he still bears about the same relation to old Ben that

Cibber does to Pope. But he has found strong and acute friends in Lamb, Hazlitt, and Hunt, and his rare merits as a poet have been felicitously presented. He is, in fact, one of the most fascinating dramatists of his generation, and, with much vulgarity and trash, has passages worthy of the greatest. He is light, airy, sportive, humane, forgetive, and possesses both animal and intellectual spirits to perfection. He seems flushed and heated with the very wine of life; throws off the sunniest morsels of wit and wisdom with a beautiful heedlessness and unstudied ease; and in his intense enjoyment of life and motion appears continually to exclaim, with his own Matheo, "Do we not fly high?" Though he experienced more than the common miseries and vexations of his class, still, like old Fortunatus, he seems to be "all felicity up to the brims;" to have "revelled with kings, danced with queens, dallied with ladies, worn strange attires, seen fantasticoes, conversed with humorists, been ravished with divine raptures of Doric, Lydian, and Phrygian harmonies." Everything in him is swift, keen, sparkling, full of quicksilver briskness and heartiness. His sentiment and his fancies run out of him in the overflowing exuberance of a happy disposition. There is something delightfully simple in his cheerfulness and humanity. His genial imagination plays with divinities. His quiver is full of those winged arrows which strike the mark in the white, though seemingly sent with a careless aim. His sympathies with nature and his kind are wide, deep, and instinctive. His mind speeds freely out among external things, with nothing to check its wide-wandering flights. His Muse leaps, laughs, and sings, of its own sweet will. Even when he condescends to what Hunt calls an "astounding coarseness," in representing the bloods and men of wit and pleasure about town, which inhabit most of the comedies of the time, there is still a sharpness and quickness of movement which carries the mind swiftly through the mud into a better region. Decker has, strictly speaking, no morality; for nothing in his works seems to depend on will or principle, but to spring from instinctive sentiments; and when these are delicate or noble he is among the purest of writers. His sweetness and humanity are exquisitely fine. Thus, one passage in his celebrated lines on Patience has become almost world-renowned.

"Patience, my lord, why, 't is the soul of peace;
Of all the virtues, 't is nearest kin to heaven;
It makes men look like gods. *The best of men*
That e'er wore earth about him was a sufferer,
A soft, meek, patient, humble, tranquil spirit,
The first true gentleman that ever breathed."

In the same spirit is his dialogue between the Christian lady and the angel, in The Virgin Martyr, a tragedy written in connection with Massinger. The refinement of the feeling is almost unmatched by any dramatist under Shakspeare. Dorothea is attended by an angel, disguised as a page, — a "smooth-faced, glorious thing," a thousand blessings "dancing upon his eyes."

"ANGELO. DOROTHEA. *The time, midnight.*

"*Dor.* My book and taper.

"*Ang.* Here, most holy mistress.

"*Dor.* Thy voice sends forth such music, that I never
Was ravished with a more celestial sound.
Were every servant in the world like thee,
So full of goodness, angels would come down
To dwell with us: thy name is *Angelo*,
And like that name thou art. Get thee to rest;
Thy youth with too much watching is opprest.

"*Ang.* No, my dear lady. I could weary stars,
And force the wakeful moon to lose her eyes,
By my late watching, but to wait on you.
When at your prayers you kneel before the altar,
Methinks I 'm singing with some quire in heaven,
So blest I hold me in your company.
Therefore, my most loved mistress, do not bid
Your boy, so serviceable, to get hence:
For then you break his heart.
"*Dor.* Be nigh me still, then.
In golden letters down I 'll set that day
Which gave thee to me. Little did I hope
To meet such worlds of comfort in thyself,
This little, pretty body, when I, coming
Forth of the temple, heard my beggar-boy,
My sweet-faced, godly beggar-boy, crave an alms,
Which with glad hand I gave, with lucky hand;
And when I took thee home, my most chaste bosom
Methought was filled with no hot wanton fire,
But with a holy flame, mounting since higher,
On wings of cherubims, than it did before.
"*Ang.* Proud am I that my lady's modest eye
So likes so poor a servant.
"*Dor.* I have offered
Handfuls of gold but to behold thy parents.
I would leave kingdoms, were I queen of some,
To dwell with thy good father; for, the son
Bewitching me so deeply with his presence,
He that begot him must do 't ten times more.
I pray thee, my sweet boy, show me thy parents;
Be not ashamed.
"*Ang.* I am not: I did never
Know who my mother was; but, by yon palace
Filled with bright heavenly courtiers, I dare assure you,
And pawn these eyes upon it, and this hand,
My father is in heaven; and, pretty mistress,
If your illustrious hour-glass spend his sand
No worse than yet it doth, upon my life,
You and I both shall meet my father there,
And he shall bid you welcome.
"*Dor.* A blessed day!"

Decker's brain was fertile in fine imaginations and choice bits of wisdom, expressed with great directness and point. We give a few specimens.

"See, from the windows
Of every eye Derision thrusts out cheeks
Wrinkled with idiot laughter; every finger
Is like a dart shot from the hand of Scorn."

"The frosty hand of age now nips your blood,
And strews her snowy flowers upon your head,
And gives you warning that within few years
Death needs must marry you; those short minutes,
That dribble out your life, must needs be spent
In peace, not travail."

"Beauty is as a painting; and long life
Is a long journey in December gone,
Tedious, and full of tribulation."

"Though mine arm should conquer twenty worlds,
There 's a lean fellow beats all conquerors."

"An oath! why 't is the traffic of the soul,
The law within a man; the seal of faith;
The bond of every conscience; unto whom
We set our thoughts like hands."

The Duchess of Malfy, and The White Devil, by JOHN WEBSTER, are among the grandest tragic productions of Shakspeare's contemporaries. They are full of "deep groans and terrible ghastly looks." "To move a horror skilfully," says Lamb, "to touch a soul to the quick, to lay upon fear as much as it can bear, *to wean and weary a life till it is ready to drop*, and then step in with mortal instruments to take its last forfeit, — this only a Webster can do." Few dramatists, indeed, equal him in the steadiness with which he gazes into the awful depths of passion, and the stern nerve with which he portrays the dusky and terrible shapes which flit vaguely in its dark abysses. Souls black with guilt, or burdened with misery, or ghastly with fear, he probes to their innermost recesses, and both dissects and represents. His mind had the sense of the supernatural in large measure, and it gives to many of his scenes a dim and fearful grandeur, which affects the soul like a shadow cast from another world. He forces the most conventional of his characters into situations which lay open the very constitution of their natures, and thus compels them to act from the primitive springs of feeling and passion. He begins with duke and duchess; he ends with man and woman. The idea of death asserts itself more strongly in his writings than in those of his contemporaries. In The White Devil, the poisoned Brachiano exclaims, —

> "On pain of death, let no man name death to me:
> *It is a word most infinitely terrible.*"

No person could have written the last line without having brooded deeply over the mystery of the grave. It belongs to that "wild, solemn, preternatural cast of grief which *bewilders* us" in Webster. He fully realized, in relation to tragic effect, that present fears are *less* than "horrible imaginings." With this sombre and unearthly hue tinging his mind, he is still not deficient in touches of simple nature, wrought out with exquisite art and knowledge, and producing effects the most pathetic or sublime. The death-scene of the Duchess of Malfy is a grand example. This proud, high-hearted woman is persecuted by her two brothers with a strange accumulation of horrors, designed, with a devilish ingenuity, gradually to break her heart and madden her brain. Lamb very truly remarks, — "She speaks the dialect of despair, her tongue has a snatch of Tartarus and the souls in bale. What are 'Luke's iron crown,' the brazen bull of Perillus, Procrustes' bed, to the waxen images which counterfeit death, to the wild masque of madmen, the tomb-maker, the bellman, the living person's dirge, the mortification by degrees!"

Vittoria Corombona, the White Devil, is a great bad character, "fair as the leprosy, dazzling as the lightning." Her conduct at her arraignment is the perfection of guilt in all its defying impudence. We have no space for extracts. Webster seems to have imitated the spirit of Shakspeare more directly than any of his brother dramatists. In the preface to this play he has a curious reference to his master, alluding to the "right happy and copious industry of Master Shakspeare, Master Decker, and Master Heywood."

Marston, Heywood, Chapman, and Middleton, are stirring names of this era. JOHN MARSTON is a bitter satirist of crime and folly, and often probes the heart to its core in his dark thrusts at evil. He shows a large acquaintance with the baseness and depravity of men, and exposes them mercilessly. His mind was strong, keen, and daring, with hot and impatient impulses, controlled by a stern will, and condensed into scorn. He seems to have borne somewhat the same relation to his contemporaries that Hazlitt did to the authors of our time. He quarrelled and fought with many of them, in metrical battles. In one of the satires of the time, he is termed a "ruffian in his style," one who

> "Cuts, thrusts, and foins at whomsoe'er he meets;"

one who in his satire is not content with "modest, close-couched terms," but uses

> "Plain, naked words, stript from their shirts,
> That might beseem plain-dealing Aretine."

We have already referred to his quarrels with Ben Jonson. He was doubtless unpopular, as most satirists must be. Jonson accuses him of envy, and other bad passions. His comic scenes, though often brilliant, have no hearty mirth; but his stern, sharp, scornful mind repeatedly touched the sources of pathos and terror, though, in his tragedy, he was too apt to shed blood as fluently as ink. We extract some short passages from his plays, clipped from their connection with character and incident, to show the strength of his powers, and their poetical side. The first has great sweetness and beauty.

> "As having clasped a rose
> Within my palm, the rose being ta'en away,
> My hand retains a little breath of sweet;
> *So may man's trunk, his spirit slipped away,*
> *Hold still a faint perfume of his sweet guest.*"

The eloquent ravings of Andrugio, in Antonio and Mellida, are replete with imagination, as when he asks, —

> "Is not yon gleam the *shuddering* Morn that flakes
> With silver tincture the east verge of heaven?"

And again: —

> "Wouldst have me go unarmed among my foes?
> Being besieged by Passion, entering lists
> To combat with Despair and mighty Grief:
> My soul beleaguered with the crushing strength
> Of sharp Impatience. Ha, Lucio; go unarmed?

Come, soul, resume the valor of thy birth;
Myself, myself will dare all opposites:
I 'll muster forces, an unvanquished power:
Cornets of horse shall press the ungrateful earth:
This hollow-wombed mass shall inly groan
And murmur to sustain the weight of arms:
Ghastly Amazement, with upstarted hair,
Shall hurry on before, and usher us,
Whilst trumpets clamor with a sound of death."

The following is very powerful and impressive, — misery dressed out in the very robes of despair, and darkening earth and heaven with its baleful gloom.

"The rawish dank of clumsy winter ramps
The fluent summer's vein; and drizzling sleet
Chilleth the wan bleak cheek of the numbed earth,
While snarling gusts nibble the juiceless leaves
From the naked shuddering branch, and pills * the skin
From off the soft and delicate aspects.
O, now methinks a sullen tragic scene
Would suit the time with pleasing congruence.

* * * * *

"But if a breast,
Nailed to the earth with grief; if any heart,
Pierced through with anguish, pant within this ring;
If there be any blood, whose heat is choked
And stifled with true sense of misery:
If aught of these strains fill this consort up,
They arrive most welcome."

The following passages tell their own story, in strong and sometimes terrible language: —

"*Day breaking.*

"See, the dapple gray coursers of the morn
Beat up the light with their bright silver hoofs,
And chase it through the sky."

* Peels.

"*One who died, slandered.*

"Look on those lips,
Those now lawn pillows, on whose tender softness
Chaste, modest Speech, stealing from out his breast,
Had wont to rest itself, as loth to post
From out so fair an Inn: look, look, they seem
To stir,
And breathe defiance to black obloquy."

"*Description of the Witch Erictho.*

"Here in this desert the great Soul of charms
Dreadful Erictho lives: whose dismal brow
Contemns all roofs, or civil coverture.
Forsaken graves and tombs (the ghosts forced out)
She joys to inhabit.
A loathsome yellow leanness spreads her face,
A heavy hell-like paleness loads her cheeks,
Unknown to a clear heaven. But if dark winds
Or black thick clouds drive back the *blinded* stars,
When her deep magic makes forced heaven quake
And thunder, spite of Jove: Erictho then
From naked graves stalks out, heaves proud her head
With long unkembed hair loaden, and strives to snatch
The night's quick sulphur."

Lamb calls THOMAS HEYWOOD, very finely, "a sort of *prose* Shakspeare," and adds, "his scenes are to the full as natural and affecting. But we miss *the poet*, that which in Shakspeare always appears out and above the surface of *the nature*. Heywood's characters, his country gentlemen, &c., are exactly what we see (but of the best kind of what we see) in life. Shakspeare makes us believe, while we are among his lovely creations, that they are nothing but what we are familiar with, as in dreams new things seem old; but we awake, and sigh for the difference." Heywood was a rapid writer, claiming, in one of his prefaces, the authorship of some two hundred and twenty plays, in which he had "either an entire hand, or at least a main finger." Of these, but twenty-five have been preserved. He appears to have been a modest, amiable man, not especially stirred by the fiercer passions, and writing with singular facility a sweet and harmonious, though not poetical, style. Hazlitt calls it "beautiful prose put into heroic metre." It is not dotted over with those sharp and fiery points of passion and fancy, nor brightened by those quick flashes of imagination, which characterized the general style of the period. A Woman Killed with Kindness is his most affecting play. The character of Mrs. Frankford in this drama has been advantageously compared with that of Mrs. Haller, in The Stranger. The Englishman of the seventeenth century is a better moralist than the German of the nineteenth. Lamb's extracts from four of Heywood's plays will give the reader a good idea of his manner and his powers. The most celebrated passage in his works is the shipwreck by drink, related in The English Traveller, in his peculiar frank, light-footed style.

George Chapman, the translator of Homer, was the author of several tragedies and comedies. Lamb places him next to Shakspeare in didactic and descriptive passages, but "he could not go out of himself, as Shakspeare could shift at pleasure, to inform and animate other existences." His genius was reflective rather than dramatic. His plays are full of striking imaginations, and stern, deep comments on life, with here and there starts of tragic passion. Hazlitt says that he "aims at the highest things in poetry, but tries in vain, wanting imagination and passion, to fill up the epic moulds of tragedy with sense and reason alone, so that he often runs into bombast and turgidity, — is extravagant and pedantic at one and the same time." This does not do justice to what Webster called "the full and heightened style of Master Chapman." Though not a man of harmoniously developed genius, there are few writers of the period, whose personal character, as stamped on their serious poetry, makes a graver and deeper impression than that of Chapman. He is the impersonation of a lofty, daring, self-centred soul, feeling within itself a right to achieve the mightiest objects of human pursuit, and reposing with a proud confidence on the sense of its own power and dignity. His feeling is Titanic, but his capacity is not up to his feeling. He resolutely plants himself on the soul, and subordinates all things to it, like some of our modern Transcendentalists; but he holds a braver, fiercer, and more defying attitude towards external things than they. In some respects he reminds us of Marlowe, but slower, more weighty, more intensely reflective and self-sustained. Perhaps he may be called the Fuseli of our old dramatists. We can imagine him, as he sat patiently and painfully fashioning, in "the quick forge and working-house of thought," his colossal and irregular shapes of power, making some such remark as Fuseli made to the pleasant gentleman who asked him if he believed in the existence of the soul: — "I don't know, sir, as you have any soul; but by —— I *know* I have." There is about Chapman a rough grandeur, firmly based, and as sufficient for itself as an old, knotty and gnarled tree, rooted in rocks, and lifting itself up in defiance of tempests, — not without fine foliage, but principally attractive from its hard vitality, its capacity of resistance, and the sullen content with which it exposes to the eye its tough, ragged, and impenetrable nodosities. He has no need of bluster or bombast to confirm his good opinion of himself, as is often the case with Marlowe and Byron; but his mind is calm, fixed, and invincible in its self-esteem. The citadel of self cannot be conquered, can hardly be attacked, though the universe marshals all its pomp and circumstance to shame him from his complacency.

> "I am a nobler substance than the stars:
> And shall the baser overrule the better?
> Or are they better since they are the bigger?
> I have a will, and faculties of choice,
> To do or not to do; and reason why
> I do or not do this: the stars have none.
> They know not why they shine, more than this taper,
> Nor how they work, nor what. I'll change my course:
> I'll piecemeal pull the frame of all my thoughts:
> And where are all your Caput Algols then?
> Your planets all being underneath the earth
> At my nativity: what can they do?"

And again, hear the brave old heathen discourse of the invulnerability of a true master spirit who has trust in himself: —

"*The Master Spirit.*

> "Give me a spirit that on life's rough sea
> Loves to have his sails filled with a lusty wind,
> Even till his sail-yards tremble, his masts crack,
> And his rapt ship run on her side so low,
> That she drinks water, and her keel ploughs air.
> *There is no danger to a man that knows*
> *What life and death is: there's not any law*
> *Exceeds his knowledge; neither is it lawful*
> *That he should stoop to any other law;*
> *He goes before them and commands them all,*
> *That to himself is a law rational.*"

The lines in Italics furnished Shelley a fit motto for his Revolt of Islam.

Chapman is supposed by Dr. Drake to be the author of those lines On Worthy Master Shakspeare and his Poems, signed J. M. S., and commencing, —

> "A mind reflecting ages past," —

the noblest and justest of the poetical tributes to Shakspeare's supreme genius. We think the conjecture a shrewd one, and borne out by the internal testimony which the lines themselves offer. They are in Chapman's labored and "enormous" manner, — the images huge and intellectual, and shown through the dusky light of his peculiar imagination. Here is a specimen: —

> "To outrun hasty time, retrieve the fates,
> Roll back the heavens, blow ope the iron gates
> Of death and Lethe, where confused lie
> *Great heaps of ruinous mortality.*"

The reputation of THOMAS MIDDLETON, with modern readers, is chiefly based on his Witch, several often quoted scenes of which have been supposed to have suggested to Shakspeare the supernatural machinery of Macbeth. If this be true, it only proves Coleridge's remark, that a great genius pays usurious interest on what he borrows. The play itself is tedious, and not particularly poetical, and the witches are introduced to effect an object very far from sublime. Lamb, after extracting copiously from the play, adds the following eloquent and discriminative remarks: —

> "Though some resemblance may be traced between the charms in Macbeth and the incantations in this play, which is supposed to have preceded it, this coincidence will not detract much from the originality of Shakspeare. His witches are distinguished

from the witches of Middleton by essential differences. These are creatures to whom man or woman plotting some dire mischief might resort for occasional consultation. Those originate deeds of blood, and begin bad impulses to men. From the moment that their eyes first meet with Macbeth's, he is spell-bound. That meeting sways his destiny. He can never break the fascination. These witches can hurt the body: those have power over the soul. — Hecate, in Middleton, has a son, a low buffoon: the hags of Shakspeare have neither child of their own, nor seem to be descended from any parent. They are foul Anomalies, of whom we know not whence they are sprung, nor whether they have beginning or ending. As they are without human passions, so they seem to be without human relations. They come with thunder and lightning, and vanish to airy music. This is all we know of them. — Except Hecate, they have no names; which heightens their mysteriousness. Their names, and some of the properties which Middleton has given to his hags, excite smiles. The weird sisters are serious things. Their presence cannot coëxist with mirth. But, in a lesser degree, the witches of Middleton are fine creations. Their power, too, is, in some measure, over the mind. They raise jars, jealousies, strifes, *like a thick scurf o'er life*." — *Lamb*, Vol. I., p. 163.

The plays of Middleton are not, in general, up to the level of the time. He rambles loosely through his work, and taxes the patience of his readers without adequately rewarding it. Numerous passages in his dramas, however, show that he had that sway over the passions, and that fertility of fancy, which seemed native to all the dramatists of the period. Hazlitt concedes to his Women beware Women "a rich, marrowy vein of internal sentiment, with fine occasional insight into human nature, and cool, cutting irony of expression." In this play occurs the noted rhapsody on marriage, spoken by one who was returning, as he supposed, to a faithful wife, but who finds her a vixen and adulteress. It reminds us of an early chapter in Goethe's Wilhelm Meister.

> "The treasures of the deep are not so precious
> As are the concealed comforts of a man
> Locked up in woman's love. I scent the air
> Of blessings when I come but near the house:
> What a delicious breath marriage sends forth!
> The violet bed 's not sweeter. Honest wedlock
> Is like a banqueting-house built in a garden,
> On which the spring's chaste flowers take delight
> To cast their modest odors.
> * * * * *
> "Now for a welcome
> Able to draw men's envies upon man:
> A kiss now, that will hang upon my lip,
> As sweet as morning dew upon a rose,
> And full as long."

Cyril Tourneur is a prominent name among the dramatists of the period. His two plays, The Atheist's Tragedy and The Revenger's Tragedy, are copiously quoted by Lamb. He has touches of the finest and highest genius. There runs through him a vein of the deepest philosophy. His tragedies evince a mind that has brooded long over its own thoughts, and sent searching glances into the unsounded depths of the soul. In his delineation of the stronger passions, he often startles and thrills the mind by terrible and unexpected flashes of truth. His diction is free, fearless, familiar, and direct, pervaded by fancy and imagination, and rarely bald and prosaic. There is one passage in The Revenger's Tragedy which is almost unequalled for tragic grandeur. Castiza is urged by her mother and her disguised brother to accept the dishonorable proposals of a duke. Vindici, the brother, whose object is simply to test the virtue of his sister, eloquently sets forth the advantages she will gain by sacrificing her honor. The mother adds: — "Troth, he says true:" and then Castiza vehemently exclaims: —

> "False! I defy you both!
> I have endured you with an ear of fire;
> Your tongues have struck hot irons on my face.
> *Mother, come from that poisonous woman there!*
> "*Moth.* Where?
> "*Cast.* Do you not see her? she's too inward, then."

At the close of this scene, there is one of those beautiful touches of nature, conveyed by allusion, in which the old dramatists excel. Vindici says: —

> "Forgive me, Heaven, to call my mother wicked!
> *O, lessen not my days upon the earth!*
> *I cannot honor her.*"

Lamb says, that the scene in which the brothers threaten their mother with death for consenting to the dishonor of their sister surpasses, in reality and life, any scenical illusion he ever felt. "I never read it," he says, "but my ears tingle, and I feel a hot blush spread my cheeks, as if I were presently about to 'proclaim' some such 'malefactions' of myself, as the brothers here rebuke in their unnatural parent, in words more keen and dagger-like than those which Hamlet speaks to his mother."

We extract one passage from this tragedy. Vindici addresses the skull of his dead lady: —

> "Here's an eye,
> Able to tempt a great man, — to serve God;
> A pretty hanging lip, that has forgot now to dissemble.
> Methinks this mouth should make a swearer tremble,
> A drunkard clasp his teeth, and not undo 'em,
> To suffer wet damnation to run through 'em.
> Here's a cheek keeps her color, let the wind go whistle:

Spout rain, we fear thee not: be hot or cold,
All 's one with us: and is not he absurd,
Whose fortunes are upon their faces set?
That fear no other God but wind and wet?
* * * * *
Does every proud and self-affecting dame
Camphire her face for this? and grieve her Maker
In sinful baths of milk, when many an infant starves
For her superfluous outside, for all this?
Who now bids twenty pound a night? prepares
Music, perfumes, and sweet-meats? all are hushed.
Thou mayst lie chaste now! it were fine, methinks,
To have thee seen at revels, forgetful feasts,
And unclean brothels: sure, 't would fright the sinner,
And make him a good coward: put a reveller
Out of his antick amble,
And cloy an epicure with empty dishes.
Here might a scornful and ambitious woman
Look through and through herself. — See, ladies, with false forms,
You deceive men, but cannot deceive worms."

Lamb, Vol. I., pp. 171, 172.

Those renowned twins of poetry, BEAUMONT and FLETCHER, long held a rank among English dramatic writers second only to Shakspeare; as, in a more profligate period, they were deemed his superiors. Though as poets, lyrical and descriptive, they are entitled to a high place for fancy and sentiment, yet they appear to us thin men, when compared with Marlowe, Jonson, Webster, Chapman, and some others. In the delineation of character, and in the exhibition of great passions, they lack solidity, depth, condensation of style, rapidity of action; and we cannot mention two prominent English writers more destitute of moral principle. Fletcher, it must be allowed, is the more volatile and fertile sinner of the two. During their lives, they enjoyed a vast reputation, for they were preëminently the panders of their generation. The commendatory verses on their works would fill a small volume. Shirley, in a preface to the folio edition of their plays, published in 1647, signs himself their "humble admirer," and pours out his admiration for their genius in the highest strain of panegyric. To mention them, he says, "is but to throw a cloud upon all other names, and benight posterity; this book being, without flattery, the greatest monument of the scene that time and humanity have produced, and must live, not only the crown and sole reputation of our own, but the stain of all other nations and languages." It would be easy to quote other eulogies almost as insanely extravagant.

Both these dramatists were men of family and education. Beaumont was born in 1586, ten years after Fletcher, and died in 1615, ten years before him. His faculties ripened early. At the age of ten, he became a gentleman commoner at college. When only sixteen, he published a translation of one of Ovid's fables; and was a close friend of Ben Jonson, and one of the lights of the Mermaid, at the age of nineteen. His "judgment" seems to have been as universally admitted as Fletcher's "fancy." Jonson, it is said, consulted him often about the plots of his plays. His partnership with Fletcher seems to have commenced when he was about twenty-two, and to have run to his death.

Fletcher was born in 1576, and was less precocious than Beaumont. There is no evidence that he wrote for the stage before 1606, when he was thirty years old. He seems to have had expensive habits, and some property; the latter probably left him in advance of the former. The fact, that during the last four years of his life he wrote eleven plays, seems to indicate a dependence on his pen for support. He died in 1625, of the plague. Of the fifty-two plays published under his and Beaumont's name, it has been contended that the latter had a part in only seventeen. Among these, however, are The Maid's Tragedy, Philaster, and King and No King, — three of the most celebrated in the collection. There is also some reason to believe that Beaumont had a share, more or less, in Valentinian, and Thierry and Theodoret; but none in The Faithful Shepherdess or The Two Noble Kinsmen. Many critics have thought they traced indubitable marks of Shakspeare's mind and manner in some scenes of the latter. Lamb countenances this conjecture from the internal evidence afforded by some of the striking Shakspearian scenes. He says that the manner of the two dramatists is essentially different. Fletcher's "ideas move slow; his versification, though sweet, is tedious; it stops every moment; he lays line upon line, making up one after the other, adding image to image so deliberately, that we see where they join. Shakspeare mingles everything; he runs line into line, embarrasses sentences and metaphors; before one idea has burst its shell, another is hatched, and clamorous for disclosure." Fletcher wrote twenty-seven plays after Beaumont's death, and, it is supposed, four before; and there are eight written in connection with other authors, which swells the whole list from fifty-two to sixty.

This speaks volumes for Fletcher's fruitfulness of fancy; and if the dramas evinced a range and depth of character corresponding to their number, it might well excite wonder. But this is not the case. The framework of Fletcher's *dramatis personæ* is generally light and thin, and he continually repeats a few types of character. What he lacks in depth and intensity of mind, he seeks to make up in point, bustle, incident, intrigue, and comic or tragic situation. If we subtract from his plays all their wit, fancy, imagination, and passion, leaving whatever is mere buffoonery, ribaldry, or exaggerated commonplace, we shall have a larger and more detestable mass of ignoble depravity and slang than could be scooped out of the works of any other man of genius. When he began to write, the morality of the fashionable and educated classes had become relaxed. The court of James the First was dissolute and intrinsically vulgar. The ears of high-born ladies did not tingle at the coarsest jests, nor their cheeks burn in viewing the most licentious situations. A change had come over the "public" taste, since the time of Sidney and Spenser. Debauchery and the maxims of libertinism were more in vogue. The line separating the gentleman from the rake had imperceptibly narrowed, not to be altogether obliterated until the reign of Charles the Second. Falsehood, folly, sin, and decay, seemed natural attendants on the Stuarts. Fletcher must be set down as a poet who wilfully or heedlessly prostituted his genius to varnish this "genteel rottenness." His mind freely obeyed external direction. Like his own Mistress Bacha, in Cupid's Revenge, he seems to say to the age: —

> "I do feel a weakness in myself
> That can deny you nothing; if you tempt me,
> I shall embrace sin as it were a friend,
> And run to meet it."

His quick animal spirits, and his absence of depth, preserve his immorality from that malignity and brutality which shock us in some of his successors at the Restoration; and as the sweetness of the poet never absolutely leaves him, he rarely exhibits their hardness of heart. But where he is better than they, it seems more the result of instinctive sentiment than any moral principle. His volatility makes his libertinism shallow, brisk, and careless, rather than hard and determined. It is Belial, with the friskiness of Puck. He was as bad as his nature would admit, — as bad as a mind so buoyant, apprehensive, and susceptible of romantic ideas and feelings, would allow him to be. Shakspeare did not yield to these corrupting tendencies of his day.

It is generally conceded that Beaumont and Fletcher are more effeminate and dissolute than the band of dramatic authors to which they must be still considered to belong. Their minds had not the grasp, tension, insight, and collected energy, which characterized others who possessed less fertility. Their tragic Muse carouses in crime, and reels out upon us with bloodshot eyes and dishevelled tresses. From this relaxation of intellect and looseness of principle comes, in a great degree, their habit of disturbing the natural relations of things in their representations of the sterner passions. The atmosphere of their tragedy is too often hot, thick, and filled with pestilential vapors. They pushed everything to excess. Their weakness is most evident when they strain the fiercest after power. Their strength is flushed, bloated, spasmodic, and furious. They pitch everything in a high key, approaching to a scream. In what has been considered the most imaginative passage in their whole works, — the speech of Suetonius to his soldiers before battle, in Bonduca, — the lines seem torn from the throat of the speaker: —

"The gods of Rome fight for ye; loud Fame calls ye,
Pitched on the topless Apennine, and blows

To all the under world, all nations,
The seas, and unfrequented deserts where the snow dwells;
Wakens the ruined monuments, and there,
Where nothing but eternal death and sleep is,
Informs again the dead bones with your virtues."

Even their heroism has generally the lightness of romance, — something framed from fancy, not from nature. Their heads grow giddy among the true horrors of tragedy, and their action becomes hurry and bustle, instead of progress. The style of their dramas, where the text is not butchered by misprinting, is sweet, colloquial, voluble, and voluptuous, but rarely condensed and powerful. It has been finely said, in respect to their agency in weakening the diction of the drama, that "Shakspeare had bred up the English courser of the air to the highest wild condition, till his blood became fire, and his sinews Nemean; Ben Jonson put a curb into his mouth, subjected him to strict *manége*, and fed him on astringent food, that hardened his nerves to rigidity; but our two authors took the reins off, and let him run loose over a rank soil, relaxing all his fibres again." The flush and hectic heat of this unbitted racing is ever observable; but the bright hoofs of the courser strike off few lightning sparks, and he is a long time arriving at his goal.

The Maid's Tragedy — which Hallam gravely says is no tragedy for maids, and one which, with all its beauties, no respectable woman can read — contains much exquisite poetry among its portentous obscenities. The character of Aspatia is the model of a love-lorn, patient maiden,

"Whose weak brain is overladen
With the sorrow of her love;"

such as we meet, in a degraded state, among the Arabella Dieways of old novels. Shirley probably refers to the vein of sentiment touched in this drama, when he says, "Thou shalt meet, almost in every leaf, a soft, purling passion, or spring of sorrow, so powerfully wrought high by the tears of innocence and wronged lovers, it shall persuade thy eyes to weep into the stream, and yet smile when they contribute to their own ruins." Lysippus thus describes Aspatia: —

"This lady
Walks discontented, with her watery eyes
Bent on the earth: the unfrequented woods
Are her delight; and when she sees a bank
Stuck full of flowers, she with a sigh will tell
Her servants what a pretty place it were
To bury lovers in; and make her maids
Pluck 'em, and strew her over like a corse.
She carries with her an infectious grief
That strikes all her beholders: *she will sing*
The mournfull'st things that ever ear hath heard,
And sigh, and sing again; and when the rest
Of our young ladies, in their wanton blood,
Tell mirthful tales in course that fill the room
With laughter, she will with so sad a look
Bring forth a story of the silent death
Of some forsaken virgin, which her grief
Will put in such a phrase, that, ere she end,
She 'll send them weeping one by one away."

Amintor, in this play, forsakes Aspatia, and marries Evadne, at the command of the king. The scene in which his wife avows herself the mistress of the monarch, and tells Amintor that her marriage with him is merely one of convenience, is wrought out in Fletcher's most characteristic manner. That, also, in which the brother of Evadne compels her to promise to murder the king, is spirited and powerful. The following scene between

Aspatia and her maidens has much softness and richness of diction and sentiment: —

"ASPATIA. ANTIPHILA. OLYMPIAS.

"*Asp.* Come, let 's be sad, my girls.
That down-cast of thine eye, Olympias,
Shows a fine sorrow; mark Antiphila,
Just such another was the nympth Œnone,
When Paris brought home Helen: now a tear,
And then thou art a piece expressing fully
The Carthage queen, when from a cold sea rock,
Full with her sorrow, *she tied fast her eyes*
To the fair Trojan ships, and having lost them,
Just as thine eyes do, down stole a tear, Antiphila.
What would this wench do, if she were Aspatia?
Here she would stand, till some more pitying god
Turned her to marble: 't is enough, my wench;
Show me the piece of needle-work you wrought.
"*Ant.* Of Ariadne, Madam?
"*Asp.* Yes, that piece.
This should be Theseus, h' as a cozening face;
You meant him for a man?
"*Ant.* He was so, Madam.
"*Asp.* Why, then 't is well enough. Never look back,
You have a full wind, and a false heart, Theseus.
Does not the story say, his keel was split,
Or his masts spent, or some kind rock or other
Met with his vessel?
"*Ant.* Not as I remember.
"*Asp.* It should ha' been so: could the gods know this,
And not of all their number raise a storm?
But they are all as ill. This false smile was well exprest;
Just such another caught me; you shall not go so, Antiphila;
In this place work a quicksand,
And over it a shallow smiling water,
And his ship ploughing it, and then a fear.
Do that fear to the life, wench.
"*Ant.* 'T will wrong the story.
"*Asp.* 'T will make the story, wronged by wanton poets
Live long and be believed; but where 's the lady?
"*Ant.* There, Madam.
"*Asp.* Fie, you have missed it here, Antiphila,

You are much mistaken, wench;
These colors are not dull and pale enough,
To show a soul so full of misery
As this sad lady's was; do it by me,
Do it again by me, the lost Aspatia,
And you shall find all true but the wild island.
I stand upon the sea-beach now, and think
Mine arms thus, and mine hair blown with the wind,
Wild as that desert, and let all about me
Tell that I am forsaken; do my face
(If thou hadst ever feeling of a sorrow)
Thus, thus, Antiphila; strive to make me look
Like Sorrow's monument; and the trees about me,
Let them be dry and leaveless; *let the rocks*
Groan with continual surges, and behind me
Make all a desolation; look, look, wenches,
A miserable life of this poor picture.
"*Olym.* Dear Madam!
"*Asp.* I have done; sit down, and let us
Upon that point fix all our eyes, that point there;
Make a dull silence, till you feel a sudden sadness
Give us new souls."

Philaster has much romantic sweetness, and deservedly takes a high rank among the joint creations of our authors. Bellario is especially beautiful. Beaumont and Fletcher's fair and fine women have been considered models of womanhood by many critics, and by some placed above those of Shakspeare,—as if their best delineations of passion or constancy approached Juliet or Cordelia! Shakspeare's women are ideal; theirs, romantic. The following passage, in which Bellario, discovered to be a woman, tells the story of her love for Philaster, is exceedingly sweet and touching:—

"My father would oft speak
Your worth and virtue, and as I did grow
More and more apprehensive, I did thirst
To see the man so praised: but yet all this
Was but a maiden longing; to be lost

As soon as found; till, sitting in my window,
Printing my thoughts in lawn, I saw a god,
I thought, (but it was you,) enter our gates;
My blood flew out, and back again as fast
As I had puft it forth and sucked it in
Like breath; then was I called away in haste
To entertain you. Never was a man
Heaved from a sheep-cot to a sceptre, raised
So high in thoughts as I; you left a kiss
Upon these lips then, which I mean to keep
From you forever; I did hear you talk
Far above singing; after you were gone,
I grew acquainted with my heart, and searched
What stirred it so. Alas! I found it love,
Yet far from lust, for could I but have lived
In presence of you, I had had my end.
For this I did delude my noble father
With a feigned pilgrimage, and drest myself
In habit of a boy, and, for I knew
My birth no match for you, I was past hope
Of having you. And understanding well,
That when I made discovery of my sex,
I could not stay with you, I made a vow
By all the most religious things a maid
Could call together, never to be known,
Whilst there was hope to hide me from men's eyes,
For other than I seemed; that I might ever
Abide with you: then sate I by the fount
Where first you took me up."

A King and No King is another play in which Beaumont and Fletcher's characteristic faults and beauties are displayed. Arbaces is well delineated, and so is Bessus, — both braggarts in different stations. Hallam and Hazlitt concur in admiring this drama. Thierry and Theodoret contains two female characters, Brunhalt and Ordella, representing the two phases under which Fletcher commonly delineated women. The latter, Lamb pronounces, we think incorrectly, to be "the most perfect idea of the female heroic character, next to Calantha, in

The Broken Heart, of Ford, that has been embodied in fiction." The former is a monstrosity, compounded of fiend and beast. Valentinian is one of the best tragedies in the collection, though the plot is absurdly managed. There are three songs in it of peculiar merit, one relating to love, another to wine, and a third, full of solemn beauty, addressed to sleep, which we extract. Valentinian is brought in sick, in a chair, and the song is introduced as an expression of the deep and silent love of Eudoxia, the empress, who leans over him.

"Care-charming Sleep, thou easer of all woes, —
Brother to Death, sweetly thyself dispose
On this afflicted prince: fall like a cloud
In gentle showers; give nothing that is loud
Or painful to his slumbers; — easy, sweet,
And as a purling stream, thou son of night,
Pass by his troubled senses: — sing his pain,
Like hollow murmuring wind, or silver rain:
Into this prince gently, oh, gently slide,
And kiss him into slumbers like a bride!"

The scene which succeeds this reminds us of the last in King John. The ravings of the poisoned emperor, however, though clothed in a drapery of similar imagery, have not the intense grandeur of the death-scene of Shakspeare's monarch.

Fletcher's comedies are light, airy, fluttering, vivacious, full of diverting situations, and often sparkling with fancy and wit; but still superficial and farcical, compared with Shakspeare's and Jonson's. They have none of that intensity of humor, little of that substantial life, which we demand in English comedy. The gentleman, as understood by Fletcher, is of a different type from that indicated by old Decker. Beaumont and Fletcher, according to Dryden, understood and imitated much better than Shakspeare "the conversation of *gentlemen*, whose wild debaucheries, and quickness of wit in repartees, no poet can ever paint as they have done." We trust that they never will be equalled in this department of character. Their "studiously protracted" indecency, and their command of all the gibberish and slang of lust and vulgarity, make their comedies curious libels on the taste and morals of their audiences. Fletcher could not escape from the foul imp that had taken possession of his imagination, even in The Faithful Shepherdess, which, with all its poetic beauty and pastoral sweetness, is still so defiled in parts as to merit Schlegel's ironical comment, of its being an immodest defence of modesty. The tone and pitch of Fletcher's mind, as compared with Milton's, may be seen in the contrast between The Faithful Shepherdess and Comus. Milton is indebted to Fletcher for the suggestion of his subject, but this debt is paid a thousand-fold in the treatment of it.

Of Massinger and Ford we have space to say but little. Hazlitt remarks, that "Massinger is harsh and crabbed, Ford, finical and fastidious;" and that he cannot find much in their works, but "a display of great strength or subtlety of understanding, inveteracy of purpose, and perversity of will." Hunt accuses them of beginning that corruption of the dramatic style into prose, "which came to its head in Shirley." Hallam, on the contrary, ranks Massinger as a tragic writer second only to Shakspeare; but Hallam is often strangely infelicitous in his judgments on the old poets. The truth seems to be, that Massinger's spirit was unimpassioned, compared with his great contemporaries; his imagination was not pervaded by that fiery essence which gives to their style its figurative condensation, its abrupt turns, and its quick, startling flights. His mind was more gentle, equable, and reflective. There is a majestic sadness in Massinger, — an indication of great energies preyed upon and weakened by inward sorrow, — a stifled anguish of spirit, — which seem to point to unfortunate circumstances in his life. There is every reason to believe that he was a disappointed man, though little of his biography is known. He was born in 1584. His father was a gentleman in the service of the Earl of Pembroke. At the age of eighteen he was sent to Oxford, and after residing there four years, left without taking a degree, and went to London, where he gained a precarious subsistence as a dramatic writer. Anthony Wood says, that while at Oxford he "gave his mind more to poetry and romance, for about four years or more, than to logic and philosophy, which he ought to have done, being patronized to that end." This shows that he offended a patron. Massinger's spirit was independent, though not fiery, and probably would not brook any exercise of power which controlled his disposition. There runs through his plays an almost republican hatred of arbitrary rule. As a man, Massinger seems to have been much esteemed for his virtues. The panegyrists of his plays address to him terms almost of endearment; he is their "beloved," "dear," "deserving," "long known," and "long loved friend." As a dramatist, however, though his plays appear to have been successful, and written at the rate of two or three a year, he never raised himself above the poor gentleman. Reynolds and Morton, at the close of the last century, generally obtained five hundred pounds for their five act farces and sentimental dramas; Massinger, in his day, could not hope to average more than fifteen for his comedies and tragedies. He is known to have written, in all, thirty-seven plays, of which sixteen and the fragment of another are extant. Eleven of them, in manuscript, were in the possession of a Mr. Warburton, whose cook found them very serviceable as waste paper, in the prosecution of culinary operations.

Massinger died on the 17th of March, 1640, at the age of fifty-six. According to Langbaine, he went to bed in good health, and was found dead in the morning. He was buried in the church-yard of St. Saviour's. No stone marks the place of his interment; and "the only memorial of his mortality," says Gifford, "is given with a pathetic brevity, which accords but too well with the obscure and humble passages of his life: 'March 20, 1639–40, buried Philip Massinger, *a stranger*.'"

Massinger did not write so closely to the heart of things as some of his contemporaries. His sweet and serious mind was better fitted for description and contemplation than for representation. Possessing neither wit nor humor in any eminent degree, he had not that quick, joyous sympathy with external things, which sent the souls of many of his brethren running genially out to animate other forms of being. His characters are framed rather in the region of the understanding and the moral sentiments, than conceived by the imagination; and though often morally beautiful, have not the free, flowing, substantial life, which we require in dramatic representation. The resistance of virtue to all temptations is his favorite theme; but the temptations are often contrived out of the natural course of things, and exist rather as possibilities to the intellect than realities to the imagination. Had he possessed a little more of spontaneous creative energy, he would have been a great dramatist. His reflective habit of mind tended at once to restrain his passionateness within the bounds of a preconceived order, and to dim that keen vision by which the poet penetrates into the inmost recesses of the soul, and lays open the finest veins of thought and sentiment. Still, Massinger is one of the most original of the old dramatists, and his plays, though they do not reach the heights nor strike the depths of some others, are sustained throughout with more skill and level power. His style has been long celebrated for its sweetness and majesty of march, and its freedom from "violent metaphors and harsh constructions." "He is read," says Lamb, "with composure and placid delight." His plays exhibit a more pervading religious feeling than those of his contemporaries; and, strange to add, a coarseness of expression, in some parts, more vulgar and disgusting than the same quality in others, because utterly wanting in wit and fancy. His indecencies seem coldly and atrociously contrived in the understanding, without the concurrence of his other powers, and only introduced in obedience to "the spirit of the age." They are most essentially of the mud, muddy. They affect us like lewdness muttered from the lips of age; and his jests must be considered, on the whole, more tragical than his pathos. We never gaze on his fine serious face, as it looks out so mournfully from the canvas, without feeling how sad and degrading, how replete with that self-contempt "bitterer to drink than blood," must have been to him the task of coining vile indecencies, and bespattering his creations with the phraseology of the fish-market. It is due to Massinger to say, that his coarseness is introduced, rather than woven, into his drama, and that the string which binds the seraph to the corpse can be easily severed.

Massinger's most powerful male characters are Sforza, in The Duke of Milan, Sir Giles Overreach, in the New Way to pay Old Debts, and Luke, in The City Madam. The second of these still keeps the stage, and the third sometimes appears in a modern version, called Riches. Luke is a fine villain, forcibly conceived and strongly sustained.

JOHN FORD, a scholar and gentleman, occupies a prominent place in English dramatic literature, as a poet of pathos and sentiment. His most splendid successes are in the handling of subjects which are, in themselves, unwritten tragedies, — the deepest distresses of the heart and the terrible aberrations of the passions. His works make a sad, deep, and abiding impression on the mind, though hardly one that is pleasing or healthy. He had little of that stalwart strength of mind, and heedless daring, which characterize the earlier dramatists. Like Massinger, he is deficient in wit and humor, and like Massinger resorts to dull indecencies as substitutes. His sentiment is soft, rich, and sensuous, informed by a mild, melancholy heroism, often inexpressibly touching, and expressed in a fine, fluent diction, which melts into the mind like music. The celebrated contention of a bird and a musician, described in The Lover's Melancholy, is a specimen of his grace and sweetness of mind. In Lamb's opinion, it almost equals the strife it celebrates.

Lamb, in a note to the last scene of The Broken Heart, ranks Ford in the first order of poets. "He sought for sublimity," he says, "not by parcels, in metaphors and visible images, but directly, where she has her full residence in the heart of man; in the actions and sufferings of the greatest minds." We do not think this is the impression that his works make as a whole; it is true only of the high-wrought grandeur of detached scenes. Ford, in manners and character, seems to have been, like Jacques, melancholy and gentleman-like. Little is known regarding his life. He is supposed to have been a lawyer, and seems to have had a dislike to the reputation of a dramatist, in so far as it confounded him with those who were authors by profession; for, as Dr. Farmer says in reference to Shakspeare, with exquisite meanness of expression, "play-writing, in this poet's time, was hardly considered a creditable employ." Ford probably had something of the vanity which Congreve manifested to Voltaire, in desiring to be considered rather as a gentleman than as a dramatist. There was much of the "nice man" in his disposition. He evidently belonged not to the school of "irregular" genius, so far as regarded worldly reputation; and we can imagine what disdain would have shot from the burning eyes of Marlowe, had that sublime vagabond lived to see a dramatist studious of conventional decorum, and fastidious in small things. A contemporary satire, The Lines, quoted by Gifford, has a thrust at Ford, which illustrates as well as caricatures his peculiarity: —

> "Deep in a dump, John Ford by himself gat,
> With folded arms and melancholy hat."

He wrote sixteen plays, four of which, in manuscript, shared, with eleven of Massinger's, the distinguished honor of being consumed by Mr. Warburton's remorseless cook, for waste-paper. He seems to have retired to the country or the grave, it is uncertain which, shortly before the breaking out of the civil wars. The date of his last published play, The Lady's Trial, is 1639.

In this hurried survey of some of the Old English Dramatists, we have not been able to do more than faintly indicate their genius and individual peculiarities. It would be impossible in our limited space to do full justice to the merits of each. Indeed, though separated by individual differences, and influenced by the changes which came over the spirit of their age, they have all a general resemblance. Fletcher and Ford, perhaps, best indicate the gradual relaxation of the old sturdy strength, — that passage of comedy from humorous character into diverting incident, of tragedy from the sterner into the softer passions, — that gradual weakening of poetic diction by too strong an infusion of sweetness, — which distinguish an age slowly sinking from the region of heroic ideas into those merely romantic. But still, all these writers have, more or less, that depth, daring, vitality, comprehension, objectiveness, — that quick observation of external life and nature, and that ready interpretation of both by inward light, — that varied power and melody of versification, at times so soft and lingering, bending beneath its rich freight of delicious fancies, at others so fierce and headlong, glowing in every part with the fire of passion, — that wide sway over the heart's deepest and most delicate emotions, — and that thoroughly English cast of nature, — which associate them all in the mind, as belonging to one era of literature, and partaking of the general character stamped upon it. It would be impossible to point out a class of authors, who have appeared in any of the Augustan ages of letters, more essentially brave and strong, — any who have spoken the language of thought and passion more directly from the heart and brain, — any who more despised obtaining fame and producing effects by elaborate refinements and petty brilliancies, — any who have stouter muscle and bone. Whenever English literature has been timid and creeping, whenever the natural expression of emotion has been debased by a feeble or feverish "poetic diction," it has been to the old dramatists that men have recurred for examples of a more courageous spirit and a nobler style.

ROMANCE OF RASCALITY.

THAT this is a great world is a maxim forced upon the attention by the moral aspect of every-day events. It is especially apparent, when we consider the room it affords for the operations of knaves. The great brotherhood of rogues, who live by cheating and corrupting the species, now occupy some of the most important posts in society, science, and letters, and, as missionaries of the devil, are threading every avenue to the heart and brain of the community. Sin, every day, takes out a patent for some new invention. One of its latest and most influential is the Romance of Rascality. To a man who knows what it is to have his pocket picked, or a knife insinuated into his ribs, there may appear little that is romantic in the operation; but to a large and increasing portion of society it is otherwise. Thieves and cut-throats have come to be considered the most important and interesting of men, and virtuous mediocrity to be valuable only as affording them subjects for experiment. There is a certain *piquant* shamelessness, a peculiarly ingenious dishonesty, in some of the forms of literary chicane, which nothing can equal in impudence; for it is practically assumed that the final cause of human society is the provision of a brilliant theatre for the exploits of its outcasts.

At one time, it was considered settled that the domain of ideality was closed to vulgar criminals, and that footpads and windpipe-slitters had no pretensions to the honors of romance. For persons to act as heroes of stirring adventures and lovers of beautiful women, the novelist was compelled to rely on gentlemen, who did nothing in the way of theft and murder which the "moral sense" of the world did not approve. If he introduced characters who carried matters with a high hand, he availed himself of respectable generals and statesmen, men who might ruin an empire, but who would not condescend to relieve a traveller of his purse or his brains. In all cases he never selected his heroes and heroines from the common herd of profligates and criminals, or sought eminence by perching himself on the gallows. But now it appears that the old class of romancers were deficient in comprehension. It has been discovered that everything in nature and life has its poetic side; that it is foreign to the spirit of the age for the Republic of Letters to tolerate any of that aristocratic exclusiveness which refuses the name of hero to the inmate of the jail and the occupant of the gibbet. Rascality is now the rage, and asserts its existence with an emphasis. It has forced the passages leading to the temple of fame, and breaks into literature as it was wont to break into houses. Things heretofore considered incapable of apology or adornment, the fixed facts of guilt and crime, which charity itself doomed to infamy or oblivion, are now thrust into our faces, candied over with panegyric, and challenging our respect. The thief and the cut-purse, the murderer and the incendiary, strut and swagger in the sunny land of romance. It is a saturnalia of complacent blackguardism and vulgar villany, tricked out in the cast-off frippery of Sir Charles Grandison and Thaddeus of Warsaw. It is Satan grown sentimental, and covering his cloven foot in a satin slipper. And from the whole comes a complex fragrance, made up of sulphur and lavender, hot pitch and *eau de Cologne.*

According to the philosophy obtaining among the romancers of rascality, the fact that an object creates physical disgust is the reason why we should take it to our arms; the fact that a man excites moral reprobation is his claim upon our sympathy. That the world is sadly out of order, is proved from the fact that all the wise men are shut up in insane asylums, and all the heroes are clanking fetters or pounding stone in prisons. The real virtue of society is to be found in the victims of "social arrangements;" and the true objects of love are those whom the law hates and persecutes. What we call law and order, are other names for injustice and oppression. Sin is a word by which bigots express their dislike of great souls and free opinions.

Again, these gentlemen are champions for what they are pleased to call nature, both in thought and conduct. They desire to have this nature presented in its proper nudity, arrayed in no conventional robes, shining with no rhetorical varnish. The taste which would dictate discrimination in the selection of objects for romantic treatment, and respect the natural relations of things, they spurn at as effeminate. It must be conceded that they have brought round a large number of readers to their views. Let an author's brain teem with monsters, and his progeny are soon cradled in the bosom, or dandled in the arms, of an "enlightened" public. Let him pile horror upon horror, revel in the description of stale enormities, draw aside the "decent drapery" which covers the nakedness of depravity, and have a pool of blood running and glistening through his compositions, and there are people who will throw up their caps in admiration of his "power," and be voluble in praise of his "insight." A literary reputation may thus be acquired by a judicious mixture of horror and stupidity, and afford, likewise, a fine medium through which all the rogues of the nation may communicate with all the gulls. That the simple and the foolish should be victimized by the knowing, is the notion which a romancer of rascality entertains of preëstablished harmony and the fitness of things.

The great compensation for all the evil which this kind of literature produces is found in the fact that it is cheap. The cheapness must be acknowledged. By the progress of science and improvement, the most economical or miserly of beings is enabled to gratify his taste for mental degradation, and his *penchant* for moral ruin, at the extremely low price of ninepence. Who will not commit suicide, when poison is cheap? What keeps people from blowing out their brains, but the high price of pistols? Formerly, it seems, self-destruction was a luxury to be enjoyed only by the rich, but now it is placed within the means of the humblest. Formerly, blasphemy was held at high rates, and few could indulge in scoffing but the purchaser of Voltaire and D'Holbach; now this elegant recreation of pride can be bought for a penny. That great doctrine of equality, for which certain old gentlemen in '76 perilled their honor, lives, and fortunes, has, it seems, been imperfectly understood until the present favored age. They fought for an equality in evil as well as good. They poured out their blood, that the people might have perdition and death at low prices. They fought against monopolies in stupidity, blasphemy, immorality, and damnation. Their most resounding declamation thundered against the enormity of allowing the rich precedence in catching at the delectable baits of sin, and not giving the poor man an opportunity of having Satan's hook fast fixed in his own bleeding gills. They wished to elevate the laboring classes, but it was by allowing them a fair competition with the lazy classes, in the great object of getting hanged. The force of this argument for cheap wretchedness and ruin will depend much on the natural disposition of those to whom it is addressed. Some men, doubtless, have a theory of human life, in which happiness is synonymous with lowness, and a journey on the road to ruin is considered a performance of the whole duty of man. On such a road it is important to have cheap fares, in order to increase the travel.

It may be objected, by the patrons of this cheap Romance of Rascality, that criminals appear in legitimate romance as much as they do in rascally romance, and that it is unfair to stigmatize their department of fiction as preëminently wicked. It must be confessed that a line of distinction should here be drawn between romances which have villanous characters, and romances of which villany is the characteristic. A dramatist, poet, or romancer, is doubtless to accommodate his creations to the truth of things. His fictions should have a basis of reality, and present a true exhibition of life, actual or possible. Now, it is unfortunately true, that no exhibition of life can be accurate, unless it exhibits a large portion of rascality; for rascality is an important element of life. The romancer, perhaps, might be justified in making most of his characters more or less wicked, without running the risk of having his production condemned as unnatural. But there is a great difference between exhibiting criminals as they are in themselves, and exhibiting criminals as proper objects of esteem and moral approbation. In the first case, a true exhibition of life is given, and truth has no adulterous connection with immorality; in the other case, a false exhibition of life is given, and falsehood is but another name for immorality. Provided a writer respects the natural relations of things, there is no danger in his delineations of criminality. Shakspeare's Iago, Scott's Rashleigh Osbaldistone, Goethe's Mephistopheles, convey no pleasant impressions of sin and the devil. They rather increase our natural abhorrence of evil, by increasing our knowledge of its essence. But if Iago were so exhibited that malignity and murder fastened on our heroic sympathies, and we sided with him against his victims, the poet of nature would have been a bungler in characterization, as well as a knave in ethics. It is the same with the others. Their renown comes from their truth; and morality of effect always results from truth of representation. It is needless to demand that a poet or novelist should have a moral purpose in his delineations. All we can require is, that he should have a healthy imagination, capable of perceiving or creating objects in accordance with their natural relations; that he should avoid making monstrosities, by refusing to connect qualities in romance which have no connection, actual or possible, in life; and that he should respect the laws of the things he describes. Such a writer may let the morality of his work take care of itself. It cannot be immoral, unless it is false or one-sided. Guilt and misery are twins, and should not be separated in romance, any more than in life.

In English literature, the poet who has done most in his writings to disturb the natural relations of things, and give to sympathy an unnatural direction, is Lord Byron. The strength of his genius is shown in his success in making rascality fashionable. He awakened the sensibility of the Anglo-Saxon race for misanthropic rakes, genteel robbers, and sentimental pirates. He preached that the height of wisdom was hatred of mankind, and that all the heroism of society was among its outcasts. This he did with such force of passion and splendor of imagination, that common sense was baffled in every attempt to reach him by invective or ridicule. Ascending higher, he at last taught that heroism consisted in opposition to law, — particularly to that which originated in the skies, — and that man's greatness consisted in resolutely bearing the tortures of the damned. This was lifting rascality to the sublime; and many ambitious gentlemen began seriously to think of turning rascals. Fortunately, however, for their morals, if not for their necks, a host of imitators commenced writing in this vein, and an opportunity was offered to see the philosophy divested of its sensibility and imagination. This worked a magical change in public sentiment. The imitators were hooted and hissed into oblivion or into their senses, and the Newgate Calendar was no longer versified. It is to the honor of Byron, that he did not cant about the rascality he preached. Instead of teaching that adultery, licentiousness and blasphemy, were right, he steadily inculcated that the flavor of sin came from disobedience to law, and that without the sense of a violated conscience, wickedness was a very flat and tasteless affair. He was incapable of justifying libertinism by a philosophy of immorality, and making reason pander will. He would have men descend into the pit with the fierce plunge of the cataract, not creep to it on all-fours. He never stooped to that cowardly perfection of intellectual meanness which represents falsehood to marriage oaths as one phase of philanthropy, and covers up sin in some moral babble about nature and conventionality.

The next man of mark who illustrated rascality for the edification of nobility and gentry was Bulwer. A man of great talents and master of a style of singular fascination, he still was deficient in health and robustness of mind. His nature was morbid; and like all morbid writers who are devoured by an ambition for fame, he sought to produce effects, not by skilful combinations of realities, but by striking exhibitions of rascalities. His romances are accordingly filled with characters, almost every one of whom deserves to be hanged or whipped, but who, in the opinion of the writer, are evidently very clever people. He endeavors hard to make rascality genteel, by converting rascals into coxcombs. He compounds a hero from Beau Brummell and Dick Turpin. He must have him flat enough to please Bond-street, and brave enough for Hounslow-Heath. At one time his hero reminds us of that exquisite who had brought his charms to such a pitch of perfection that he was compelled to carry a club in the streets "to keep off the women;" at another, he seems just the man to make a picturesque appearance on the gallows. Through incident, description, character, there runs one perceptible vein of rascality. Let a reader of healthy mind judge of Bulwer's books by particular portions or by the impression of the whole, and he will see a radical defect in the writer's mode of looking at life. He distorts objects instead of representing them, and at best achieves but eloquent falsehoods.

Bulwer introduced romantic rascality into drawing-rooms, and aimed to make it the companion of people of rank and fashion. He cared little for the poor mob of readers. It remained for Ainsworth, and other novelists of a low order of talent, to debauch the popular mind, and manufacture romance for the vulgar. Jonathan Wild, Jack Sheppard and Dick Turpin, were the results of an attempt to give the people a romance of rascality for themselves. Their success stimulated a study of the records of the hanged to obtain heroes for "intense" novels; and the romancer emerged from his researches rich in the spoils of the prison and gallows. The result was a general jail delivery into literature of the convicts of centuries. The popular imagination was laden with the exploits of robbers and murderers. This was stimulating the intellect of the people with rum and gin, and it succeeded. The romances were eagerly reprinted here, and eagerly purchased. There was but one thing wanting to complete the evil, and that was a morality which justified rascality, and made it philosophical as well as romantic. This was supplied by France.

The vice of the French mind is its tendency to run into extremes. It abhors a just medium between opposite faults. With regard to religion, it rests in superstition or atheism; in government, it flies from servility to license; in literature, it passes from cold correctness to convulsive deformity. France is almost the only country which could have produced the Massacre of St. Bartholomew and the writings of the Encyclopædists. It is either in the repose of despotism or the frenzy of revolution. It adored Louis XIV., and butchered Louis XVI.

It is the politest nation in the world, and the nation in which the greatest brutalities have been practised. In literature it once worshipped Corneille and Racine, and called Shakspeare a barbarian. With a revolution in government came a revolution in literature, and it rushed into every extreme of license. The old idols were dashed to pieces, to be replaced with monsters. For the cold sculptural figures reproduced from classic models, were substituted furies from the mad-house, or wretches from the prison. The French romance of rascality has a peculiar recklessness of its own, which the Anglo-Saxon mind is not capable of reaching. In its subjects, the worst excesses of the English school are exaggerated to hideous caricature, and its representations provoke a kind of shuddering laughter.

The improvement, however, which the French romancers have added to the English school, is in connecting immorality with an ethical system. The leading idea of French romance is opposition to law and obedience to desire; and its mode of proceeding is to exaggerate the defects of social institutions, in order to obtain plausible arguments for the violation of social duties. Thus it practically sides with every form of criminality, and holds up crime, not to hatred, but sympathy. Sometimes it apologizes and extenuates, sometimes defends, but in all cases it attempts to confuse our moral perceptions. As it is very inconvenient for some minds to violate conscience, conscience must be smothered in sophistries, compounded of the Satanic and the sentimental. As these sophistries give a degree of respectability to wickedness, and allay the irritation of moral wounds and bruises, they at last convince the mind which framed them, and what originated in hypocrisy ends in faith.

The French romancers pretend to see deeper than others into the sources of sin and error; and have discovered the cause of the misery they produce, in legal and moral restraint. They accordingly argue that it is the duty of philanthropists to remove these restraints; and invite all men and women to commence the enterprise, and not be disheartened by the martyrdom it calls for at first. To assail prejudice naturally draws down obloquy upon the assailant. Great souls must not mind such annoyances. We perceive in this the French tendency to extremes. From the defects or imperfection of social institutions, such writers argue for their total overthrow. Marriage, for instance, is often a fertile source of misery to husband and wife. If either party chooses to break the connection, let the act, they would say, not be stigmatized as adultery, but hailed as indicating a mind superior to common prejudices. It is the same with other institutions. Because they are abused, they would dispense with their use. But robbery, adultery, blasphemy, and the like, are disrespectable; being under the social ban, they occasion other vices; make them respectable, and you make them beneficent. The object of these French romances is to exhibit characters who practise all that society calls sin, and yet are better than the society by whom they are denounced. This is the perfection ot sentimental rascality.

Now, this literary compound of English ruffianism and French ethics has invaded the United States in large force; and it comprises at present a considerable portion of the literature which the people read. This literature would not be read unless it were attractive; and what is attractive is influential. Its effect upon character can hardly be estimated. Doubtless such matters as cheap literary rascalities may be of small moment to the smooth scholar; but they should be of more importance than any other form of literature to the patriot and statesman. Good books are the most precious of blessings to a people; bad books are among the worst of curses. The romance of rascality in the imagination will be followed by the reality of rascality in the conduct. It contains in itself principles of demoralization which will inevitably be felt in action. This country is the only country where everybody reads. It is of much importance to know what everybody is reading. How much of this reading is ninepenny immorality, ninepenny irreligion, ninepenny stupidity, ninepenny deviltry? It might not be gratifying to the national pride of "the most enlightened people on earth" to answer this question.

THE CROAKERS OF SOCIETY AND LITERATURE.

In modern society there are innumerable obstacles in the way of obtaining or preserving a healthy condition of the heart and brain. The ten thousand prejudices, resulting from peculiarities of individual constitution, or those which are insensibly imbibed in social life, are apt to distort the mind, and vitiate the judgment and feelings. Society is cursed with so much deep-seated mental disease, and such a number of psychological epidemics, that it has been petulantly fleered at by some as a huge "Hospital of Incurables." There is no nonsense so transparent, no crotchet so ridiculous, no system so unreasonable, that it cannot find advocates and disciples. The maladies of the body, produced by artificial modes of living, reäct upon the mind, and infect the reason and sentiments; and many a spurious philosophical system is the product, not of induction, but dyspepsia; and many a plan of reform, assuming to come from the brain, has its true origin in the bile. A sickening feebleness covers its imbecile elegance, under the name of refinement, and the energy of disease and madness struts and fumes in the habiliments of power. Nothing is rarer than to see, among the vast mass of men, a healthy, strong-minded, simple man. From amiable weaknesses down to unamiable insanities, there are unnumbered disorders and infirmities which stunt the free growth and development of our natures.

One of the most melancholy productions of this condition of life is the sniveller, — a biped that infests all classes of society, and prattles from the catechism of despair on all subjects of human concern. The spring of his mind is broken. A babyish, nerveless fear has driven the sentiment of hope from his soul. He cringes to every phantom of apprehension, and obeys the impulses of cowardice as though they were the laws of existence. He is the very Jeremiah of conventionalism, and his life one long and lazy lamentation. In connection with his maudlin brotherhood, his humble aim in life is to superadd the *snivelization* of society to its civilization. He snivels in the cradle, at the school, at the altar, in the market, on the death-bed. His existence is the embodiment of a whine. Passion in him is merely a whimper. He clings to what is established as a snail to a rock. He sees nothing in the future but evil, nothing in the past but good. His speech is the dialect of sorrow; he revels in the rhetoric of lamentation. His mind, or the thing he calls his mind, is full of forebodings, premonitions, and all the fooleries of pusillanimity. He mistakes the tremblings of his nerves for the intuitions of his reason. Of all bores he is the most intolorable and merciless. He drawls misery to you through his nose, on all occasions. He is master of all the varieties of the art of petty tormenting. He tells you his fears, his anxieties, his opinions of men and things, his misfortunes and his dreams, as though they were the most edifying and delightful of topics for discourse. Over every hope of your own he throws the gloom of his despondency. He is a limping treatise on ennui, who invades sanctuaries to which no mere book could possibly gain admittance.

It must be confessed that all snivellers do not attain this height of their ideal, and that there are many degrees of foolery among the class. It requires a peculiar mental and bodily constitution, and an uncommonly bad experience of life, so to pervert the object of our being and the laws of our nature as to produce a finished whimperer. But still there is no community free from a multitude of croakers and alarmists, who display with greater or less completeness the qualities we have pointed out, and who afflict the patience and conscience of all good Christians within the reach of their influence. They are of various kinds, and exercise their misery-making propensities in manifold ways. We find them among lawyers, physicians, politicians, merchants, farmers, and clergymen, as well as among poets and old women. Wherever man, sin, and the gallows are, there is the sniveller. As a citizen and politician, he has, for the last three hundred years, opposed every useful reform, and wailed over every rotten institution as it fell. He has been and is the foe of all progress, and always cries over the memory of the "good old days." He is ever fearful of the present. His slough of despond of to-day is his paradise of to-morrow. As a clergyman, he has no force of reasoning or unction, but whines dubiously about the sin of the world, and the impossibility of checking it; he tells his congregation that the earth is a vale of tears, that they should do nothing but lament over their degeneracy, and hints the probability that few of them can be saved from the fire that is not quenched. He makes the house of mourning more mournful, and tolls the funeral bell of his voice as he joins loving hands in marriage.

But it is in literature that the sniveller is most unendurable, for in composition he can give full expression to much which human nature would prevent him from displaying in conduct. Reader, have you not seen or read many a snivelling poet? — those weak manikins and dapper authorlings who mistake indigestion for inspiration? Heaven save us all from such an infliction! There is nothing so bad as the slave of despondency when he attempts to dance in the chains of rhyme. He sets his groans and grumblings to a kind of squeaking tune, and forces innocent types to be the pander of his passion for melancholy. He goes about the streets of the intellectual republic, wearing "his heart upon his sleeve," and praying all charitable persons to drop into his hat some coppers of commiseration and crumbs of consolation. He wishes to make the whole world his confidant, — to paste up the placards of his misery in the public markets, — to inform all men and women that his heart is dust, that his hopes are blighted, and that unhappiness is his portion, — to exhibit the most recondite secrets of his bosom to the gaze of tattlers and sneerers, with the expectation of sympathy; and, with effeminate plaints of fictitious woes, to snivel away his life in a vain attempt to turn his metrical drivelling into the current coin of the land. He trusts that if hard, cold, inhuman man refuses a hearing to his maudlin miseries, the tender heart of angelic woman will pity and purchase his misfortunes. All the "little feeblenesses" generated in the atmosphere of "conventionalism's air-tight stove," which make his mind the seat of more infirmities than the pharmacopœia dreams of, he expects will find an answering response in a sex which has always enough old women of its own.

The poets who thus snivel in rhyme generally labor under the hallucination that their mawkish foolery finds sympathizing hearers. Bound up and circumscribed by their own petty world of consciousness, and brooding over their own little sorrows and cares, they are incapable of giving any free and fresh expression to natural thought and emotion. They hug the phantom of their conceit close to their breasts, and deem it of universal interest and love. Everything which occurs to themselves, from a pain in the heart to a pain in the head, they deem worthy of commemoration in metre. Their idiosyncrasies, follies, maladies, moonshine, and misery, are never satisfied until they have been tortured into rhyme. The public take interest in the psychological history of great poets, because those poets have earned their title to such distinction by works of great genius, in which all can sympathize. Shakspeare's sonnets are invaluable, because we desire to know everything which can be learned of the author of Hamlet and Macbeth. But the class of metrical snivellers would reverse this, and have the world's curiosity excited for the mental diseases of complaining mediocrity. All the "decent drapery" that decorum casts over those private meditations which every healthy intellect dislikes to divulge, they throw off with the utmost carelessness, and glory in an indelicate exposure of mind. Every little event of their mental or bodily life they deem worthy of being celebrated in a poem. If a thought happens accidentally to stray into their craniums, they rush instantly into rhyme. A sonnet to them is a soothing-syrup, and lyrics flow from their lamentations. They would turn their whine into a warble. They mistake their mental diseases for general laws. They would re-construct life after the image of their own sick imaginations, and make a nation of snivellers. An inelegant imbecility, like the mingling of moonbeams with fog, drearily illumines the intense inane of their rhetoric.

When we consider the importance of energy and hope in the affairs of the world, and contemplate the enfeebling if not immoral result of indulging in a dainty and debilitating egotism, we cannot but look upon the snivellers of social life as great evils. Even when the habit of selfish lamentation is accompanied by talent, it should be treated with contempt and scorn. There are so many inducements in our time to pamper it, that there is no danger that the opposition will be too severe. Whithersoever we go, we meet with the sniveller. He stops us at the corner of the street to intrust us with his opinion on the probability that the last measure of Congress will dissolve the Union. He fears, also, that the morals and intelligence of the people are destroyed by the election of some rogue to office. He tells us, just before church, that the last sermon of some transcendental preacher has given the death-blow to religion, and that the waves of atheism and the clouds of pantheism are to deluge and darken all the land. Next he informs us of the starvation of some poor hack, engaged as assistant editor to a country journal, and infers from it that, in the United States, literature cannot flourish. In a time of general health, he speaks of the pestilence that is to be. The mail cannot be an hour late but he prattles of railroad accidents and steamboat disasters. He fears that his friend who was married yesterday will be a bankrupt in a year, and whimpers over the trials which he will then endure. He is ridden with an eternal nightmare, and emits an eternal wail.

Recklessness is a bad quality, and so is blind and extravagant hope; but neither is so degrading as inglorious and inactive despair. We object to the sniveller, because he presents the anomaly of a being who has the power of motion without possessing life. His insipid languor is worse than tumid strength. Better that a man should rant than whine. The person who has no bounding and buoyant feelings in him, whose cheek never flushes at anticipated good, whose blood never tingles and fires at the contemplation of a noble aim, who has no aspiration and no great object in life, is only fit for the hospital or the band-box. Enterprise, confidence, a disposition to believe that good can be done, an indisposition to believe that all good has been done — these constitute important elements in the character of every man who is of use to the world. We want no wailing and whimpering about the absence of happiness, but a sturdy determination to abate misery. The world should have too much work on its hands to lend its ear to the plaints of its individual members. The laborers should have no mercy for the do-nothings. The man of serious purpose has no time to be miserable. Into the very blood and brain of our youth there should be infused energy and power. The literature of the country should breathe the bracing air of a healthy inspiration, not the hot atmosphere of a spurious spiritualism and silly sentimentality. Instead of brooding over his own diseased consciousness, and aggravating the malady which enfeebles his mind, the jaded *blasé* should cure his unhappiness by ministering to the comfort of others. And we would say to the poor sniveller, whether he dawdles in a drawing-room or tottles in a tavern, in the words of the sagacious Herr Teufelsdröckh, — "Produce! produce! were it but the pitifullest infinitesimal fraction of a product, produce it in God's name! 'Tis the utmost thou hast in thee; out with it, then. Up, up! whatsoever thy hand findeth to do, do it with thy whole might. Work, while it is called to-day, for the night cometh wherein no man can work."

BRITISH CRITICS.*

THE British reviews and reviewers of the early part of the present century are closely connected with the history of English literature, not only on account of the influence they exerted on public opinion, but for the valuable contributions which a few of them made to literature itself. Some of the most masterly disquisitions in the whole range of English letters have appeared in the three leading periodicals of the time,—the Edinburgh Review, the Quarterly Review, and Blackwood's Magazine. Almost all systems of philosophy, theology, politics and criticism, have been vehemently discussed in their pages. They have been the organs through which many of the subtlest and strongest intellects have communicated with their age. In classifying historical events under ideas and principles, in tracing out the laws which give pertinence to seemingly confused facts, in presenting intellectual and historical epochs in vivid pictures, they have been especially successful. But

* 1. Contributions to the Edinburgh Review. By Francis Jeffrey, now one of the Judges of the Court of Sessions in Scotland. London: Longman & Co. 4 vols. 8vo.

2. Wiley & Putnam's Library of Choice Reading: Characters of Shakspeare. By William Hazlitt. New York. 16mo.

3. Imagination and Fancy. By Leigh Hunt. New York: Wiley & Putnam. 16mo.—*North American Review, October*, 1845.

although containing papers of the greatest merit, their general tone has been too much that of the partisan. Being political as well as literary journals, their judgments of authors have often been determined by considerations independent of literary merit. In criticism, they have repeatedly violated the plainest principles of taste, morality, and benevolence. Their dictatorial "we" has been assumed by some of the most unprincipled hacks that ever lifted their hoofs against genius and virtue. Though they did good in assisting to purge literature of much mediocrity and stupidity, it is questionable whether their criticism on contemporaries was not, on the whole, productive of evil. The rage for strong writing, which the success of their example brought into fashion, at one time threatened to destroy all discriminating criticism. An article was more effective by being spiced with sarcasm and personalities, and the supply was equal to the demand. The greatest poets of the day found themselves at the mercy of anonymous writers, whose arrogance was generally equalled only by their malice or ignorance, and by whom a brilliant libel was considered superior to the fairest *critique.*

It is impossible to look over the current criticism of that day, and observe the meanness and injustice which so often characterize it, without a movement of indignation. This is mingled with surprise, when we discover in it traces of the hand of some distinguished man of talent, who has lent himself to do the dirty work of faction or prejudice. The great poets of the period were compelled to suffer, not merely from attacks on their writings, but from all that malice could bring against their personal character, and all that party hostility could bring against their notions of government. It was unfortunate, that the same century in which an important revolution occurred in the spirit and character of poetry, was likewise that in which political rancor raged and foamed almost to madness. The exasperated passions growing out of the political dissensions of the time, which continually brought opposite opinions in a rude shock against each other, and turned almost every impressible spirit into a heated partisan, gave a peculiar character of vindictiveness to literary judgments. The critics, being politicians, were prone to decide upon the excellence of a poet's images, or a rhetorician's style, by the opinion he entertained of Mr. Pitt and the French Revolution. The same journal which could see nothing but blasphemy and licentiousness in the poetry of Shelley, could find matter for inexpressible delight in the poetry of John Wilson Croker. Criticism, in many instances, was the mere vehicle of malignity and impudence. Whigs libelled tory writers, tories anathematized whigs. Eminence in letters was to be obtained only by men gifted with strong powers of endurance or resistance. The moment a person became prominent in the public eye, he was considered a proper object of public contempt or derision. As soon as his head appeared above the mass, he was certain that some journal would deem him worthy of being made the butt of merciless satire or scandalous personalities. Every party and *clique* had its organ of "public" opinion; and, in disseminating its peculiar prejudices or notions, exhibited a plentiful lack of justice and decorum. The coarseness and brutality which party spirit thus engendered brought down the moral qualifications of the critic to a low standard. Every literary bully, who was expert in the trade of intellectual assassination, could easily find employment both for his cowardice and his cruelty. The public looked admiringly on, month after month, as these redoubtable torturers in the inquisition of letters stretched some bard on the rack, and insulted his agonies with their impish glee. If the author denied, in meek or indignant tones, the justice of the punishment, the reply which they sometimes condescended to make was in the spirit of the taunt with which the judges in "The Cenci" mocked the faltering falsehoods of their tortured victim: —

> "Dare you, with lips yet white from the rack's kiss,
> Speak false? Is it so soft a questioner,
> That you can bandy lovers' talk with it,
> Till it wind out your life and soul?"

From this insolence and vindictiveness few British periodicals have been free, though there are wide differences in the ability and learning of the contributors, and in the artistical form which their bad qualities have taken. No eminent man, of any party, has escaped criticism of the kind we have noticed, — criticism having its origin in the desire to pamper a depraved taste, in envy, and hatred, and political bigotry, — a criticism which considered the publication of a book merely as an occasion to slander its author. Insignificance was the only shield from defamation.

But perhaps the authors of the time suffered less vexation from those critical structures directly traceable to malevolence and political fanaticism, than from those which were dictated from a lack of sympathy with the spirit of their works. There can hardly be a more exquisite torture devised for a sensitive man of genius, than to have the merit of his compositions tested by canons of taste which he expressly repudiates, and dogmatically judged by one who cannot comprehend the qualities which constitute their originality and peculiar excellence. If the critic has the larger audience of the two, and his decisions are echoed as oracular by the mob of readers, the thing becomes doubly provoking. The personal feelings of the poet are outraged, and his writings are, for the time, prevented from exerting that influence which legitimately belongs to them. As an earnest man, conceiving that he has a message of some import to deliver to the world, he must consider his critic as doing injury to society, as well as to himself. This impression is apt to engender a morbid egotism, which makes him impatient even of just censure, and to render the gulf between him and the public wider and more impassable. Much of the narrowness and captiousness, which we observe in ludicrous connection with some of the noblest thoughts and most exalted imaginations of the poets of the present century, had their source in the stings which vindictive or flippant reviewers had planted in their minds. Thus unjust or ignorant criticism subverts the purpose it proposes to accomplish, and makes the author suspicious of its capacity to detect faults, where it is so plainly incompetent to apprehend beauties. Besides, though it seems to annihilate its object, its effect is but transitory. That silent gathering of thought and sentiment in the minds of large bodies of people, which, when it has assumed distinct shape, we call public opinion, reverses the dicta of self-constituted literary tribunals; indeed, it changes the tone of the tribunals themselves. In 1816, the Edinburgh Review assumes an attitude of petulant dictatorship to Wordsworth, and begins a *critique* on "The Excursion" with,— "This will never do;" in 1831, it prefaces an objection to one characteristic trait of his descriptions of nature with the words, — "In spite of the reverence we feel for the genius of Mr. Wordsworth!"

Among the essayists and reviewers of the time, FRANCIS JEFFREY occupies a prominent position. He was one of the projectors of the Edinburgh Review,—the earliest, ablest, and most influential of the periodicals of the nineteenth century, — and from 1803 to 1829 its editor. A selection from his contributions, occupying four octavo volumes, has been lately published under his own superintendence. These evince a mind of versatile talents and acquirements, confident in its own capacity, and delivering unhesitating judgments on all matters relating to politics, literature and life, without the slightest self-distrust. It would be useless to deny that many of the opinions in these volumes are unsound and presumptuous, that they are far in the rear of the critical judgments of the present day, and that some of their most dogmatic decisions have been reversed in the journal where they originally appeared, — some by himself, but more by Macaulay, Carlyle, Hazlitt, and others. The influence of very few of his articles has been permanent. Written for the most part to serve a transitory purpose, and deficient in fixed and central principles, their influence has ceased with the controversies they excited. With a few exceptions, they will be read rather for the merits of their style and the peculiar individuality they embody, than for any additions they have made to thought or knowledge. When we consider that their author assumed to show the poets and thinkers of a whole generation how to write and to think, and that he has not left behind him a single critical principle connected with his name, his pretensions are placed in a disadvantageous contrast with his powers.

A prominent defect of Jeffrey's literary criticism arose from his lack of earnestness, — that earnestness which comes, not merely from the assent of the understanding to a proposition, but from the deep convictions of a man's whole nature. He is consequently ingenious and plausible, rather than profound, — a man of expedients, rather than of ideas and principles. In too many of his articles, he appears like an advocate, careless of the truth, or sceptical as to its existence or possibility of being reached, and only desirous to make out as good a case for his own assumed position as will puzzle or unsettle the understandings of his hearers. His logical capacity is shown in acute special pleading, in sophistical glosses, more than in fair argument. He is almost always a reasoner on the surface; and the moment he begins to argue, the reader instinctively puts his understanding on guard, with the expectation of the ingenious fallacies that are to come. He cannot handle universal principles, founded in the nature of things, and he would not, if he could; for his object is victory rather than truth. When a proposition is presented to his mind, his inquiry is not whether it be true or false, but what can be said in its favor or against it. The sceptical and refining character of his understanding, leading him to look at things merely as subjects for argument, and the mockery and *persiflage* of manner which such a habit of mind induces, made him a most provoking adversary to a man who viewed things in a more profound and earnest manner.

As an effect of this absence of earnestness, and of the consequent devotion of his faculties to the mere attainment of immediate objects, we may mention this subordination of principle to tact, both in his own writings and in his management of the Review. There is no critic more slippery, none who can shift his position so nimbly, or who avoids the consequences of a blunder with such brilliant dexterity. He understood to perfection the art of so mingling praise and blame, that, while the spirit and effect of the *critique* was to represent its object as little better than a dunce, its mere letter was consistent with a more favorable view. Thus, while it was the fashion to underrate and ridicule any class of poets, there was none who could do it with more consummate skill than Jeffrey, — none who could gain more reputation for sense and acumen in the position he assumed; but whenever public feeling changed, he could still refer confidently to his course, and prove that he had always acknowledged the extraordinary gifts of his victims, and only ridiculed or mourned their misdirection. He thus made his writings oracular among all talkers about taste and letters, among all who felt and thought superficially. He was popular with them, not because he gave them deeper principles by which to judge of merit, but because he reconciled them to their own shallowness. The lazy and the superficial, who consider everything as nonsense which they have not the sense to perceive, are especially gratified with the writer who confirms their own impressions by plausible arguments, and expresses them in brilliant language. Profound and earnest feeling, sentiments of awe, wonder, and reverence, a mind trained to habits of contemplation on man and the universe, were needed in the critic who should do justice to Wordsworth and Coleridge. These Jeffrey did not possess; but instead, he had a subtle understanding, considerable quickness of apprehension, sensibility, and fancy, a great deal of wit, a most remarkable fluency of expression, and, with little insight beyond the surface of things, an acute perception of their practical and conventional relations. In the exercise of these powers on their appropriate subjects, he appears to great advantage. No one could demolish a dunce more effectively, or represent in clearer light the follies and crimes of knavish politicians. But when he came to discuss the merits of works of high and refined imagination, or to criticize sentiments lying deeper than those which usually appear in actual life, he did little more than express brilliant absurdities. It is here that we discover his lack of power to perceive the thing he ridicules; and accordingly his wit only beats the air.

In saying this, we are by no means insensible to the charm of Jeffrey's wit, nor to the facile grace of his diction. The reviews of Wordsworth's different works are masterpieces of impertinence. The airiness and vivacity of expression, the easy arrogance of manner, the cool and provoking dogmatism, the insulting tone of fairness, the admirable adaptation of the sarcasm to tease and irritate its object, the subordination of the praise of particular passages to the sweeping condemnation passed on the whole poem, and the singular skill with which the loftiest imaginations are represented as commonplace or nonsensical, are good examples of Jeffrey's acuteness and wit. Of "The Excursion" he remarks:—"It is longer, weaker, and tamer, than any of Mr. Wordsworth's other productions; with less boldness of originality, and less even of that extreme simplicity and lowliness of tone which wavered so prettily, in the Lyrical Ballads, between silliness and pathos. We have imitations of Cowper, and even of Milton, here, engrafted on the natural drawl of the Lakers, — and all diluted into harmony by that profuse and irrepressible wordiness which deluges all the blank verse of this school of poetry, and lubricates and weakens the whole structure of their style."

Then the critic informs us, that, if he were to describe the volume very shortly, he should characterize it "as a tissue of *moral and devotional ravings,* in which innumerable changes are rung upon a very few simple and familiar ideas; but with such an accompaniment of long words, long sentences and unwieldy phrases, and such a hubbub of strained raptures and fantastic sublimities, that it is often difficult for the most skilful and attentive student to obtain a glimpse of the author's meaning — and altogether impossible for an ordinary reader to conjecture what he is about. . . . . The fact accordingly is, that in this production he is more obscure than a Pindaric poet of the seventeenth century; and more verbose 'than even himself of yore;' while the wilfulness with which he persists in choosing his examples of intellectual dignity and tenderness exclusively from the lowest ranks of society, will be sufficiently apparent from the circumstance of his having thought fit to make his chief prolocutor in this poetical dialogue, the chief advocate of Providence and Virtue, an *old Scotch pedler* — retired indeed from business, but still rambling about in his former haunts, and gossiping among his old customers, without his pack on his shoulders. The other persons of the drama are, a retired military chaplain, who has grown half an atheist and half a misanthrope — the wife of an unprosperous weaver — a servant-girl with her natural child — a parish pauper, and one or two other personages of equal rank and dignity."

After condemning some of the most splendid and some feeble passages in the poem, and extracting a few which are thought really beautiful or pathetic, this honest critic concludes thus: —

"The absurdity in this case, we think, is palpable and glaring; but it is exactly of the same nature with that which infects the whole substance of the work — a puerile ambition of singularity engrafted on an unlucky predilection for truisms; and an affected passion for simplicity and humble life, most awkwardly combined with a taste for mystical refinements, and all the gorgeousness of obscure phraseology. His taste for simplicity is evinced by sprinkling up and down his interminable declamations a few descriptions of baby-houses, and of old hats with wet brims; and his amiable partiality for humble life, by assuring us that a wordy rhetorician, who talks about Thebes, and allegorizes all the heathen mythology, was once a pedler — and making him break in upon his magnificent orations with two or three awkward notices of something that he had seen when selling winter raiment about the country — or of the changes in the state of society, which had almost annihilated his former calling."

In the review of "The White Doe of Rylstone," Jeffrey is even more emphatic in his censures. He had given up Wordsworth, on the appearance of "The Excursion," as beyond the reach of his teachings; and accordingly, in this article, he merely libels and parodies the poem. We are told that, "In the Lyrical Ballads, he was exhibited, on the whole, in a vein of very pretty deliration; but in the poem before us he appears in a state of low and maudlin imbecility, which would not have misbecome Master Silence himself, in the close of a social day. . . . . . The seventh and last canto contains the history of the desolated Emily and her faithful doe; but so very discreetly and cautiously written, that we will engage that the most tender-hearted reader shall peruse it without the least risk of any excessive emotion. The poor lady runs about indeed for some years in a very disconsolate way, in a worsted gown and flannel night-cap: but at last the old white doe finds her out, and takes again to following her — whereupon Mr. Wordsworth breaks out into this fine and natural rapture," &c., &c.

The importance which should attach to criticism like this may be estimated by a short contrast of the character and pursuits of the poet and critic: Wordsworth, living amid the most magnificent scenery, impressed with a mysterious sense of the spiritualities of things, pure, high-minded, imaginative, contemplative, earnest; — Jeffrey, passing his life in the bustle of politics and courts of law, brisk, vivacious, plausible, sarcastic, practical, available. Was ever poet matched with critic so well calculated to discern excellences, so capable of correcting faults?

In his articles on the poetry of Crabbe, Campbell, Byron, Scott, Moore, Keats, Rogers, and Mrs. Hemans, although we think he has not always perceived their highest merits, or accurately estimated their relative position, Jeffrey still appears to considerable advantage. The happy facility of his expression, the neatness and precision of his thinking, his occasional glow of feeling and fancy, and his sly, stinging wit, make them very fascinating compositions. But we see nothing in them that indicates the highest taste, — nothing that gives evidence of profound feeling or thought. They are kept studiously within the tone of "good society." Though vigorous and brilliant, they rather sparkle than burn, and have little of the living energy of earnest feeling.

Though Jeffrey evidently felt contempt for the taste of Wordsworth and Coleridge, none of his articles on poetry can be compared, in point of true insight into critical principles, with their prefaces and essays on the same theme. But these articles still have a charm, apart from their critical value; and we have no doubt that they will long be read for their shrewdness and point, and their peculiar sweetness and grace of diction. The practical remarks are always acute, and evince uncommon power of distinct expression. The review of Moore's "Lalla Rookh"— a work just calculated to display his qualities of mind and manner in their best light— is full of fancy and observation, conveyed in a style of exuberant richness. There is one sentence which well illustrates the affluence and ease of expression which he had so readily at command. "There are passages," he says, "and those neither few nor brief, over which the very Genius of Poetry seems to have breathed his richest enchantment,— where the melody of the verse and the beauty of the images conspire so harmoniously with the force and tenderness of the emotion, that the whole is blended into one deep and bright stream of sweetness and feeling, along which the spirit of the reader is borne passively away, *through long reaches of delight.*"

The passage on Shakspeare, in the review of Hazlitt, is another instance of his sweetness and luxuriance of diction. Though it is well known, we cannot resist the inclination to quote it.

"In the exposition of these is room enough for originality,— and more room than Mr. Hazlitt has yet filled. In many points, however, he has acquitted himself excellently;— partly in the development of the principal characters with which Shakspeare has peopled the fancies of all English readers— but principally, we think, in the delicate sensibility with which he has traced, and the natural eloquence with which he has pointed out, that familiarity with beautiful forms and images — that eternal recurrence to what is sweet or majestic in the simple aspects of nature — that indestructible love of flowers and odors, and dews and clear waters, and soft airs and sounds, and bright skies, and woodland solitudes, and moonlight bowers, which are the material elements of poetry — and that fine sense of their undefinable relation to mental emotion, which is its essence and vivifying soul, and which in the midst of Shakspeare's most busy and atrocious scenes, falls like gleams of sunshine on rocks and ruins, contrasting with all that is rugged and repulsive, and reminding us of the existence of purer and brighter elements, which he alone has poured out from the richness of his own mind, without effort or restraint, and contrived to intermingle with the play of all the passions and the vulgar course of this world's affairs, without deserting for an instant the proper business of the scene, or appearing to pause or digress from love of ornament or need of repose; — he alone, who, when the object requires it, is always keen, and worldly, and practical — and who yet, without changing his hand, or stopping his course, scatters around him, as he goes, all sounds and shapes of sweetness, and conjures up landscapes of immortal fragrance and freshness, and peoples them with spirits of glorious aspect and attractive grace — and is a thousand times more full of fancy, and imagery, and splendor, than those who, for the sake of such qualities, have shrunk back from the delineation of character or passion, and declined the discussion of human duties and cares. More full of wisdom, and ridicule, and sagacity, than all the moralists and satirists in existence, — he is more wild, airy, and inventive, and more pathetic and fantastic, than all the poets of all regions and ages of the world — and has all those elements so happily mixed up in him, and bears his high faculties so temperately, that the most severe reader cannot complain of him for want of strength or of reason, nor the most sensitive for defect of ornament or ingenuity. Everything in him is in unmeasured abundance, and unequalled perfection — but everything so balanced and kept in subordination, as not to jostle, or disturb, or take the place of another. The most exquisite poetical conceptions, images and descriptions, are given with such brevity, and introduced with such skill, as merely to adorn, without loading, the sense they accompany. Although his sails are purple and perfumed, and his prow of beaten gold, they waft him on his voyage, not less but more rapidly and directly than if they had been composed of baser materials. All his excellences, like those of Nature herself, are thrown out together; and instead of interfering with, support and recommend each other. His flowers are not tied up in garlands, nor his fruits crushed into baskets — but spring living from the soil, in all the dew and freshness of youth; while the graceful foliage in which they lurk, and the ample branches, the rough and vigorous stem, and the wide-spreading roots on which they depend, are present along with them, and share, in their places, the equal care of their Creator."

Every reader will appreciate the voluble beauty of this loving description; and passages almost equal to it, in richness and melody, are not infrequently found in the multifarious *critiques* of the author. The elaborate disquisition on Beauty, though founded on a mistaken theory, is written with a grace and unstudied ease which cannot fail to interest and charm. We could not, without trespassing beyond our limits, enter into a discussion to test the force of its reasoning or the pertinence of its illustrations; but we think that no poet, who ever created new beauty, could subscribe to Jeffrey's theory without doing violence to his nature. By making beauty dependent on the association of external things with the ordinary emotions and affections of our nature, by denying its existence, both as an inward sense and as an outward reality, he substantially annihilates it. His theory of "agreeable sensations" would find but little toleration from any whose souls had ever been awed before the presence of the highest Beauty which the mind can recognize. Jeffrey has not made out his case even from his own point of view; and a reader, who carefully follows the ingenious twists and turns of his argument, finds that the theory is radically superficial, or continually supposes the very principles it aims to reason away. He misconceives the nature and processes of the imagination, or, rather, in the dazzling fence of his rhetoric, imagination is used more as a meaningless word than as that power which,

> "Like to the fabled Cytherea's zone,
> Binding all things with beauty,"

is not only the bond which unites the soul with external objects, and gives the feeling and sense of beauty, but likewise suggests a loveliness grander than both, compared with which all finite beauty is insignificant. The contempt with which he refers to a "rapturous Platonic doctrine as to the existence of a Supreme Good and Beauty, and of a certain internal sense, by which both beauty and moral merit are distinguished," shows that his consciousness had never been disturbed by a class of phenomena vitally important to a settlement of the question he discusses. Carlyle, in an article in the Edinburgh Review, published in 1829, entitled "Signs of the Times," quietly sneers at the editor's whole theory, we believe, without condescending to expend any argument upon it. The same writer has contradicted, in the Edinburgh Review, Jeffrey's estimate of Goethe, of German literature in general, and of Burns, with the most provoking coolness.

Perhaps the ablest and most interesting contributions of Jeffrey to the review were those in which he portrayed the characters of eminent authors and politicians, such as his articles on Swift, Warburton, Burns, Franklin, Alfieri, Mackintosh, Curran, Richardson, and Cowper. The impeachment of Swift of high crimes and misdemeanors, before the bar of history, is a masterpiece of its kind, and has obtained deserved celebrity. The vices of his character are exposed with tremendous force, and, considered as an argument drawn simply from the actions of the man, the article is conclusive. But even in this able and powerful paper the deficiencies of Jeffrey are still apparent. In delineating character, he did it from the "skin inwards, and not from the heart outwards." His own character was the test he ever applied. He had not imagination enough to identify himself with another, and look at things from his point of view. Thus, all the palliations which bad or questionable actions might receive from original temperament or mental disease were not taken into consideration; but the individual was judged from an antagonist position, according to the very letter which killeth. This is the mode of the advocate, rather than of the critic. In the case of Swift, the feeling that the article excites against the man is one of unmitigated detestation. A more profound knowledge of his internal character might have modified the harshness of this feeling with one of commiseration. A similar remark is applicable to the judgment expressed of Burns. As regards Warburton, however, we think Jeffrey was essentially right. Nothing can be finer than the castigation he gives the insolent and vindictive bishop, at the same time that he acknowledges his talents and erudition.

Jeffrey's political articles are very spirited compositions, full of information and ability, displaying an admirable practical intellect and talent for affairs, and great command over the weapons both of logic and sarcasm. The course of the Edinburgh Review, in opposing with courage and skill the numerous political crimes and corruptions of the day, and the vigor with which it scourged tyranny and its apologists, though too often alloyed by wilful injustice to authors who happened to be classed with the tory party, will always be remembered in its favor. The part which the editor took in the political warfare of the time was honorable to his talents and his integrity. Though the extreme practical view he takes of government and freedom is not always to our taste, and though we could have wished that he possessed a deeper faith in human nature, and principles deeper grounded in right and less modified by expediency, it would be unjust to deny his claim to be considered among the most prominent of those who, in small minorities and with the whole influence of the government against them, warred for years, with inflexible zeal, to overthrow great abuses, and remove pestilent prejudices.

The critical and historical essays contributed to the Edinburgh Review by THOMAS BABINGTON MACAULAY have obtained a wide celebrity. Compared with Jeffrey, he may be said to have more earnestness, industry, learning, energy of feeling, more intellectual and moral hardihood, and a wider range of argumentation, but less grace, ease, subtilty, and sweetness. There are few contemporary writers more purely masculine, more free from all feminine fastidiousness of taste and sentiment, more richly endowed with the qualities of a hard and robust manhood, than Macaulay. His diction and style of thinking indicate physical as well as mental strength, and a contemptuous impatience of all weak emotions. He never commits himself on any subject until he has fully mastered it, and then he writes like a person who neither expects nor gives quarter, — who shows no mercy for the errors of others, because he cares not to have any shown to his own. Though a good analyst, his chief strength lies in generalization. He would hardly condescend, like Jeffrey, to pause and play with the details of a subject, or fritter away his acuteness in petty refinements; but he always aims to grasp general principles. He has one power that Jeffrey lacks, — the capacity to learn from other minds. Accustomed to look before and after, to view a literary or a political revolution in its connection with general history, his taste and judgment are comprehensive in the sense of not being fettered by conventional rules. He has considerable rectitude of intellect, and a desire to ascertain the truth of things. His literary criticism refers to the great elements or the prominent characteristic of an author's mind, not to the minutiæ of his rhetoric or his superficial beauties and faults. With Jeffrey, the reverse is often true. His wit and acuteness are so continually exercised in detecting and caricaturing small defects, that the result of his representation is to magnify the faults of his author into characteristics, and to consider his excellences as exceptions to the general rule. Macaulay, by taking a higher point of view, by his willingness to receive instruction as well as to administer advice, contrives to give more effect to his censures of faults, by keeping them in strict subordination to his warm acknowledgment of merits. The skill with which he does this entitles him to high praise as an artist. He has attempted to delineate a large number of eminent men of action and speculation, many of whose characters present a seemingly tangled web of virtues and vices; and he has been almost always successful in preserving the keeping of character, and the relation which different qualities bear to each other. He places himself in the position of the man whose character and actions he judges, seizes upon his leading traits of mind and disposition, and ascertains the relation borne to them by his other powers and feelings. As his object is to represent his subject pictorially to the imagination, as well as analytically to the understanding, and at all events to stamp a correct portrait on the mind of the reader, he sometimes epigrammatically exaggerates leading traits, in order that the complexity of the character may not prevent the perception of its individuality. This epigrammatic manner has often been censured as a fault, — in some instances justly censured; but we think that his use of it often evinces as much wisdom as wit; for his object is to convey the truth more vividly, by suggesting it through the medium of a brilliant exaggeration. No person is so simple as to give the epigram a literal interpretation; and all must acknowledge, that at times it is an arrow of light, sent directly into the heart of the matter under discussion.

There is probably no writer living who can hold up a great criminal to infamy with such terrible force of invective and sarcasm as Macaulay. Scattered over his essays, we find references to men and events that have become immortal through their criminality; and he has allowed few such occasions to pass without a flash of scorn or an outbreak of fiery indignation. All instances of bigotry, meanness, selfishness, and cruelty, especially if they are overlaid with sophistical defences, he opposes with a force of reason and energy of passion which render them as ridiculous as they are infamous. He is especially severe against those panders to tyranny who attempt to reason base actions into respectability, and to give guilt the character of wisdom. He crushes all such opponents with a kind of merciless strength. Even when his view of a person is on the whole favorable, he never defends any crime he commits. This is the case in the most difficult and delicate task he ever undertook, — the character and actions of Warren Hastings. No one can be more severe than he on Mr. Gleig, the biographer and apologist of Hastings. Every instance of oppression and cruelty which comes under his notice he condemns with the utmost indignation; but in summing up the character, he balances great crimes against great difficulties and strong temptations. The reader is at liberty to take an opposite view, and, indeed, is supplied with the materials of an impartial moral judgment. Macaulay's admiration for great intellectual powers and talent for administration is preserved amid all the detestation he feels for the crimes by which they may be accompanied. This is the amount of his toleration for Warren Hastings. In the case of Barère, however, he had to do with a man as mean in intellect as he was fiendlike in disposition; and his delineation of him is masterly. The skill with which the essential littleness of the man is kept in view amid all the greatness of his crimes, the mingled contempt and horror which his actions inspire, and the felicity with which his cruelty is always associated with his cowardice and baseness, are in Macaulay's finest manner.

We have introduced this notice of Macaulay rather to illustrate the objection to Jeffrey, than from any hope or intention to give his various writings a strict review; and we accordingly pass to another eminent essayist and critic, Sir James Mackintosh. His miscellaneous compositions are now in the course of publication in London. He is known as the author of various political, literary, and philosophical articles, in the Edinburgh Review. It would be difficult to mention any writer, whose name has been connected with the literary journals of the nineteenth century, who has carried into the task of criticism so much fairness and moderation as Mackintosh. His nature was singularly free from asperity and dogmatism. To a large understanding, and boundless stores of knowledge, he united candor, and even humility, in their employment. His mind was eminently judicial. From the character of his intellectual powers, and the moral qualities from which they received their direction, it was natural for him to look at things with an impartial desire to arrive at truth, and to view both sides of every question. He had no intellectual pride, no love for principles simply because they were his by discovery or adoption. His mind was always open to new truth. As far as his perceptions extended, he ever did full and complete justice to all systems of philosophy or legislation which came under his notice. He was incapable of misrepresenting a personal enemy or a political opponent. We have sometimes thought that an argument for the whig party of Great Britain might be built on the simple fact that their general principles and conduct were warmly approved by a man of so much comprehensiveness of heart and understanding, and so much freedom from partisanship, as Sir James Mackintosh.

The intellectual and moral character of this eminent man are so closely connected that it is difficult to view them separately. We do not think his works are fair and full exponents of his nature; and his reputation was always justly greater for what he was than for what he performed, valuable as were most of his performances. His friends and associates were among the greatest intellects of his time, and he was respected and venerated by them all. His name always carried with it a moral influence; and wherever heard, it was always associated with sound and weighty views of philosophy, with liberal principles of government, with learning, humanity, justice, and freedom. His influence was great, although it was not so palpable as that of many among his contemporaries; and it will be permanent. A man of so much uprightness and virtue, placed in such a prominent position, and mingling daily with his contemporaries as a practical statesman and philosopher, could not fail to wield unconsciously great power over the opinions and actions of his generation; and the beauty of his character will long continue to exert an influence, in insensibly moulding the minds of scholars and statesmen, and giving a humane and moral direction to their powers.

Among the critical essays contributed by Mackintosh to the Edinburgh Review, the most distinguished are his two articles on Dugald Stewart's review of the "Progress of Ethical, Metaphysical, and Political Science." These are eminently characteristic of his mind and character, being remarkable rather for largeness of view than strength of grasp, and free altogether from the fanaticism of system. The sketches of Aquinas, Bacon, Descartes, Hobbes, Locke, Boyle, Leibnitz, Machiavel, Montaigne, Grotius, Puffendorf, Barrow, and Jeremy Taylor, abound in profound remark, and often in delicate criticism. The different thinkers who pass before him for review he treats with admirable fairness, and sets forth their leading principles in a clear light. Though the style is elegant and condensed, it is at times languid, as if it paused in its movement with the pauses of the writer's judgment, or its pace was retarded by the mass of thought and erudition it conveyed. Occasionally it becomes a little verbose, from the introduction of words to restrain the full force of general epithets, or to indicate minute distinctions. A large number of striking thoughts might be quoted from these articles. They can be read again and again, with pleasure and instruction. The weight, solidity, and coolness of understanding, of which Mackintosh's disquisitions give so marked an example, remind the reader more of the judicial minds of the old English prose writers, than of the pugnacious and partisan intellects of the moderns. They lack the fire both of passion and prejudice; but their mingled gravity and sweetness of feeling, and amplitude of comprehension, will always preserve their interest. His miscellaneous essays and reviews, when collected, will occupy, we think, a permanent place in the higher literature of the generation of thinkers to which he belongs.

The various disquisitions of Sir William Hamilton seem to have attracted but little attention on this side of the Atlantic, from the fact that they deal with subjects somewhat removed from popular taste and popular apprehension; yet it would be difficult to name any contributions to a review which display such a despotic command of all the resources of logic and metaphysics as his articles in the Edinburgh Review on Cousin, Dr. Brown, and Bishop Whately. Apart from their scientific value, they should be read as specimens of intellectual power. They evince more intense strength of understanding than any other writings of the age; and in the blended merits of their logic, rhetoric, and learning, they may challenge comparison with the best works of any British metaphysicians. He seems to have read every writer, ancient and modern, on logic and metaphysics, and is conversant with every philosophical theory, from the lowest form of materialism to the most abstract development of idealism; and yet his learning is not so remarkable as the thorough manner in which he has digested it, and the perfect command he has of all its stores. Everything that he comprehends, no matter how abstruse, he comprehends with the utmost clearness, and employs with consummate skill. He is altogether the best trained reasoner on abstract subjects of his time. He is a most terrible adversary, because his logic is unalloyed by an atom of passion or prejudice; and nothing is more merciless than the intellect. No fallacy, or sophism, or half-proof, can escape his analysis, and he is pitiless in its exposure. His method is to strike directly at his object, and he accomplishes it in a few stern, brief sentences. His path is over the wreck of opinions, which he demolishes as he goes. After he has decided a question, it seems to be at rest forever, for his rigorous logic leaves no room for controversy. He will not allow his adversary a single loop-hole for escape. He forces him back from one position to another, he trips up his most ingenious reasonings, and leaves him at the end naked and defenceless, mournfully gathering up the scattered fragments of his once symmetrical system. The article on "Cousin's Course of Philosophy," and that on "Reid and Brown," are grand examples of this gladiatorial exercise of intellectual power.

Hamilton is not only a great logician, but a great rhetorician. His matter is arranged with the utmost art; his style is a model of philosophical clearness, conciseness, and energy. Every word is in its right place, has a precise scientific meaning, can stand the severest tests of analysis, and bears but one interpretation. He is as impregnable in his terms as in his argument; and with all the hard accuracy of his language, the movement of his style is as rapid, and sometimes as brilliant, as that of Macaulay. It seems to drag on the mind of the student by pure force. The key to a whole philosophical system is often given in a single emphatic sentence, whose stern compression has sometimes the effect of epigram, — as when he condenses the results of the Scotch philosophy into these few words: — "It proved that intelligence *supposed* principles, which, as the *conditions* of its activity, could not be the *results* of its operation; and that the mind contained notions, which, as primitive, necessary, and universal, were not to be explained as generalizations from the contingent and particular, about which alone our external experience was conversant. The phenomena of mind were thus distinguished from the phenomena of matter, and if the impossibility of materialism were not demonstrated, there was, at least, demonstrated the impossibility of its proof." The mastery of his subject, which Hamilton possesses, the perfect order with which his thoughts are arranged, and his exact knowledge of terms, free him altogether from that comparative vassalage to words which so often confuses the understandings of metaphysicians. His style has the hard brilliancy of polished steel; its lustre comes from its strength and compactness.

Among his contributions to the Edinburgh Review, besides those already enumerated, are the articles on the "Universities of England," on "Recent Publications on Logical Science," and on "Johnson's Translation of Tenneman's History of Philosophy." The most pleasing to the general reader would be the article on Cousin, although that on the Philosophy of Perception displays to greater advantage his immense stores of metaphysical learning and his intensity of thought. None of his articles have ever been answered. Indeed, on logical principles, they are probably unanswerable. The disquisition on Cousin, which comprehends not only a review of his philosophy, but a consideration of the whole ground of Rationalism, and a course of argument directed against all philosophical theories of the Infinite, is admirably calculated for the present state of speculation in this country, however unpalatable may be its doctrines. He takes the position, that our knowledge is restricted within the domain of the finite, — that we have no immediate knowledge of things, but only of their phenomena, — and that, in every attempt to fix the absolute as a positive in knowledge, "the absolute, like the water in the sieves of the Danaides, has always hitherto run through as a negative into the abyss of nothing." As a specimen of the style, we extract his statement of the opinions "which may be entertained regarding the unconditioned as an immediate object of knowledge and thought."

"These opinions may be reduced to four: — 1. The unconditioned is incognizable and inconceivable; its notion being only negative of the conditioned, which last can alone be positively known or conceived. 2. It is not an object of knowledge; but its notion, as a regulative principle of the mind itself, is more than a mere negation of the conditioned. 3. It is cognizable, but not conceivable; it can be known by sinking back into identity with the absolute, but is incomprehensible by consciousness and reflection, which are only of the relative and the different. 4. It is cognizable and conceivable by consciousness and reflection, under relation, difference, and plurality.

"The first of these opinions we regard as true; the second is held by Kant; the third by Schelling; and the last by our author.

"1. In our opinion, the mind can conceive, and consequently can know, only the *limited and the conditionally limited.* The unconditionally unlimited, or the *infinite,* the unconditionally limited, or the *absolute,* cannot positively be construed to the mind; they can be conceived at all only by a thinking away, or abstraction, of those very conditions under which thought itself is realized; consequently the notion of the unconditioned is only negative, — negative of the conceivable itself. For example, on the one hand, we can positively conceive neither an absolute whole, that is, a whole so great that we cannot also conceive it as a relative part of a still greater whole; nor an absolute part, that is, a part so small that we cannot also conceive it as a relative whole, divisible into smaller parts. On the other hand, we cannot positively represent to the mind an infinite whole, for this could only be done by the infinite synthesis in thought of finite wholes, which would itself require an infinite time for its accomplishment; nor, for the same reason, can we follow out in thought an infinite divisibility of parts. The result is the same, whether we apply the process to limitation in space, in time, or in degree. The unconditional affirmation of limitation — in other words, the *infinite* and the *absolute, properly so called* * — are thus equally inconceivable to us.

"As the conditionally limited (which we may briefly call the conditioned) is thus the only object of knowledge and of positive thought, thought necessarily supposes conditions; to think is therefore to condition, and conditional limitation is the fundamental law of the possibility of thought. How, indeed, it could ever be doubted that thought is only of the conditioned, may well be deemed a matter of the profoundest admiration.

* "It is proper to observe, that though we are of opinion that the terms Infinite and Absolute, and Unconditioned, ought not to be confounded, and accurately distinguish them in the statement of our own view; yet, in speaking of the doctrines of those by whom they are indifferently employed, we have not thought it necessary, or rather we have found it impossible, to adhere to the distinction."

Thought cannot transcend consciousness; consciousness is only possible under the antithesis of a subject and object of thought, known only in correlation and mutually limiting each other; while, independently of this, all we know either of subject or object, either mind or matter, is only a knowledge in each of the particular, of the different, of the modified, of the phenomenal. We admit that the consequence of this doctrine is, that philosophy, if viewed as more than a science of the conditioned, is impossible. Departing from the particular, we admit that we can never, in our highest generalization, rise above the finite; that our knowledge, whether of mind or matter, can be nothing more than a knowledge of the relative manifestations of an existence which, in itself, it is our highest wisdom to recognize as beyond the reach of philosophy: — *Cognoscendo ignorari, et ignorando cognosci.*"

A collection of Sir William Hamilton's articles, as far as they are generally known, might easily be contained in a moderately sized volume, and we trust it will soon be made. Such a book could not fail to be successful, even in the publisher's notion of that word; and it would familiarize the minds of our students with far more rigorous habits of thinking and investigation than are now in vogue. Three or four of the ablest of these papers have already been translated into French, and published in a single volume at Paris.

William Gifford, the editor of the Quarterly Review, seems to have united in himself all the bad qualities of the criticism of his time. He was fierce, dogmatic, bigoted, libellous, and unsympathizing. Whatever may have been his talents, they were exquisitely unfitted for his position — his literary judgments being contemptible, where any sense of beauty was required, and principally distinguished for malice and word-picking. The bitter and snarling spirit with which he commented on the excellence he could not appreciate; the extreme narrowness and shallowness of his taste; the labored blackguardism in which he was wont to indulge, under the impression that it was satire; his detestable habit of carrying his political hatreds into literary criticism; his gross personal attacks on Hunt, Hazlitt, and others who might happen to profess less illiberal principles than his own; made him a dangerous and disagreeable adversary, and one of the worst critics of modern times. Through his position as the editor of an influential journal, his enmity acquired an importance due neither to his talents nor his character. His notoriety was coëxtensive with his malignity; his fame consisted in having the power to wound better men than himself; and consequently, from being a terror and a scourge, he has now passed into oblivion, or is only occasionally rescued from it to be an object of wondering contempt. As far as his influence in the management of the review extended, it was employed to serve the meanest and dirtiest ends of his party, and the exploded principles of a past literary taste; and it was owing to no fault of his, that the journal did not become a synonyme of malignant dulness and ferocious illiberality, and feed to the full the vulgar appetite for defamation. Nothing but the occasional contributions of eminent writers and scholars prevented it from sinking to the dead level of his intellect and prejudices. The blindness which partisan warfare produces, even in men of education and courtesy, could alone have permitted the organ of a great party to be under the management of this critical Ketch, this political Quilp. His acumen was shown in his profound appreciation of works which died as soon as puffed, and in his insensibility to those whose fame was destined to begin with his oblivion; and his statesmanship, in the low abuse of individuals, in a resolute defence of the rotten parts of toryism, and in assiduous libels on foreign countries. It is to him, we presume, that we are indebted for the lies and blunders about the United States for which the Quarterly was once distinguished.

To Gifford for a time belonged the equivocal fame of killing John Keats; but we are glad that a disclosure of the facts has lately robbed him of this laurel of slander. It is quite a satisfaction to know, that even the tenderest and most sensitive of poets was beyond the reach of his envenomed arrows. Shelley, in a monody on the death of Keats,—then supposed to have been accelerated by the brutal article in the Quarterly,—has, in a strain of invective hot from his heart, fixed a brand on Gifford's brow, which may keep it above the waters of oblivion for some years to come.

"Live thou, whose infamy is not thy fame!
Live! fear no heavier chastisement from me,
Thou noteless blot on a remembered name!
But be thyself, and know thyself to be!
And ever at thy season be thou free
To spill the venom, when thy fangs o'erflow:
Remorse and Self-contempt shall cling to thee;
Hot Shame shall burn upon thy secret brow,
And like a beaten hound tremble thou shalt—as now.

"Nor let us weep that our delight is fled
Far from these carrion-kites that scream below:
He wakes or sleeps with the enduring dead;
Thou canst not soar where he is sitting now,—
Dust to the dust! but the pure spirit shall flow
Back to the burning fountain whence it came,
A portion of the Eternal, which must glow
Through time and change, unquenchably the same,
Whilst thy cold embers choke the sordid hearth of shame."

The various critical writings of William Hazlitt are laden with original and striking thoughts, and indicate an intellect strong and intense, but narrowed by prejudice and personal feeling. He was an acute but somewhat bitter observer of life and manners, and satirized rather than described them. Though bold and arrogant in the expression of his opinions, and continually provoking opposition by the hardihood of his paradoxes, he does not appear to have been influenced so much by self-esteem as sensibility. He was naturally shy and despairing of his own powers, and his dogmatism was of that turbulent kind which comes from passion and self-distrust. He had little repose of mind or manner, and in his works almost always appears as if his faculties had been stung and spurred into action. His life was vexed by many troubles, which rendered him impatient and irritable, prone to opposition, and inclined to take delight in the mere exercise of power, rather than to produce the effects for which alone power is valuable. Contempt and bitterness too often vitiate his notions of men and measures; and his political writings, especially, often exhibit him as one who courts and defies opposition, and who is more desirous of making enemies than converts. He would often give the results of patient reasonings in headlong assertions, or paradoxical impertinences. In attacking ignorance and prejudice, he did not distinguish them from positive vices. If any one of his opinions was more heretical than another, he sought to enunciate it with a startling abruptness of expression, in order that it might give the more offence. There was bad temper in this, and it made him violent enemies, and subjected his character and writings to the most unscrupulous attacks.

The element in which Hazlitt's mind was most genially developed was literature. If he was lacking in love for actual human nature, or viewed men in too intolerant a spirit, his affections clustered none the less intensely around the "beings of the mind." His best friends and companions he found in poetry and romance, and in the world of imagination he lived his most delightful days. As a critic, in spite of the acrimony and prejudice which occasionally dim his insight, he is admirable for acuteness, clearness, and force. His mind pierces and delves into his subject, rather than gracefully comprehends it; but his labors in the mine almost always bring out its riches. Where his sympathies were not perverted by personal feeling or individual association, where his mind could act uninfluenced by party spirit, his perceptions of truth and beauty were exquisite in their force and refinement. When he dogmatizes, his paradoxes evince a clear insight into one element of the truth, and serve as admirable stimulants to thought. His comments on passages of poetry or traits of character which have struck his own imagination forcibly, are unrivalled for warmth of feeling and coloring. His criticism inspires the reader with a desire to peruse the works to which it refers. It is not often coldly analytical, but glows with enthusiasm and "noble rage." His style is generally sharp and pointed, sparkling with ornament and illustration, but almost altogether deficient in movement. Though many of his opinions are unsound, their unsoundness is hardly calculated to mislead the taste of the reader, from the ease with which it is perceived, and referred to its source, in caprice, or a momentary fit of spleen. He is a critic who can give delight and instruction, and infuse into his readers some of his own vehement enthusiasm for letters, without making them participants of his errors and passions.

Some of the most distinguished of Hazlitt's critical writings are, — "Lectures on the Comic Writers," "Spirit of the Age," "Characters of Shakspeare's Plays," "Lectures on the Age of Elizabeth," "Lectures on the English Poets," and "Criticisms on Art." These cover a wide ground, and are all more or less distinguished by his characteristic merits and faults. They all startle the reader from the self-complacency of his opinions, and provoke him into thought.

Leigh Hunt is well known as the author of a large number of agreeable essays, and for his friendly connections with many of his eminent contemporaries. He has been more a victim of criticism than a critic. It has been truly said of him by Macaulay, "that there is no man living whose merits have been more grudgingly allowed, and whose faults have been so cruelly expiated." In his character there is such a union of pertness and kindliness, that he is always open to attack. He made the public his confidant, poured into its ear his little frailties and fopperies, expressed his opinions on all subjects with the most artless self-conceit, and at times exhibited a kind of Richard Swiveller order of good feeling, in speaking of such men as Shelley and Byron. These follies, though most of them venial, made him a continual butt for magazine scribblers; and the fine qualities of heart and intellect, which underlie his affectations, have not, until lately, been generally acknowledged. He is, in truth, one of the pleasantest writers of his time, — easy, colloquial, genial, humane, full of fine fancies and verbal niceties, possessing a loving if not a "learned spirit," with hardly a spice of bitterness in his composition. He is an excellent commentator on the minute beauties of poetry. He has little grasp or acuteness of understanding, and his opinions are valueless where those qualities should be called into play; but he has a natural taste, which detects with nice accuracy what is beautiful, and a power of jaunty expression, which conveys its intuitive decisions directly to other minds. He surveys poetry almost always from a luxurious point of view, and his criticism therefore is merely a transcript of the fine and warm sensations it has awakened in himself. He is a sympathizing critic of words, sentences, and images, but has little success in explaining the grounds of his instinctive judgments, and is feeble and jejune in generalization. He broods over a dainty bit of fancy or feeling, until he overflows with affection for it. He dandles a poetic image on his knee as though it were a child, pats it lovingly on the back, and addresses to it all manner of dainty phrases; and, consequently, he has much of the baby-talk, as well as the warm appreciation, which comes from affection. This billing and cooing is often distasteful, especially if it be employed on some passages which the reader desires to keep sacred from such handling; and we cannot see him approaching a poet like Shelley without a gesture of impatience; but generally it is far from unpleasant. His "Imagination and Fancy" is a delightful book. "The Indicator" and "Seer" are filled with essays of peculiar excellence. Hunt's faults of style and thinking are ingrained, and cannot be weeded out by criticism; and to get at what is really valuable in his writings, considerable toleration must be exercised towards his effeminacy of manner and daintiness of sentiment. That, with all his faults, he has a mind of great delicacy and fulness, a fluent fancy, unrivalled good-will to the whole world, a pervading sweetness of feeling, and that he occasionally displays remarkable clearness of perception, must be cheerfully acknowledged by every reader of his essays.

In these hurried remarks on some of the essayists and critics of the time, we have not noticed two, who are well entitled to an extended consideration. We refer to Thomas Carlyle and John Stuart Mill. The influence of Carlyle on the whole tone of criticism at the present day has been powerfully felt. Mill is principally known on this side of the Atlantic by his work on Logic; but he has been for a number of years a writer for the Westminster Review, over the signature of A, and his articles, especially his masterly disquisition on Jeremy Bentham, evince uncommon solidity, fairness, penetration, and reach of thought. These are worthy of a more elaborate review than our limits will now permit; but we trust at some early period to repair the deficiency.

RUFUS CHOATE.*

To give a strict analysis of a mind so complex, various, and richly gifted, as that of Mr. Choate, we feel to be a difficult and delicate task. What is peculiar in his genius and character is provokingly elusive; and though an unmistakable individuality characterizes all his productions as a lawyer, orator, and statesman, it is an individuality so modified by the singular flexibility of his intellect, that it can be more easily felt than analyzed. We propose to give a few dates illustrating his biography; to allude to some of his masterly expositions of national policy as a statesman; and to touch slightly that rare combination in his character of the poet and the man of affairs, by which the graces of fancy and the energies of impassioned imagination lend beauty and power to the operations of his large and practical understanding.

Mr. Choate was born in Ipswich, Mass., on the 1st day of October, 1799. He entered Dartmouth College in 1815, and was distinguished there for that stern devotion to study, and that love of classical literature, which have accompanied him through all the distractions of political and professional life. Shortly after graduating he was chosen a tutor in college; but, selecting the law

* *American Review, January*, 1847.

for his profession, he entered the Law School at Cambridge, and afterwards completed his studies in the office of Judge Cummins, of Salem. He also studied a year in the office of Mr. Wirt, Attorney-General of the United States. He commenced the practice of his profession in the town of Danvers, in 1824. But a considerable portion of the period between his first entry into his profession and his final removal to Boston, in 1834, was passed in Salem. He early distinguished himself as an advocate. His legal arguments, replete with knowledge, conducted with admirable skill, evincing uncommon felicity and power in the analysis and application of evidence, blazing with the blended fires of imagination and sensibility, and delivered with a rapidity and animation of manner which swept along the minds of his hearers on the torrent of his eloquence, made him one of the most successful advocates at the Essex bar. In 1825, he was elected a representative to the Massachusetts Legislature; and in 1827 he was in the Senate. He took a prominent part in the debates, and the energy and sagacity which he displayed gave him a wide reputation. In 1832 he was elected member of Congress from the Essex district. He declined a reëlection, and in 1834 removed to Boston, to devote himself to his profession. He soon took a position among the most eminent lawyers at the Suffolk bar, and for seven years his legal services were in continual request. In 1841, on the retirement of Mr. Webster from the Senate, he was elected to fill his place by a large majority of the Massachusetts Legislature, — an honor which Massachusetts bestows on none but men of signal ability and integrity. Since Mr. Choate resigned his seat in the Senate, he has been more exclusively devoted to his profession than at any previous period of his life. The only public office he now holds is that of Regent of the Smithsonian Institute. The country is principally indebted to his efforts for the promising form which that institution has now assumed.

Mr. Choate's powers as a statesman are to be estimated chiefly by his course while a member of the United States Senate, especially by his speeches on the Tariff, the Oregon question, and the Annexation of Texas. These appear to us among the ablest which were delivered during the agitation of those inflammable questions. Beneath an occasional wildness of style, there can easily be discerned a sagacious and penetrating intellect, well trained in dialectical science; capable of handling the most intricate questions arising under the law of nations and constitutional law; keen to perceive the practical workings of systems of national policy; possessed of all the knowledge relating to the topics under discussion; fertile in arguments and illustrations, and directing large stores of information and eloquence to practical objects. In his speech, March 14, 1842, on the right and duty of Congress to continue the policy of protecting American labor, he presents a lucid and admirable argument to prove that Congress has the constitutional power "so to provide for the collection of the necessary revenues of Government as to afford reasonable and adequate protection to the whole labor of the country, agricultural, navigating, mechanical, and manufacturing, and ought to afford that protection;" and in the course of the argument he gives a review of the opinions current on the subject about the period of the adoption of the Constitution. This displays an extensive acquaintance with the political history of the time, the result of original research. In this speech he declares the origin of the objection to the protective policy, based on the assumption of its unconstitutionality, to have arisen in "a subtle and sectional metaphysics;" and adds, in a short paragraph, well worthy to be pondered by all who are exposed to the fallacies springing up in the hot contests of party, that "it is one of the bad habits of politics, which grow up under written systems and limited systems of government, to denounce what we think impolitic and oppressive legislation as unconstitutional legislation. The language is at first rhetorically and metaphorically used; excited feeling, producing inaccurate thought, contributes to give it currency; classes of states and parties inweave it into their vocabulary, and it grows into an article of faith."

The best and most characteristic of his speeches on the tariff, however, is that delivered in the Senate on the 12th and 15th of April, 1844. It shows a most intimate acquaintance with the history of our legislation on the question; the subject is taken up in its principles and details, and exhibited in new lights; it glows with enthusiasm for the honor, glory, and advancement, of the nation; and its illustrations, allusions, and arguments, have the raciness of individual peculiarity. The philosophy of the manufacturing system is given with great clearness in respect to principles, and at the same time is presented to the eye and heart in a series of vivid pictures. The problem, he says, which the lawgiver should propose to himself is this, — "How can I procure that amount of revenue which an economical administration of government demands, in such manner as most impartially and most completely to develop and foster the universal industrial capacities of the country, of whose vast material interests I am honored with the charge?" We should like to quote the whole of that passage in which he enforces the importance of manufactures, on the ground that they give the laborer the choice between many occupations, and do not absolutely confine him to one or two. "In a country," he says, "of few occupations, employments go down by an arbitrary, hereditary, coërcive designation, without regard to peculiarities of individual character. But a diversified, advanced, and refined mechanical and manufacturing industry, coöperating with those other numerous employments of civilization which always surround it, offers the widest choice, detects the slightest shade of individuality; quickens into existence and trains to perfection the largest conceivable amount and utmost possible variety of national mind." He proceeds to illustrate this idea by supposing a family of five sons, who, in some communities, would all be compelled to follow one occupation, as fishermen, or farmers, or servants. He then sketches the history of four of these sons, in a community where the diversified employments of civilization give scope to the ruling passion of each. The allusion to the fifth boy is as honorable to the statesman as the poet. "In the flashing eye, beneath the pale and beaming brow, of that other one, you detect the solitary first thoughts of genius. There are the sea-shore of storm or calm, the waning moon, the stripes of summer evening cloud, traditions, and all the food of the soul, for him. And so all the boys are provided for. Every fragment of mind is gathered up. The hazel-rod, with unfailing potency, points out, separates, and gives to sight every grain of gold in the water and in the sand. Every taste, every faculty, every peculiarity of mental power, finds its task, does it, and is made the better for it."

We should like to refer, at some length, to Mr. Choate's speech on the bill to provide further remedial justice in the courts of the United States, delivered in the Senate, May, 1842. It is one of the most ingenious, learned, and vehement of his speeches. Replete with logical passion, rapid, animated, high-toned, it at one moment transfixes an objection with those radiant shafts which speed from the mind only in periods of excited reasoning, and at another overthrows an antagonist proposition by a series of those quick, trampling interrogations by which argument is gifted almost with muscular power. There is one passage, illustrating the idea that the condition of national existence is to be under the obligations of the law of nations, from which we quote a characteristic sentence or two: "You may cease to be a nation; you may break the golden unseen band of the constellation in which we move along, and shoot apart, separate, wandering stars, into the infinite abyss; you may throw down the radiant ensign, and descend from the everlasting and glittering summits of your freedom and your power; but while you exist as now you do, the only nation of our system known to the other nations, you are under, you must obey, and you may claim upon the common code of all civilized and Christian commonwealths."

The closing passage of the speech is even more passionately imaginative: "The aspect," he says, "which our United America turns upon foreign nations, the aspect which our constitution designs she shall turn upon them, the guardian of our honor, the guardian of our peace, is, after all, her grandest and her fairest aspect. We have a right to be proud when we look on that. Happy and free empress-mother of states themselves free! unagitated by the passions, unmoved by the dissensions, of any one of them, she watches the rights and fame of all; and reposing, secure and serene, among the mountain summits of her freedom, she holds in one hand the fair olive-branch of peace, and in the other the thunderbolt of reluctant and rightful war. There may she sit forever; the stars of union upon her brow, the rock of independence beneath her feet!" This image has the splendor and energy of one of Burke's, with a slight touch, perhaps, of Mr. Jefferson Brick. The shock it may give to the finer filaments of taste is owing to the ridicule which has been cast on the sentiment of national exaggeration, through the nonsense and bombast of fifth-rate declaimers. In this connection we may as well allude to Mr. Choate's sympathy with those general feelings of patriotism, as they are felt, not by tasteful students, but by great bodies of people. Though one of the first classical scholars in New England, and a diligent student of the great productions of English genius and taste, he is still exceedingly open to impressions from the common mind and heart, and has none of that daintiness, which, in the man of letters, contemptuously tosses aside all sentiment, expression, and imagery, which the pharisees of scholarship may choose to consider vulgar and ungenteel. The greatest English statesmen have always addressed these common sentiments of large classes of the people — have often spoken in their speeches as Dibdin wrote in his songs — and have been indebted for a great deal of their influence to passages which wrinkle with scorn the lips of elegant scholars and contributors to the reviews.

The speech delivered by Mr. Choate on March 21,

1844, on the Oregon question, in reply to Mr. Buchanan, is dotted all over with splendid sentences: the general course of the argument is well sustained and happily enforced; and there is a joyous spring in the style, even in its occasional inflation, which seems to indicate that most of it was delivered without any more preparation than the facts and arguments demanded. It is an exceedingly spirited and brilliant speech, but has the inequalities of merit common to purely extemporaneous productions, in which argument is diversified by personal matters of reply and retort. The tone of most of the speech is that of excited conversation, with the exaggeration, both of passion and wit, common in colloquial disputes. The invective, provoked by a remark that the American people cherish a feeling of deep-rooted hatred to Great Britain, is perhaps its intensest passage. "No, sir," he indignantly observes, "we are above all this! Let the Highland clansman, half naked, half civilized, half blinded by the peat-smoke of his cavern, have his hereditary enemy and his hereditary enmity, and keep the keen, deep, and precious hatred, set on fire of hell, alive if he can; let the North American Indian have his, and hand it down from father to son, by Heaven knows what symbols of alligators, and rattlesnakes, and war-clubs smeared with vermilion and entwined with scarlet; let such a country as Poland, — cloven to the earth, the armed heel on the radiant forehead, her body dead, her soul incapable to die, — let her remember the wrongs of days long past; let the lost and wandering tribes of Israel remember theirs — the manliness and the sympathy of the world may allow or pardon this to them: but shall America, young, free, and prosperous, just setting out on the highway of heaven, 'decorating and cheering the elevated sphere she just begins to move in, glittering like the morning star, full of life and joy,'—shall she be supposed to be polluting and corroding her noble and happy heart, by moping over old stories of stamp-act, and tea-tax, and the firing of the Leopard on the Chesapeake, in time of peace? No, sir; no, sir; a thousand times no! * * * * We are born to happier feelings. We look on England as we look on France. We look on them from our new world,—not unrenowned, yet a new world still,—and the blood mounts to our cheeks, our eyes swim, our voices are stifled with the consciousness of so much glory; their trophies will not let us sleep: but there is no hatred at all—no hatred; all for honor, nothing for hate! We have, we can have, no barbarian memory of wrongs, for which brave men have made the last expiation to the brave."

We have not by us the great speech of Mr. Choate on the Annexation of Texas, but we remember being impressed at the time with its strength and felicity; and the position taken in it regarding the consequences of the measure have been realized almost to the letter. He was one of the most ardent opponents of annexation, and both in the Senate and in addresses to the people, made his resistance felt.

In what we have said regarding his other speeches, we have not, of course, done justice to their merit as arguments, or stated the wide variety of topics and principles they discuss. We have merely, in our quotations, given prominence to a few sentences which illustrate the essential solidity and correctness of his views of national policy, amid all the exaggeration and ornament of their expression. It is one of his peculiarities, and a very striking one, that he combines a conservative intellect with a radical sensibility; and those irregular impulses of fancy and passion, which usually push men into the adoption of reckless, desperate, and destructive principles of legislation, he employs in the service of the calmest, most comprehensive, and most practical political wisdom, rooted deep in reason and experience. His fire *seems* to be of that kind which sweeps, in a devouring flame, to blast and desolate what is established and accredited; but it really is that heat, which infuses energy and breathing life into maxims and principles, which are in danger of becoming ineffective, from their usual disconnection with the sensibility and imagination. He is a kind of Mirabeau-Peel.

In what we have now to say in regard to Mr. Choate's mind and character, we shall have to consider him chiefly as a lawyer and advocate, and only incidentally as a statesman. His greatest triumphs have been at the bar; and to unfold from any central principle the character of that genius by which he often works such wonders — to give anything like the philosophy of his influence — is a task full of difficulty. We desire to present a portrait which shall suggest to the reader the character and qualities of the man, but we feel able to do it but imperfectly.

Mr. Choate's mind is eminently large, acute, flexible, vigorous, versatile, enriched with the most various acquirements, and displaying in its exercise a rare union of understanding and imagination, shrewdness and sensibility, tact and fire. He is one of the most sagacious, as well as one of the most brilliant and impassioned, of orators. An unwearied fire seems to burn in the very centre of his nature, penetrating every faculty, flaming out in almost every expression; yet his intellect preserves its clearness of view, amid his most fervent declamation, and he is never himself whirled along in that rush of passion which hurries away the minds of all who come within its influence. With the keenest sensitiveness to impressions, he is distinguished as much for his power of self-control as his power of self-excitation; and his emotions, like well-trained troops, "are impetuous by rule." In this singular combination of qualities the puzzle of his character seems to lie; and it brings us at once to the prominent characteristic of his mind — his swift sympathy with any given events and persons, by force of imagination. Facts and principles are not with him abstract data for an abstract conclusion; but he instinctively grasps them in the concrete, and realizes them to his own mind as living things. The most careless glance at his productions will reveal this tendency of his intellect to the most superficial reader. Whatever may be the subject or object of his speech, he endows it with personal life. Thus he speaks of the system of American manufactures as a "refined, complicated, *sensitive* industry." He ever impersonates the country, and sections of the country, whenever he alludes to them. They appear always to rise up to his mind as personal existences. Thus, New York, with him, is not simply a city distinguished for commercial energy, but a city which "with one hand grasps the golden harvests of the West, and with the other, like Venice, espouses the everlasting sea." Again he observes, that after we came out of the war of 1812, "the baptism of fire and blood was on our brow, and its influence on our spirit and legislation."

The most inanimate things start into life beneath his touch. We recollect that he once objected to the reception of an illiterate constable's return of service, bristling all over with the word *having*, on the ground that it was bad. The judge remarked that though inelegant and ungrammatical in its structure, the paper still seemed to be good in a legal sense. "It may be so, your honor," replied Mr. Choate, "but it must be confessed he has greatly *overworked* the participle," — a humorous imagination worthy of old Dr. Fuller. Again, in referring to the misgovernment and weakness of the Confederation, he remarked that, "when at last the Constitution was given to the longing sight of the people, they threw themselves upon it like a famished host on miraculous bread." But, perhaps, the finest specimens of his imaginative power are those little minor touches, which are occasionally inserted in the throng and impatient pressure of his fanciful illustrations, and to a critical eye are more pleasing than his most splendid and flaring images. They evince that an acuteness and intense clearness of mind ever accompanies, if it be not the result of, his most vehement excitement. This is an important point of separation between the orator and the mere declaimer.

From this power of intense conception comes the force of Mr. Choate's eloquence, and also its seeming exaggeration. A vivid insight into one particular fact or truth, and a statement of it in corresponding warmth of language, practically draws it out of its natural relations, and converts the less into the greater reason. This is the advantage which the great advocate holds over the merely learned and logical lawyer. He can make the little have the effect of the great by his power of impressing it upon the mind; and it requires a corresponding intensity of conception on the part of his opponent, to restore the intrinsically more important fact to its rightful precedence. Force in the orator often compensates for deficiencies in the evidence. When this force, this power of giving prominence to facts and principles which are really of secondary importance, is wielded by one who controls the restless faculties of imagination and sensibility by which it is performed, the effect is proportionably increased. The dramatic poet is all the more powerful in delineating character, when he intensely sympathizes with the passions he creates, without being blinded and borne away on their impetuous flood. A prominent characteristic of genius, says John Foster, "is the power of lighting its own fire."

The object of Mr. Choate, in the discussion of a question, and the object of every great orator, is not primarily to convince the intellect or please the fancy, but to influence the will. He attempts to storm the citadel of the mind. His arguments, consequently, do not address the understanding alone, nor his passion the sensibility alone, but fact, argument, fancy, and passion, are fused together in one glowing mass, and boldly directed at the very springs of action and volition. Though, for the purposes of classification, we speak of the mind as a collection of sentiments and faculties, we should never forget that it is still not an aggregation but a unit, and that its unity is its leading and vital characteristic, amidst all the variety of its manifestation. Though this fact is commonly overlooked by the logician, the great reasoner, no less than the great orator, keeps it constantly in view, when his object is to produce a practical effect upon the will of his audience. There is little force in abstract principles, but immense power in living ideas. It is the commonest of truisms that men do not necessarily act from the barren commonplaces to which their understandings may yield assent. Many of Queen Elizabeth's most peaceable subjects were Roman Catholics, who believed they would be justified in being her assassins. Many of the bishops who assisted in driving James the Second from his throne were champions of the divine right of kings, and believers in the doctrine of non-resistance to their authority. The orator, therefore, instinctively appreciating the difference between notions which are civilly assented to by the intellect, and operative ideas which produce corresponding action, addresses the whole nature of his audience, and moves as well as convinces. Mr. Choate possesses this power in a large measure; and it is especially seen in his legal arguments.

This fiery and fusing imagination lies at the centre of his flexible nature, and constitutes, in fact, the real characteristic of his eloquence, and is the chief source of his power. But the most obvious characteristic of his mind is fancy; and certainly it is one of exhaustless opulence and almost unbounded range. For every idea, event, or action, which comes into his mind, he has a fancy to suggest something which bears to it a seeming likeness. His analogical power, indeed, both of understanding and fancy, is immense, and it is difficult in the rush of his eloquence always to distinguish real from apparent analogies, — analogies in the nature of things, from analogies in the appearances of things. The latter class are profusely scattered over his various speeches, and lend to his style a character of gorgeous, but often ungraceful ornament. His productions should be viewed with reference to the fact that they were intended to be spoken, and spoken by the orator himself. To a cool taste, the printed orations, disconnected from the excitement under which they were delivered, and the purpose they were intended to serve, would seem occasionally turgid in style and meretricious in metaphor. Even in this respect, however, his ornament is not of that kind which makes the speeches of Counsellor Phillips a continual shock to taste, nor that style of elaborated frenzy and careful tawdriness which stiffens the diction of Sheridan's speeches; but there is behind all a force and fire hurrying the mind onwards, and never allowing it to stop for criticism. His most exaggerated images seem forced from him in moments of excitement, and are all infused with the life of the occasion. His eloquence, fierce, rapid, and bold, conscious of power, and feeling a kind of wild delight in its exercise, dares everything, forces the minds of the hearers into appropriate moods, and at times accomplishes its object by main strength. He fires the whole mass of his facts, arguments and images, until they blaze, and the grotesque flashes of flame which sometimes impatiently dart from the main body are hardly noticed as incongruous. It would be easy to adduce specimens of his fierce and exaggerated fancies — comparisons clutched in moments of raised passion, and made to harmonize with the thought or feeling of the moment. In an argument before a Committee of the Massachusetts Legislature, on the petition for a new railroad from Salem to Boston, he drew a very vivid picture of the different towns the present road did *not* pass through, and referred especially to Danvers, which is only two or three miles from Salem. "Her people," he said, "were just near enough to hear the whistle of the locomotive, and gaze at the sparks of that flying giant; yet, for all practical purposes, they might as well stand under the sky at midnight, gazing at a *firmament of falling meteors*."

Mr. Choate's fancy usually accompanies, and sometimes almost blends with, the exercise of his imagination; but it is still to be distinguished from its nobler companion. By imagination he apparently exaggerates a thing through the intensity which he conceives it; by fancy, he really magnifies it by comparison with larger objects. From the manner in which these two powers of his mind play into each other's processes, and also from his frequent practice of overtopping an imagination with a fanciful decoration, the charge of exaggeration against his eloquence has its foundation. The phrase "clothed upon," which is often applied to the operations of imagination, is more properly applicable to those of fancy; and in Mr. Choate's productions, the shining garment of comparison, which he has placed upon his vital thought, may easily be disconnected from it, and leave the original idea, grasped and modified by imagination, in its own intense and living beauty. Even if the fancy, as is sometimes the case with him, grows out of the imagination, it can be severed from it without striking at the life of its parent,—as we can lop the luxuriant foliage from a tree without injuring its root and trunk. The truth is, that, in respect to ornament, fancy is more effective than imagination, because it is more readily apprehended; and Mr. Choate's real poetic power has generally suffered most from the praises of such as have been captivated by his swollen comparisons and flaring illustrations.

Mr. Choate has a peculiar kind of mirth in his composition, and also that readiness which commonly accompanies ludicrous perception; but his wit is rather witty fancy, and his humor, humorous imagination. He has a kind of playful sympathy with the ludicrous side of things, and is often exceedingly felicitous in its expression. Such is his grotesque image, in his speech on the Oregon question, of the Legislature putting its head out of the window, and, in a voice audible all over the world, speaking to the negotiators of the impending treaty, bidding them God-speed, but insinuating that if they did not give up the whole subject in dispute, it would be settled by main strength. But perhaps his best passage in this way is his picture of a New England summer, introduced in his second speech on the tariff, to illustrate the idea that irregularity is not ruin.

"Take the New England climate in summer; you would think the world was coming to an end. Certain recent heresies on that subject may have had a natural origin there. Cold to-day; hot to-morrow; mercury at 80° in the morning, with wind at south-west; and in three hours more a sea-turn, wind at east, a thick fog from the very bottom of the ocean, and a fall of forty degrees of Fahrenheit; now so dry as to kill all the beans in New Hampshire; then floods carrying off the bridges of the Penobscot and Connecticut; snow in Portsmouth, in July; and the next day a man and a yoke of oxen killed by lightning in Rhode Island. You would think the world was twenty times coming to an end! But I don't know how it is: we go along; the early and the latter rain falls, each in its season; seed-time and harvest do not fail; the sixty days of hot corn weather are pretty sure to be measured out to us. The Indian Summer, with its bland south-west, and mitigated sunshine, brings all up; and on the twenty-fifth of November, or thereabouts, being Thursday, three millions of grateful people, in meeting-houses, or around the family board, give thanks for a year of health, plenty, and happiness."

The reader of Mr. Choate's speeches will readily call to mind many sentences in which the serious and the ludicrous shake hands as cordially, and with as little detriment to each other, as in the preceding extract.

This peculiar sportiveness, which Mr. Choate can command at pleasure, is an element in the general impression conveyed by his genius, and it makes the character complete. Will, understanding, imagination, passion, fancy, humor, subtlety in the perception of distinctions, subtlety in the perception of resemblances, sympathy with the ideal, and sympathy with the familiar; these, both in their separate exercise, and their subtle interpenetration, are resources which he commands and blends at will. In this play and interchange of imagination and humor, in this union of the high with the common, there is established in his mind a kind of fellowship with the things he describes and the persons he addresses. Through this he contrives, in his legal arguments, to lift the familiar into the ideal, by the strength of his conception of both; and when his materials are at all tractable, he can achieve the task without suggesting the ludicrous. When they are not, he does it by pure force and determination. He discerns, instinctively, the unconscious poetry in characters and actions which are prosaic to the common eye; and he does not, perhaps, so often superadd as evolve. His arguments have often the artistical effect of a romantic poem, even when they are most firmly based on law and evidence. His client is the hero of the narrative; and spectators, if not juries, always desire that the hero of Mr. Choate's epic argument may not come to an end "by edge of penny cord and vile reproach." The immense fertility of his mind, in possibilities and plausibilities, enables him to account for every action on other principles than those which are obvious; and the warm blood never glows and rushes through his sentences with more intensity than when he is giving to the secondary the prominence and life of the primitive. There is a constant appeal, in his arguments, to generous sentiment, — an implied assumption that men will always act honestly and without prejudice, — that a jury will as heartily pronounce in favor of his client, as the reader of a romance in favor of persecuted virtue. And, for the time, the orator himself is earnest and sincere. By force of sympathy, he has identified himself with his client, and realized everything to his own mind. He pleads as if his own character or life was at stake. Ideas, suppositions, possibilities, drawn into his own imagination, are vitalized into realities, and he sees them as living things, — sees them as Dante saw Farinata rise from his glowing tomb, — as Shakspeare saw Cordelia bending over Lear. And while thus giving breathing life to characters and events, he does not overlook a single particle of evidence, or neglect to urge a single point of law, which bears upon the case. Indeed, a legal argument, as conceived and delivered by Mr. Choate, has the merit of combining an influence upon the will and understanding, with an artistical effect upon the imagination. He makes no parade of logic; the skeleton is not always forcing itself through the flesh, as in the arguments of men of dryer brains and less skill; yet he ranges his case with consummate art around its great leading points, to which he binds, in the strictest sequence, and with a masterly power of concentration, every fact and every argument. His fancy leads him into no illogical discursions, but plays like heat-lightning along the lines of his argument, while his imagination, interpenetrating and working with his logic, at once condenses and creates.

It is needless to say that his arguments cannot be

reported. In a newspaper, they have the effect of "champagne in decanters, or Herodotus in Beloe's version."

It would be impossible to convey an idea of this power of Mr. Choate by single passages, as it is something which animates, unites, and vivifies the whole argument. It is *imagination*, not a series of *imaginations*, which produces the result. Sentences cut apart from the main body of one of his productions can only suggest his manner through the process of caricature. Thus, we recollect that an honest master-mason, in one of his arguments, rose to the dignity of "a builder and beautifier of cities." In another, he represented the skipper of a merchant vessel, who had been prosecuted by his crew for not giving them enough to eat, as being busily studying some law-book, while passing the island of St. Helena, to find out his duty in case the vessel was short of provisions. "Such," said Mr. Choate, "were his meditations, as the invisible currents of the ocean bore him by the grave of Napoleon." A witness once testified, in reference to one of his clients, that he had called upon him on Friday evening, found him crying, and, on asking him what was the matter, received in answer,—"I'm afraid I've run against a snag." This was rendered by Mr. Choate somewhat in this way:—"Such were his feelings, and such his actions, down to that fatal Friday night, when at ten o'clock, in that flood of tears, his hope went out like a candle."

These instances convey an idea of the process by which Mr. Choate makes "strange combinations out of common things," but a little more accurate than an intentional parody of his manner.

The style of Mr. Choate is the style of an orator, not

of an author. It will hardly bear a minute criticism, founded on general principles of taste, but must be judged with reference to the character of the speaker and the object of his speech. The tone of his diction is pitched on too high a key for written composition. The same splendid oration which thrilled a popular assembly, or influenced the verdict of a jury, would lose a very important portion of its charm when subjected to the calm, cold judgment of the reader. Besides, it must be admitted that Mr. Choate's immense wealth of language, and opulence of fancy, urge him into redundance of expression, and sometimes overload his style with shining words. This is principally seen in his use of adjectives. He will pour out in one breath five or six of them, sometimes because he has not time to choose the most expressive one, sometimes from the desire to point out all the qualities of the thing defined. It has been said of him, that he "drives a substantive and six." He is often exceedingly felicitous in this accumulation of epithets, and really condenses where he seems to expand. Thus he once spoke of the Greek mind, as "subtle, mysterious, plastic, apprehensive, comprehensive, available" — a page of disquisition in one short sentence. But commonly, we think, it tends to weaken his diction, especially when it is disconnected from his peculiar manner of speaking. It is the vice of a fertile intellect, always in haste, and rusting to its own wealth to supply at the moment the words which are wanted. Perhaps this peculiarity has been unconsciously caught from a study of the later writings of Burke, especially those on the French Revolution. Burke often "drives a substantive and six," but he has his reins upon them all, and each performs a service to which all the others would be inadequate. His epithets do not clog his style, however they may modify the rapidity of its movement. They are selected *by* his mind; Mr. Choate's seem to occur *to* his mind.

We cannot conclude these hurried observations on some of the characteristics of Mr. Choate, without expressing the hope that his large, fertile, and available intellect, so rich in experience and scholarship, may be directed, at some period, to the production of a work, in which his genius and acquirements may be fairly expressed. Everything which he has performed, heretofore, has been done on the spur of the occasion, and to serve some particular object connected with his party or his profession. He is capable of producing a work which will give his name that literary prominence to which his great powers seem to point. In the prime of life, and in the vigor of his genius, having achieved early the highest political and professional objects of a manly ambition, we trust that his splendid intellect will not pass away, without leaving behind something which shall embody its energies, and reflect honor upon the literature of his country.

PRESCOTT'S HISTORIES.*

THE publication of Mr. Prescott's "Peru" affords us an opportunity for which we have long waited, to attempt an estimate of his powers as a historian, and to give some account of his works. To him belongs the rare distinction of uniting solid merit with extensive popularity. He has been exalted to the first class of historians, both by the popular voice and the suffrages of the learned. By avoiding all tricks of flippancy or profundity to court any class of readers, he has pleased all. His last history is devoured with as much avidity as the last novel; while, at the same time, it occupies the first place in the pages of the reviews. His fame, also, is not merely local, or even national. It is as great at London, Paris, and Berlin, as at Boston or New York. His works have been translated into Spanish, German, French, and Italian; and into whatever region they have penetrated, they have met a cordial welcome, and done much to raise the character of American letters and scholarship. In England his success has probably been beyond that of any other American author. The tone of the English press towards our publications has too often been either patronizing or insolent. But Mr. Prescott's histories have been spared both the impertinence of condescension and the impertinence of abuse, and judged according to their intrinsic merits. The best evidence, perhaps, of

* *Methodist Quarterly Review, January,* 1848.

his transatlantic reputation is to be found in his membership of numerous literary associations abroad. We perceive that since the publication of The Conquest of Peru, he has been chosen a member of the Royal Society of Literature, and also of the Society of Antiquaries. The last honor he shares with but one other American.

It is needless to say that a reputation so extensive could only result from sterling excellences. Some of Mr. Prescott's popularity may, doubtless, be attributed to the peculiar disadvantages under which he has prosecuted his historical researches. That a man nearly blind should collect a large mass of rare chronicles and MSS., and attempt the composition of histories requiring the utmost industry, sagacity, and toil, is of itself sufficient to awaken attention, and almost to confer fame. But Mr. Prescott's works require no apology founded on the obstacles he has surmounted. They can stand the tests we apply to similar compositions without any call upon the charity of reader or reviewer. Indeed, though the historian cannot dispense with the use of his eyes without being subjected to numberless annoyances which might well discourage the most patient and energetic of men, the value of his history must come, after all, from his own mind and character. It is not the channel through which facts and authorities pass into the head, but the shape in which they come out of the head, which is of the most importance. The real difficulties which Mr. Prescott has surmounted are intellectual, and inherent in his subjects and materials. These difficulties can hardly be appreciated by a superficial reader of his histories. They are not perceived until we consider out of what obstinate materials he has drawn his consistent, animated, and picturesque narrative, and reflect upon that peculiar combination of qualities by which he has been enabled to perform it with such splendid success.

The distinguishing merit of Mr. Prescott is his power of vividly representing characters and events in their just relations, and applying to them their proper principles. He thus presents a true exhibition of the period of time he has chosen for his subject, enabling the reader to comprehend its peculiar character, to realize its passions and prejudices, and at once to observe it with the eye of a contemporary, and judge it with the calmness of a philosopher. To succeed in this difficult object of historical art, requires not only mental powers of a high order, but a general healthiness of moral and intellectual constitution, which is uncommon, even among historians who evince no lack of forcible thought and intense conception. History is false, not only when the historian wilfully lies but also when facts, true in themselves, are forced out of their proper relations through the unconscious operation of the historian's feelings, prejudices, or modes of thought. He thus represents, not his subject, but his subject as modified by his own character. Certain facts and persons are exaggerated into undue importance, while others are unduly depressed, in order that they may more readily fall within the range of his generalizations, or harmonize with his preconceived opinions. He may have a system so fixed in his mind, or a passion so lodged in his heart, as to see facts in relation to it, instead of seeing them in relation to each other. An honest sectarian or partisan, an admirable moralist or philanthropist, might make his history a tissue of fallacies and falsehoods, without being justly chargeable with intentional untruth. This is done by confounding individual impressions with objective facts and principles.

Now, Mr. Prescott's narrative of events and delineations of character are characterized by singular objectiveness. By a fine felicity of his nature, he is content to consider his subject as everything, and himself as nothing. Objects stand out on his page in clear light, undiscolored by the hues of his own passions, unmixed with any peculiarities of his own character. This disposition and power to see things as they are in themselves, when joined to a corresponding capacity to convey them to other minds in their true proportions, indicates a finely balanced as well as largely endowed nature, and implies moral as well as intellectual strength. The moral qualities evinced in Mr. Prescott's histories, though they are seen in no ostentation of conscience and parade of noble sentiments, are still of a fine and rare order, and constitute no inconsiderable portion of his excellence as a historian. These are modesty, conscientiousness, candor, toleration, — a hatred of wrong, modified by charity for the wrong-doer, — a love of truth, expressed not in resounding commonplaces, but in diligence in seeking it out, — and a comprehension of heart which noiselessly embraces all degrees of the human family, just and merciful to all, looking at motives as well as actions, and finding its fit expression in a certain indescribable sweetness of tone pervading his style like an invisible essence. It is one of the greatest charms of his compositions, that these qualities are so unostentatiously displayed that they can be best described in negatives. Thus we speak of his absence of egotism, of intolerance, of narrowness, of rancor, of exaggeration, rather than of the positive qualities through which such faults are avoided.

The intellectual power displayed in Mr. Prescott's works has a similar character of unobtrusiveness and reserve. It would, doubtless, appear to many readers much greater were it asserted with more emphasis, and occasionally allowed to disport itself in the snapping contrasts of antithesis, or the cunning contortions of disputation. A writer may easily gain the reputation of a strong and striking thinker, by sacrificing artistical effect to momentary surprises, or by exhibiting his thoughts in their making, before they have attained precision and definiteness, and taken their place in the general plan of his work. To the generality of readers, depth of thought is confounded with confusion of thoughts. Events and ideas, heaped and huddled together, and lit up here and there with flashes of wit and imagination, are often received in their chaotic state as indications of greater mental power than they would be if reduced to order and connection by the stringent exercise of a patient, penetrating, and comprehensive intellect. Now, pure force of understanding is principally shown in so grappling with the subject as to educe simplicity from complexity, and order from confusion. According to the perfection with which this is done will be the apparent ease of the achievement; and a thinker who follows this method rarely parades its processes. His mind, like that of Mr. Prescott, operates to the reader softly and without noise. Any strain or contortion in thought or expression would indicate imperfect comprehension of his subject, and exhibit the pains of labor instead of its results. Far from desiring to tickle attention by giving undue prominence to single thoughts or incidents, such a thinker would be chiefly solicitous to keep them in subjection to his general purpose; for it is violating the first principle of art to break up the unity of a subject into a series of exaggerated individual parts.

The moment we consider the materials which form the foundation of Mr. Prescott's elaborate histories, we perceive the high degree of intellect they imply in the writer, and are able to estimate that healthiness of mind by which he shunned the numerous temptations to brilliant faults which beset his path. In the collection of these materials he has displayed all the industry and diligence of an antiquary. With the utmost indifference to labor and expense, he has gathered from every quarter all books and MSS. which could elucidate or illustrate his subjects, and nothing which could cast the minutest thread of light into any unexplored corner of history seems to have escaped his terrible vigilance. With all his taste for large views, which comprehend years in sentences, the most mole-eyed analyst has not a keener sight for the small curiosities of history. No chronicle or personal history, happy in the consciousness of its insignificance, can hide itself from his quick eye, if it chance to contain a single fact which he needs. He has shown more industry and acuteness than almost any other contemporary resurrectionist in the grave-yards of deceased books. Yet he has not one of the faults which cling so obstinately to most antiquaries. He does not estimate the importance of a fact or date by the trouble he experienced in hunting it out. He does not plume himself on the acquisition of what has baffled others. None of the dust of antiquity creeps into his soul. His style glides along with the same unassuming ease in the narration of discoveries as of common facts.

Indeed, it is not so much in the collection as in the use of his materials that Mr. Prescott claims our regard as a historical artist. These materials are, it is true, original and valuable beyond any which have fallen into the hands of any contemporary historian; but to analyze them, and to compose accurate histories from their conflicting statements, required judgment in its most comprehensive sense. They are the productions of men who looked at persons and events from different points of view. They are vitiated with the worst faults of bad historians. They all reflect their age in its common passions and prejudices, and each is disfigured by some unconscious or wilful misrepresentations, springing from personal bias or imperfect comprehension. They are full of credulity and bigotry, of individual and national prejudices, — sometimes the mere vehicles of private malice, almost always characterized by a bad arrangement of facts and confusion of principles. Together they present so strange a medley of shrewdness and fanaticism, of fact and fiction, and throw over the subject they are intended to illustrate such a variety of cross lights, and entangle it in such perplexing contradictions, that to sift out the truth requires the most cautious consideration and comparison of authorities. The testimony of kings, statesmen, scholars, priests, soldiers, philanthropists, each inaccurate after a fashion of his own, Mr. Prescott was compelled to estimate at its exact worth, disregarding all the exaggerations of pride, interest, and sensibility. To do this, he was necessarily obliged to study the personal history of his authorities, to examine the construction of their minds, and to consider all inducements to false coloring which would result from their position and character. Those who have carefully read the critical notes of his authorities, subjoined to each division of his histories, must admit that Mr. Prescott has shown himself abundantly capable of performing this difficult and delicate task. He analyzes the mental and moral constitution of his veterans with singular acuteness, laying open to the eye their subtlest excellences and defects, and showing in every sentence that in receiving their statements of facts, he has allowed much for the medium through which they have passed. This portion of his duty, as a historian, demanded a judgment as nice in its tact as it was broad in its grasp. The scales must have been large enough to take in the weightiest masses of details, and perfect enough to show the slightest variation of the balance.

Mr. Prescott's understanding is thus judicial in its character, uniting to a love for truth diligence in its search and judgment in its detection. But this does not comprehend all his merits as a historian of the past; and, indeed, might be compatible with an absence of life in his narrative, and vitality in his conceptions. Among those historians who combine rectitude of purpose with strength of understanding, Mr. Hallam stands preëminent. All his histories have a judicial character. He is almost unexcelled in sifting testimony, in detecting inaccuracies, in reducing swollen reputations to their proper dimensions, in placing facts and principles in their natural order. He has no prepossessions, no preferences, no prejudices, no theories. He passes over a tract of history sacred to partisan fraud and theological rancor, where every event and character is considered in relation to some system still acrimoniously debated, without adopting any of the passions with which he comes in contact. No sophistical apology for convenient crime, no hypocrite or oppressor pranked out in the colors of religion or loyalty, can deceive his cold, calm, austere, remorseless intellect. He sums up each case which comes before him for judgment with a surly impartiality, applying to external events or acts two or three rigid rules, and then fixing on them the brand of his condemnation. The shrieks of their partisans he deems the most flattering tribute to the justice of his judgment. This method of writing history has, doubtless, its advantages; and, in regard to Mr. Hallam, it must be admitted that he has corrected many pernicious errors of fact, and overthrown many absurd estimates of character. But, valuable as his histories are in many important respects, they generally want grace, lightness, sympathy, picturesqueness, glow. From his deficiency of sensibility and imagination, and from his habit of bringing everything to the tribunal of the understanding, he rarely grasps character or incidents in the concrete. Both are interesting to him only as they illustrate certain practical or abstract principles. He looks at external acts without being able to discern inward motives. He cannot see things with the same eyes, and from the same position, as did the persons whom he judges; and, consequently, all those extenuations and explanations of conduct which are revealed in an insight into character are of little account with him. He does not realize a past age to his imagination, and will not come down from his pinnacle of judgment to mingle with its living realities. As he coldly dissects some statesman, warrior, or patriot, who at least had a living heart and brain, we are inclined to exclaim with Hamlet, "Has this fellow no feeling of his business?" It is the same in his literary criticisms. He gives the truth as it is *about* the author, not as it is *in* the author. He describes his genius in general terms, not in characteristic epithets. Everything that is peculiar to a particular writer slips through his analysis. That mysterious interpenetration of personality with feelings and powers which distinguishes one man's genius from another's escapes the processes of his understanding. Persons, in Mr. Hallam's hands, commonly subside into general ideas, events into generalizations. He does not appear to think that persons and events have any value in themselves, apart from the principles they illustrate; and, consequently, he conceives neither with sufficient intensity to bring out always the principles they really contain.

We have already said that this mode of writing history has its advantages, but it is still so over-informed with understanding as to sink representation in reflection. Now, the historian should address the eye and heart, as well as the understanding, to enable the reader really to understand his work. Mr. Prescott possesses the qualities by which this object is attained, and he possesses them in fine harmony with the qualities of his understanding. He has a quick sensibility, and a high degree of historical imagination — an imagination which, though it cannot create character and events which never existed, can still conceive facts in the concrete, and represent them instinct with their peculiar life. In studying a past age, he is not content with appending to a rigid digest of facts certain appropriate reflections, but he brings the age up to his mind in its characteristic form, costume, and social condition. He, in a manner, sees and feels its peculiar life, and comprehends, with his heart, as well as his head, the influences which shaped character, and supplied motives and palliations of conduct. He distinguishes between crimes which result from wickedness of heart and crimes which result from accredited error, and discerns those intricate operations of the mind by which superstition hallows vices into virtues, and prejudice obliquely justifies inhumanity and persecution. By conceiving character, also, as a whole, his page is filled with men instead of monstrosities. He sees that the progress of opinion has stamped with reprobation many practices which were once commanded by conventional morality and perverted religion; and he discriminates between evil performed from a false idea of duty, and evil performed from selfish passion. At the same time, he understands all those unconscious hypocrisies of selfishness by which vice and error are gradually sanctified to the conscience and ennobled to the imagination. He comprehends, likewise, that apparent anomaly in human nature, the commission of great crimes by persons who are not destitute of elevated sentiment and disinterested action; and in the delineation of men whose lives present a strange medley of folly and wisdom, virtue and wickedness, he presents complete and consistent portraits, recognized at once as harmonizing with the principles of our common nature. History, as often written, is false in the impressions it conveys, from an absence of this vitality, vividness, and picturesqueness. We do not perceive the connection between past and present events; and do not meet the actors in them on the common ground of humanity. Mr. Prescott always recognizes one nature in the different personages of history, however strange may be the combination of its elements, however novel the circumstances among which it is placed.

Connected with this power of pictorial representation and imaginative insight, he possesses a large share of sensibility; and from the combination of these arises, in a great degree, the peculiar charm and interest of his histories. By the readiness with which he himself sympathizes with his incidents and characters, he awakens the sympathies of the reader, and bears him willingly along the stream of narrative. Take, for instance, the histories of the conquest of Mexico and Peru. Almost everything seems presented directly to the imagination, — the physical characteristics of the countries, the character and varying fortunes of the conquerors and their motley followers, the manners, customs, government, religion, of the conquered race. With exquisite artistical effect, our sympathies are made to gather round each in its turn, and to realize each in its peculiar form of life. Scenery, persons, and events, are thus fixed in the imagination in their proper relations, and together make up a comprehensive whole, the contemplation of which exercises almost every faculty and feeling of the mind. The same thing presented simply to the understanding, divested of its coloring and characterization, would certainly lose as much in instruction as attractiveness. Mr. Prescott understands what has made historical novels so much more readable than histories, and he has succeeded in making history as fascinating as romance. In accomplishing this, it was not necessary that he should introduce anything fictitious. The nearer his narrative approached the truth of the matter, the more complete would be the interest it would awaken. But he had the sagacity to perceive that a mere detail of events however remarkable, and a mere estimate of persons however eminent, did not constitute history until they had been informed again with their original life.

In performing this difficult task, Mr. Prescott has avoided another fault, scarcely less injurious than its opposite extreme; we mean the fault of producing confusion of objects by the intensity with which each is conceived and expressed. Michelet, a man of splendid talents and accomplishments, is an illustration of this brilliant defect. His histories are as intense as Childe

Harold or Manfred. He writes, as old John Dennis would say, in a perfect "fury and pride of soul." He conceives character and events with such vividness as to adopt the passions of the age he describes, blending them with his own life, and making their expression a matter of personal concern. He is whirled away by the spirits he has evoked. "Thierry," he once remarked, "called history narration; and M. Guizot, analysis. I have named it *resurrection*, and it will retain the name." This remark conveys a fair impression of his historical method. He wakes from the sleep of ages kings, statesmen, warriors, and priests, and they start up into convulsive life. Each individual object glares upon the reader with eyes of fire, distracting his attention from relations. The historian is not upon an eminence surveying the whole field, but amid the noise and dust of the *melée*. There are in his histories detached sentences of extraordinary depth, single impersonations of wonderful grandeur, but the calm and comprehensive judgment, unfolding events and characters in their true connection, is generally wanting. Much of his finest narrative is disfigured by bursts of declamation which would be deemed extravagant in a political meeting, with drizzles of mysticism which would puzzle a transcendentalist. He has whole chapters which display a strange combination of qualities, made up of Lord Byron, Jacob Behmen, and Mr. Jefferson Brick. Mr. Prescott, perhaps, has nothing in his histories equal to Michelet's delineations of Joan of Arc, Charles of Burgundy, Hannibal, or Cæsar. But if he is not so vivid and powerful in detached parts, he excels him in the unity and proportion of his whole matter, and the sustained life and interest of his narrative. The healthy combination and balance of powers in Mr. Prescott's mind are more valuable to him, as an accurate historian, than would be the impassioned imagination of Michelet, or the judicial understanding of Mr. Hallam.

The style of Mr. Prescott's works, as might be expected from his character, is manly, perspicuous, picturesque, lucid, equally removed from stateliness and levity, disdaining all tawdry ornaments and simulated energy, and combining clearness and simplicity with glow. In the composition of a long work, it is a delicate matter to fix upon a proper form. The style which would delight in an essay might grow intolerably tedious in a volume. When brilliancy or dignity, intensity or melody, become monotonous, they tire nearly as much as dulness or discord. The only safe style for a long history is one without peculiarities which call attention to itself, apart from what it conveys. It must be sufficiently elevated to be on a level with the matter, or its meagre simplicity and plainness would distract attention as much as luxuriant ornament, while it must vigorously resist all temptations to display for the mere sake of display. Mr. Prescott has been compared with Robertson in respect to style. The comparison holds as far as regards luminous arrangement of matter and clearness of narration; but, with the exception, perhaps, of passages in "America," not in the graces of expression. The manner of Robertson is a fair representation of his patient, passionless, elegant mind. Its simplicity is often too prim, its elegance too nice. The smooth-rubbed mind of the Scotchman risks nothing; is fearful of natural graces, fearful of English verbal criticism, fearful of violating the dignity of history. His diction loses sweetness and raciness in its effort after correctness, and, as a general thing, is colorless, characterless, without glow or pictorial effect. The water is clear, and mirrors facts in beautiful distinctness, but it neither sparkles nor flows. His diction, however, has the rare quality of never being tedious, and fixes the pleased attention of the reader when the labored splendor of Gibbon would fatigue from its monotony. Mr. Prescott has the characteristic merits of Robertson, with other merits superadded. His style is flowing, plastic, all alive with the life of his mind. It varies with the objects it describes, and is cautious or vehement, concise or luxuriant, plain or pictorial, as the occasion demands. It glides from object to object with unforced ease, passing from discussion to description, from the council-chamber to the battle-field, without any preliminary flourishes, without any break in that unity which declares it the natural action of one mind readily accommodating itself to events as they rise. Such a style is to be judged not from the sparkle or splendor of separate sentences or paragraphs, but from its effect as a whole. A person can only appreciate it by following its windings through a long work. Of course, we speak of Mr. Prescott's style, in this connection, in its general character, after his powers of composition had been well trained by exercise. The diction of the earlier chapters of "Ferdinand and Isabella" displays an effort after elegance, and an occasional timidity of movement, natural to a man who had not learned to dare, and mistook elegant composition for a living style. He soon worked himself free from such shackles, and left off writing sentences. With the exceptions we have mentioned, there is no fine writing — no writing for the sake of words instead of things — in Mr. Prescott's works. His mind is too large and healthy for such vanities. Perhaps the perfection of his style, in its flowing movement, is seen in The Conquest of Peru. There are passages in that which seem to have run out of his mind, clear as rills of rock water. They are like beautiful improvisations, where passions and objects so fill the mind that the words in which they are expressed are at once perfect and unpremeditated.

We have thus attempted to pass beneath the surface of Mr. Prescott's works, to show out of what combination of elements, moral and intellectual, they have taken their present form. It is only in this way that we can estimate the amount of industry, candor, intellect, and command of expression, he brought to bear upon his difficult labors. The analysis would have been easier had his mind presented more positive points, or his works displayed more stubborn individual traits. The different powers of his mind so interpenetrate each other, that the critic is puzzled to hit the right point which exhibits their relative size and strength. It is needless to say that intellects like that of Mr. Prescott are often underrated, from the very harmony of their proportions. It is only by going carefully over their processes that we appreciate their results.

Mr. Prescott's first work was the History of the Reign of Ferdinand and Isabella. It was the labor of ten years, and of ten years well spent. He was as fortunate in the selection of his subject as in its treatment. It was in this reign that the Spanish monarchy may be said to have been organized, and the Spanish character permanently formed. Yet, either from the paucity of materials, or from an under-estimate of its importance, European writers left to an American the honor of first writing a classic history of the period. Two inconsiderable compilations, one in French by Mignot, the other in German by Becker, were the only records of an attempt to grapple with the subject as a whole. At the time Mr. Prescott selected it, the materials for its proper treatment were more numerous and available than at any preceding period. The researches of Llorente, Marina, Sempere, Capmany, Conde, Navarette, and Clemencin, had cleared up the darkness which previously enveloped some of the most important and interesting features of the subject. Through friends abroad and at home, he was able to collect almost everything, both in a printed and MS. form, which could illustrate the period, comprehending chronicles, memoirs, private correspondence, legal codes, and official documents. Then occurred an untoward circumstance, which cannot be better related than in his own words: —

"Soon after my arrangements were made, early in 1826, for obtaining the necessary materials from Madrid, I was deprived of the use of my eyes for all purposes of reading and writing, and had no prospect of again recovering it. This was a serious obstacle to the prosecution of a work, requiring the perusal of a large mass of authorities in various languages, the contents of which were to be carefully collated and transferred to my own pages, verified by minute reference. Thus shut out from one sense, I was driven to rely exclusively on another, and to make the ear do the work of the eye. With the assistance of a reader, uninitiated, it may be added, in any modern language but his own, I worked my way through several venerable Castilian quartos, until I was satisfied of the practicability of the undertaking. I next procured the services of one more competent to aid me in pursuing my historical inquiries. The process was slow and irksome enough, doubtless, to both parties, at least till my ear was accommodated to foreign sounds, and an antiquated, oftentimes barbarous phraseology, when my progress was more sensible, and I was cheered with the prospect of success. It certainly would have been a far more serious misfortune to be led thus blindfold through the pleasant paths of literature; but my track stretched for the most part across dreary wastes, where no beauty lurked to arrest the traveller's eye and charm his senses. After persevering in this course for some years, my eyes, by the blessing of Providence, recovered sufficient strength to allow me to use them with tolerable freedom in the prosecution of my labors, and in the revision of all previously written."

The range of Mr. Prescott's subject was extensive, and its different portions had to be taken up in their order, and their relative importance and influence rigidly preserved. In a long and labored Introduction, embodying a large amount of thought and research, he gives a view of the Castilian monarchy before the fifteenth century, and a review of the constitution of Aragon to the middle of the same period. This comprehends a luminous survey of all those manners, customs, and institutions, which represent national life and character; and it places the readers at once among the people of Spain as they were in the fifteenth century. His history, then, naturally divides itself into two parts; the period when the different kingdoms of Spain were first united under one monarchy, and a thorough reform introduced into their internal administration, and the period when, the interior organization of the monarchy having been completed, the nation entered on its schemes of discovery and conquest. The first part illustrates the domestic policy of Ferdinand and Isabella, and the second their foreign policy. Both are filled with great events and striking personages. In the first we have a detail of those measures by which two kingdoms, distracted by civil feuds or foreign wars, and seemingly without even the elements of national greatness and power, were united, reformed, and enabled to act with such effect abroad as eventually to threaten the liberties of Europe. This part covers all those events in Castile and Aragon which preceded the marriage of Isabella with Ferdinand; the war with Portugal which followed; the measures by which the overgrown privileges and possessions of the nobles were reduced, the laws rigidly enforced, and the powers and revenues of the crown increased; the establishment of the modern Inquisition; the war of Granada, and the addition of that kingdom to the Castilian possessions, after a desperate struggle of ten years; the application of Columbus to the Spanish court, and his first and second voyages; the expulsion of the Jews; and a general view of Castilian literature.

The second part, which is about half of the whole work, opens with a masterly view of the affairs of Europe at the close of the fifteenth century, and the first invasion of Italy by Charles VIII. of France. This we think unexcelled for that clearness of statement by which the most complex relations of states are rendered intelligible to the least informed reader. The narrative of the Italian wars then follows, and the steps are minutely traced by which the policy of Ferdinand, and the valor and ability of Gonsalvo de Cordova, eventually succeeded in expelling the French from Naples, and adding that kingdom to Spain. The rise of Cardinal Ximenes, his ecclesiastical reforms, the terrible zeal with which he persecuted the conquered Moors of Granada into insurrection, and the wonderful conversions he effected by the logic of fire and sword; the third and fourth voyages of Columbus, and the general character of the colonial policy of Spain; the death of Isabella; the dissensions of Ferdinand with Philip, his son-in-law, with regard to the regency of Castile; the reign and death of Philip, and regency of Ferdinand; the conquests of Ximenes in Africa, and his foundation of the University of Alcala; the wars and politics of Italy, arising from the League of Cambray; the conquest of Navarre, by which the only remaining independent kingdom in Spain was blended with the Spanish monarchy; the death of Ferdinand and the administration of Ximenes; and a general review of the administration of Ferdinand and Isabella, — are the leading subjects of the second portion of Mr. Prescott's history.

Great events generally arise from the conjunction of powerful natures and fitting opportunities. We call a man great when he has the sagacity to perceive these opportunities, and the will to execute what they teach. Individual character never appears in such strength as when it works in harmony with the spirit of the age. It is strong not only in its own strength, but in the accumulated energies of vast masses of men. There is a mysterious power urging it on, which, for want of a more accurate name, we call the general tendency of the time. No human mind can possibly grasp all the elements which enter into the spirit of an age; for this spirit is but one expression of the general life of humanity, one step in its progress or retrogression, and holds inscrutable relations to everything which has preceded it. To give a perfect philosophy of an age, would be to understand the philosophy of God's providence, and to know the history of the future as well as the past. The nearest approximation to correctness in history is where circumstances and men are properly connected in respect to the production of events. It will not do to refer events wholly to individual character, or to the spirit of the age. In the one case, the man is isolated from humanity; in the other, a tendency is confounded with an act. Thousands of men have opportunities and inspirations to perform great things, but men of genius are none the less rare. The Almighty seems to endow some persons with the power to anticipate the progress of events, and to produce at once what the operation of a general tendency upon a generation of men would postpone for years. A historian, therefore, fairly to describe an age, must have the powers of characterization and generalization so related as to operate harmoniously.

The general tendency of the age which forms the subject of Mr. Prescott's history was, in the domestic affairs of European nations, to a concentration of power; and, in their external relations, to combinations for conquest or defence, and contests for preëminence. The sovereigns under which this revolution in the domestic and foreign system of the European states was accomplished were admirably suited to their task. By the union of Castile and Aragon under Ferdinand and Isabella, the subsequent conquests of Granada, Navarre, and Naples, the acquisition of a new world in America, and the marriage of the heiress of the Spanish dominions with the son of the Emperor Maximilian, Spain, under the house of Austria, became the most important power in Europe, and long threatened its liberties. Robertson, in his History of the Emperor Charles the Fifth, has taken up the history at about the period where Mr. Prescott's ends, and exhibited the Spanish-Austrian power in its most colossal form. Our countryman has traced it from its commencement, and developed the causes of its growth. To understand Robertson, such a history was wanted; and certainly its subject would not yield in interest to that of the reign of Charles the Fifth. As the period which Mr. Prescott selected was that in which the modern system of Europe may be said to have taken its rise, and was in an especial degree encumbered with falsehood and sophistry, it was a subject which seemed at once to tempt the historian by its importance and repel him by its difficulties.

The History of Ferdinand and Isabella shows that Mr. Prescott thoroughly comprehended the revolution to which we have referred; and his exposition of it is admirable. His work accurately reflects the spirit of the age and the character of its prominent actors; and we have been especially struck with his felicity in developing character, not in an isolated analysis of qualities, but in the narration of the events which called them forth. He so blends character with events that their mutual relation is distinctly seen. The reader instinctively connects persons with actions,—what they are with what they perform; and, in doing this, he has not merely an idea of their external conduct, but a clear insight into their inward aims and motives. Thus to diffuse the results of analysis through the very veins of narration, and picture forth character to the imagination, is a fine triumph of art. That mechanical delineation of character, which consists in summing up a man's various qualities at the end of a narration of his objects and actions, Mr. Prescott also possesses; but in him it seems like a repetition of what he has continually suggested throughout his whole narrative. In his accounts of events we are able to estimate better the degree of power in the actors, by his exhibiting the actors as following or resisting current tendencies.

Among the wide variety of persons and events to which

Mr. Prescott's first history relates, five characters stand prominently forth: — Isabella, Ferdinand, Columbus, Gonsalvo de Cordova, and Ximenes. The character of Isabella Mr. Prescott has skilfully developed, through all her various relations, as queen, wife, and mother. It seems to us that her moral qualities were fully equalled by her intellectual, and that she excelled Ferdinand in both. Indeed, the important events of the reign are all traceable, in a greater or less degree, to her. She obtained the crown of Castile as much by her virtue, prudence, and sagacity, as her right. Her intellect, as well as her affection, was shown in her selection of Ferdinand as her husband. It was she who made force yield to law in Castile, and the reforms in its administration refer to her as their source. The conquest of Granada might not have been achieved, had it not been for her providence, forecast, and determination. At the time almost every one despaired, it was her indomitable resolution that infused new life into the army. It was she who appreciated and aided Columbus, when the sharp, wily intellect of Ferdinand was blind to the grandeur and practicability of his plan; and to her it was owing that the new world was added to the dominions of Spain. Against the advice and entreaty of Ferdinand, she raised Ximenes to the see of Toledo, and provided a fitting station for the development of his vast energies. Her sagacity detected the military genius of Gonsalvo de Cordova, when he was acting in a subordinate capacity in the war of Granada, and to her it was owing that he had the command of the army in the Italian wars. It is conceded that her influence was paramount in the domestic policy of the kingdom, in all those measures which gave it power to act with vigor abroad; but it appears to us that, in her selections of Columbus and Gonsalvo, she was also the spring of the foreign acquisitions of Spain. Ferdinand, with all his capacity as a warrior and statesman, and with all that unscrupulousness which gave him a command of the whole resources of perfidy and craft, was too selfish ever to be wisely and greatly politic. He did the dirty work of government and conquest with inimitable ability and appearance of cleanliness. His dark and cunning mind fairly circumvented every crowned and triple-crowned contemporary plotter. But he had not sufficient elevation of character to comprehend a great nature. The great navigator, the great captain, the great priest, whose genius the genius of Isabella instinctively recognized, were all treated by him with suspicion and ingratitude. The faults of Isabella were faults engrafted on her nature by superstition; and the persecutions she allowed or countenanced arose from a mistaken sense of religious duty, stimulated by a bigoted confessor. Ferdinand had no more religion than Machiavelli, and was a persecutor from policy or interest. The greatest satire on the Catholicism of the period is contained in his title of Ferdinand the Catholic. We are aware of no female sovereign with whom Isabella can be compared in the union of energy and intelligence with grace, sweetness, and humane feeling. Mr. Prescott has instituted an ingenious parallel between her and Elizabeth of England, in which he happily traces their points of resemblance and contrast. The Castilian queen differed from the great English virago in being a woman in reality as well as name.

In all of Mr. Prescott's histories he has to do with Spanish character, and this he has profoundly studied both in itself and as it was gradually moulded by religious and political institutions. He has considered the Spaniard in his character as crusader and oppressor, and skilfully developed the connection of his religion with his rapacity. Spain was especially calculated to be the Catholic country of Europe; for there Catholicism was associated with the national existence and glory, and with the gratification of every selfish passion. For seven or eight hundred years previous to the reign of Ferdinand and Isabella, Spain had been the theatre of a fierce "holy" war between Christian and Mussulman, for the possession of the country. Under the banner of the cross the infidel had been gradually beaten back from position to position, until his power was confined within the kingdom of Granada. All the passions which Christianity rebukes, all the passions which war stimulates, Catholicism sanctified. There was a fatal divorce between religion and morality. Lust, avarice, cruelty, murder, all raged under a religious garb. Every devout Christian might practise any enormity upon the heretic or infidel; and devout Christians might plunder each other, if the church sanctioned the robbery. The mischievousness of the system was, that the imagination and religious sentiments of the people were affected, as well as their bad passions, and strong faith sided with devilish lusts. It is doubtful whether the Spaniard could have endured the privations which accompanied his conquests in America, unless he had been sustained by some religious fanaticism: yet his zeal did not stay his hand from pillage and massacre. His bigotry was strong enough to deceive his humanity, and endowed the wolf with the heroism of the missionary.

In the History of Ferdinand and Isabella we perceive

the religion of Spain, France, and Italy, in connection with public affairs, and are able to estimate the degree of moral control it exercised over the action of states. In the Histories of the Conquest of Mexico and Peru we see it more directly in its influence upon individuals, taken from various classes of society, and pretty well representing their age. No reader who profoundly studies both aspects of this phenomenon can fail to acknowledge the wonderful flexibility and power of adaptation of Catholicism. He will see clearly reflected, in Mr. Prescott's page, the ductility with which it adapted itself to the natural disposition of its believers, binding equally saints and sinners to its communion, and strong with the strength of the worst and best men of the time. The policy of Spain, during the reign of Ferdinand and Isabella, was to have all its enterprises stamped with a religious character. Its relations with the Pope are among the most curious points in its history. It is hardly a paradox to say that Spain would have seceded from the church, had its interests or passions been crossed instead of aided by the Papacy. Ferdinand's dealings with the Pope are exceedingly characteristic. When the latter interfered with the internal affairs of his kingdom, or opposed him abroad, he had no scruples in covering him with public disgrace, or in making war upon him. He found the Pope a very convenient person to use, but he took care not to be used by him.

The second work of Mr. Prescott, the History of the Conquest of Mexico, appeared in six years after the publication of his first. The materials for this were such as no other historian had ever enjoyed. From Madrid alone he obtained unpublished documents, consisting of military and private journals, contemporary chronicles, legal instruments, correspondence of the actors in the conquest, etc., amounting to eight thousand folio pages. From Mexico he gleaned numerous valuable MSS., which had escaped the diligence of Spanish collectors. These, with what he derived from a variety of other sources, including the archives of the family of Cortés, placed in his possession a mass of materials sufficient to give a basis of undoubted facts to his wonderful narrative, and subdue the scepticism of the modern reader by the very accumulation of testimony. It is needless to add that he also obtained everything in a printed form which had reference to his subject. The result of all his labors, of research, thought and composition, was a history possessing the unity, variety, and interest, of a magnificent poem. It deals with a series of facts, and exhibits a gallery of characters, which, to have invented, would place its creator by the side of Homer; and which to realize and represent, in the mode Mr. Prescott has done, required a rare degree of historical imagination. It may be that the imperfection of the historian's eyes was one cause of his success. He was compelled to develop his memory to the full extent of its capacity; but memory depends, to a considerable degree, upon understanding, sensibility, and imagination. To recollect facts, they must be digested, methodized and realized. The judgment must place them in their natural order; the heart must fasten its sympathies to them; the imagination must see them as pictures. They are then a possession forever. To the inward vision of the mind they are as much living realities as though they were present to the outward eye.

In our limited space we cannot give anything which would approach to an account of this work. In its general plan and composition, it illustrates what we have previously said of Mr. Prescott's processes as a historian. We had marked our copy on every page, intending to notice numerous passages for comment or quotation; and certainly the work is full enough of strange facts and wonderful adventures to awaken new views of the powers and perversions of human nature. Mr. Prescott first introduces the reader to the people and country of Mexico, and gives a luminous view of the ancient Mexican civilization. In the space of two hundred pages he comprehends a survey of the races inhabiting the country, and brings before us their character, history, government, religion, science, arts, domestic manners, everything, in short, necessary to a comprehension of their intellectual, moral, and political condition, at the period Cortés commenced his enterprise. This introduction is mostly confined to the Aztecs, as they were the fiercest, most sanguinary, most intelligent, and most powerful, of the Mexican races; and as it was against their empire that the efforts of the conquerors were principally directed. Then follows the story of the conquest, with all its remarkable features of heroism and cruelty. Cortés is, of course, the central figure of the group, — the soul, and almost the body, of the enterprise; and around him are gathered some of the bravest warriors that romance ever imagined, encountering dangers and surviving miseries which, in a romance, would be pronounced impossible. The picture presents the meeting of two civilizations, brought in a rude shock against each other, and the triumph of the race which was superior in craft and science. In the followers of Cortés we have what we would now call a gang of thieves, pirates, ravishers, and assassins, yet displaying in their worst excesses the courage and endurance of heroes, and sustained in their worst calamities by what they were pleased to call their religion. The pagan Aztec gave the first place in his bloody pantheon to his terrible war-god, and with a cannibal appetite devoured the body of his captive. We have some consolation for this in knowing the Aztec was a heathen, and his god a chimera. But the deity the Spanish Catholic worshipped, and to whom he prayed for aid in his schemes of avarice, lust, and murder, was also of Mexican origin, however much he may have deceived himself into the belief he was addressing the Christian's God. Moloch, Mammon, and Belial, were the inspiration of his schemes of conquest and deeds of massacre.

The great checks upon rapacity are conscience and natural humanity. It is one of the objects of true religion to strengthen and increase these natural obstacles to crime. When, however, bigotry sides with rapacity against human feeling, and breaks, instead of tightening, the bond of brotherhood, it produces those monstrosities of action so difficult to reconcile with the common principles of human nature. We can conceive of men as becoming demons, but the difficulty is to conceive of them as performing demoniacal acts from motives partly religious, and preserving any humanities in their character after the performance. Yet this we are compelled continually to do, in following the Spaniards in their American conquests. It is one of the charms of Mr. Prescott's history, that his worst characters are so fully developed that we perceive their humanity as well as their rascality. They never appear as bundles of evil qualities, but as men.

Mr. Prescott places his readers in a position to understand the moral condition of his personages, as that condition was influenced by the current practices of their age, and by their individual lives. Crimes, in their effect upon character, change their nature as the conventional standard of morals varies. To commit any delinquency whatever exercises a pernicious effect upon character; but its effect is not so pernicious, when it is hailed as the sign of the hero, as when it is hooted at as the brand of the felon. In the one case a man may discharge many of the social and public duties of life, and preserve that degree of morality and religion conveyed in the phrase of "a respectable citizen;" in the other case, he sinks into the common herd of profligates and criminals, and makes war upon respectable citizens. In one sense, shedding blood in battle is murder; yet there is still a great difference in the moral character of General Scott and Jonathan Wild. No well-minded person can now follow the career of Cortés without an expression of horror and indignation; yet the countrymen of Cortés applauded his exploits, as our countrymen applaud those of the victor of Monterey and Buena Vista.

There is another very important fact to be considered in our estimate of the Spaniards. The Pope, in whom was lodged the power to dispose of the kingdoms of the heathen, had given the new world to Spain, to be conquered and converted. Cortés, as a devout Catholic, had no scruples about the right of conquest. Mexico was clearly his, or his sovereign's, provided he could get it. Now, assuming the right of conquest, all the crimes in which he was directly implicated might be extenuated by the right of self-defence. The truth is, he had no right to Mexico at all; and the chief crime he committed was in its invasion: but the head of Christendom had decided for him that this was not a crime, but a right. Many good Catholics might have been, and doubtless were, shocked at the barbarities which accompanied the conquest: but Cortés might have replied that what he did was necessary to obtain his rightful objects; that the question simply was, whether he and his followers should be sacrificed to the Mexican gods, or a certain number of Aztecs should be massacred. We know that his cruelties sprang from no disregard of his religion, such as it was. For that religion he was ready to die at any moment; for that religion he repeatedly risked the success of his enterprise; and it required all the address of Father Almedo to prevent his zeal for the conversion of the natives and the overthrow of their gods from involving himself and his cause in a common ruin.

Cortés was in all respects a remarkable man, whether we consider the strength or the versatility of his genius. He attempted an enterprise as daring as ever entered the head of a maniac, and brought it to a successful result by the resources of his own mind. He was at once the most enthusiastic and most prudent of men, — a heart all fire, and a head all ice. His intellect was large, flexible, capacious of great plans, inexhaustible in expedients, and preserving, in the fiercest inward excitement of his passions, a wonderful coolness, clearness, and readiness. He seems to have been naturally a man of quick sensibility, rather than of deep feeling, — a cavalier elegant in person, lax in morals, with much versatility but little concentration of power, and chiefly distinguished for qualities which captivate, rather than command. It was not until his mind had been possessed by one dominant idea that the latent powers of his nature were displayed. This idea he held with the grasp of a giant, and it tamed his volatile passions, and concentrated his flashing powers, and put iron into his will. Everything, including life itself, was to him of little importance, compared with the conquest of Mexico. In his darkest hours of defeat and despondency, when hope appeared to all others but the insanity of folly, he never gave up his project, but renewed his attempts to perform the "impossible" with the coolness of one setting about a commonplace enterprise. It is needless to say that this idea made him unscrupulous, and silenced all objections ,to the commission of convenient crime. He was not cruel by nature; that is, he took no pleasure in viewing or inflicting pain: but his mind was remorseless. Like other conquerors, he never allowed his feelings to interfere with his plans, and carelessly sacrificed friends and foes to the success of a project. His hand executed at once what his mind conceived, not so much because he excelled other men in vigor, but because he was not deterred from action by any scruples. Remorselessness is almost ever the key to that vigor which is so much praised in great warriors and statesmen. If human nature consisted simply of intellect and will, the world would be full of vigorous characters; but the vigor would be demoniacal. To a cruel man the bloodshed which attended the conquest of Mexico would have been pleasant of itself; to Cortés, who was its cause, it was a mere means to an end. The desolation of a province and the butchery of its inhabitants were merely processes of working out a practical problem. The remorselessness of thought produces more suffering than the cruelty of passion. The latter may be glutted with a few victims at a time; the former may scatter firebrands arrows, and death, over an empire. Cortés, in this respect, was not worse than a hundred others whose "vigor" is the admiration of the world, and the inspiration of the devil.

No general ever excelled Cortés in the command he exercised over the minds and hearts of his followers. He knew them better than they knew themselves, and his ready eloquence reached the very sources of their volitions. He was at once their commander and companion. He could bring them round to his plans against the evidence of their five senses, and make them dance in the very chains of famine and fatigue. The enterprise would have been repeatedly abandoned, had it not been for his coolness, intrepidity, and honeyed eloquence. His whole lawless and licentious crew he held by a fascination for which they could not themselves account. They suspected him of making their lives and fortunes subsidiary to his ambition; they taxed him with deceit and treachery; they determined again and again to leave him; and yet they followed him — followed him, against their desires and reason, to encounter the most appalling dangers, for an object which receded as they advanced, and which they constantly pronounced a chimera. The speeches of Cortés, given by Mr. Prescott, are master-pieces of practical eloquence. Indeed, wherever Cortés was, there could be but one will; and what authority was unable to do, he did by finesse and persuasion.

Cortés was brave in almost every sense of the term. He combined the courage of the knight-errant and the martyr. His daring in battle, perhaps, was not greater than that exhibited by some of his officers, — Alvarado, for example; but he excelled all in the power of endurance. His constancy of purpose had the obstinacy of sheer stupidity, and seems almost incompatible with his fiery valor. Famine, fatigue, pestilence, defeat, every extreme of mental and physical wretchedness, could present no arguments sufficiently strong to shake his purpose of conquest. What depressed his followers only called forth his courage in its most splendid light. When he himself had most cause for despondency, his serene valor not only mounted above his own miseries, but enabled him to use all the resources of his fertile mind in cheering his followers. Wounded, bleeding, wasted by famine, broken down by disease and despair, there was always one voice whose magical tones could make their hearts leap with their old daring, and send them again on their old enterprise of peril and death.

We cannot follow the genius of Cortés as it was developed in the events of the conquest, and attempt an abstract of what Mr. Prescott has performed with such fulness, richness, and power. Rarely has so splendid a theme been treated by a historian so fortunate at once in the possession of requisite materials and requisite capacity. Among the many characteristics of the work, that which will be most likely to strike and charm the general reader is its picturesqueness of description, both as regards incidents and scenery. The freshness and vividness with which everything is presented is a continual stimulant to attention; and there is a nerve in the movement of the style which gives to the narrative a continual vitality. Among these descriptions we would particularize the account of the retreat from Mexico, in the second volume, and the battles which preceded its final conquest and destruction, in the third, as being especially pervaded by intense life. The critical reader, also, will not fail to perceive that the interest of particular passages is subservient to the general effect of the whole, and that the author has produced a work of art as well as a history. That quality of objectiveness, which we have mentioned as characterizing the mind of Mr. Prescott, and favorably distinguishing him from many eminent historians, is especially obvious when we contrast the representations in "Ferdinand and Isabella" with those in the "Conquest of Mexico." The objects are different, and in each case they are presented in their own form, life, and character. We can conceive of the two histories as the production of separate minds. But few historians are thus capable of representing objects in white light. To see anything through the medium of another mind, is too often to see it caricatured. Objects, to the egotist, whether he be called thinker or coxcomb, are commonly mirrors which more or less reflect himself. Nature, events, and persons, are considered as deriving their chief importance from their relation to him. This relation, and not their relation to each other, he is prone to call the philosophy of history.

PRESCOTT'S CONQUEST OF PERU.*

THIS work has probably been the most extensively popular of Mr. Prescott's histories, though the subject would not seem to admit so many elements of interest as the others. In "Ferdinand and Isabella" he had a period of time crowded with important events and striking characters, a period which witnessed the organization of a powerful nation out of seemingly discordant elements, and which opened to the historian the whole field of European politics during one of the most important epochs of modern civilization. In the "Conquest of Mexico" he had an epic story, capable of the strictest artistic treatment, with that strangeness in incidents and scenery which fastens most readily on the attention. If he has made the present work more interesting than the others, it must be owing to greater felicity in its treatment. This felicity does not arise from a departure from his historical method, or from the adoption of a new form of composition, but is the result of a more complete development of his method and his style. In the "Conquest of Peru" his characteristic merits are displayed in their best aspect, exhibiting the effects of time and experience in giving more intensity to his conceptions, and

* History of the Conquest of Peru, with a Preliminary View of the Civilization of the Incas. By William H. Prescott. 8vo. 2 vols. New York: Harper & Brothers. —*Methodist Quarterly Review, April,* 1848.

more certainty to his language. Accordingly, we have not here to chronicle a decay of power, but its freer and more vigorous expression.

Mr. Prescott's leading excellence is that healthy objectiveness of mind which enables him to represent persons and events in their just relations. Of all his histories, we think that the present, while it illustrates this characteristic merit, approaches nearest to the truth of things, and presents them with the most clearness and vividness. The scenery, characters, incidents, with which his history deals, are all conceived with singular intensity, and appear on his page instinct with their peculiar life. The book, on this very account, has been charged in some quarters with exaggeration, with giving more importance to the subject than its relative position in history will warrant. This objection we consider as implying its greatest praise. We admit that the Conquest of Peru does not take that place in the history of the world, as commonly written, which it assumes in Mr. Prescott's narrative; but we think that history, as commonly written, conveys but a feeble notion of persons and events. Undoubtedly the wars between Charles V. and Francis I. were more important than the skirmishes of the Spaniards with the Peruvians: but we by no means acknowledge that this is indicated in Robertson; and we think it a strange blunder of criticism to demand that the historian shall place his work in relation to other histories, instead of making it a mirror of his subject; and, because the usual description of the battle of Pavia conveys no idea of an engagement, require that the account of the capture of Atahualpa shall convey no idea of a massacre. The truth is, Mr. Prescott has done, in this matter, all that criticism can sensibly desire, in observing the natural relations of the characters and events with which he deals, and in varying the intensity of his representation with the varying importance of the different parts of his History. If he had capriciously given prominence to some things which would naturally fall in the background, or exaggerated others out of their proper connections, his work would have been inconsistent with the truth, and justly amenable to criticism; but, instead of this, he has reproduced, with vivid accuracy, the whole course of the conquest, solicitous only to convey clear impressions of actual things, and to print them on the mind in their true character and vital relations. If in doing this he has shown more force of conception and felicity of narration than the class of dignified historians; if he has avoided all verbal forms and barren generalities in the surrender of his mind to the objects which impressed it; if, in short, he has been more desirous to exhibit his subject than to make a show of himself, we protest against his being judged by rules which he does not pretend to follow, and having his excellence tested by principles drawn from the defects of other historians.

Indeed, the great merit of the work consists in its representing a portion of universal history as a living, appreciable reality. The comparative narrowness of the subject, and fewness of the characters, enabled him to perform this with the greater completeness. There was less room for generalization, and more for individualization; more space for pictures, and less for propositions. Accordingly, everything is realized; everything stands out in its distinct shape and dimensions, and moves on with the general movement of the narration. We become acquainted, not only with the leaders, but with their individual followers; discerning their motives, the complex action of their passions, the strange jumble of ferocity, valor, superstition, and diabolism, which went to make up their characters. It must be confessed, we are placed in the company of a herd of graceless rascals, who, with all their valorous vice and heroic baseness, richly deserve the gallows; but we are still not among demons or monstrosities, but among bad men. It is human nature, we perceive, though human nature in a form so perverted as to make us almost ashamed of it. An insight so vivid into the character of the soldiers of Pizarro and Almagro, and of the conventional morality of the age, gives us a knowledge of the period which we can easily apply to persons of more historical importance, and events of greater magnitude. In Peru we have, as it were, a microcosm, wherein we can see Catholic Europe as it was at the commencement of the sixteenth century; the little world is a fair diminutive of the great world, and more comprehensible from its compression. Its study enables us to understand somewhat the nature of that moral confusion which springs from a violation of eternal laws; from the skirmishes of Pizarro we can infer the character of those awful wars which we read of in history with so even a pulse; and from the cruelty and rapacity of the Spaniards we see how thin is often the partition which separates the regular soldier from the proficient in rapine, massacre, and lust. We believe, if history were written throughout with this truth to things, that, in increasing our knowledge, it would improve our moral judgments. The reason that the gigantic vices of the powerful do not commonly draw down upon their heads a corresponding load of infamy, is owing to the feebleness with which those vices are commonly conceived. We are sensible of the energies such men display, and glow in the recital of their exploits; but we overlook the guilt and baseness of the means they often employ. In order that a historian should rightly affect us in this matter, it is not necessary that he should set certain commonplaces at stated distances in his narrative, declaring how naughty it is for men to cut each other's throats and blow out each other's brains; but it is important that, in representing a battle, he should make us realize the sufferings it occasions, and the demoniacal passions it unleashes. This cannot be done by expressing the dead and wounded in a row of figures. We have read accounts of Austerlitz and Leipsic which inspired us with less sympathy than the account given by Mr. Prescott of some contest where hardly a hundred were killed. In the "Conquest of Peru" we gain some notion of the fathomless baseness of brazen selfishness and rapacity, and no great energies developed by the conquerors can possibly lift it into respect. If the contemplation urges us to fix a darker and more indelible brand of reprobation on the impudent enormities of all public criminals, of all robbers and murderers on a great scale, there will be some check given to that absurd apotheosis of colossal depravity, that idolatry of great men who have warred against the interest of the race, which now fills the temple of fame with Titans from the shambles, and inspires emulation instead of horror among the energetic spirits of every age.

It seems to us that Mr. Prescott thus produces morality of effect by truth of representation. This is as much better than moralizing, as the perfume which escapes from a rose is better than rose-water. If the historian has the heart and brain to grasp the truth, he may safely leave the rest to the reader's moral instincts. But this power of truthful representation is not a common quality. It implies the possession of a healthy mind, with large powers harmoniously balanced; it demands capacity as well as conscience, freedom from prejudice as well as freedom from fraud. It is not ever the prize of good intentions. It balks even the honest and intelligent, when force of conception is not accompanied by a corresponding felicity of style. In the case of Mr. Prescott that combination of powers, analytical, reflective, and representative, which constitutes his truthfulness, is expressed altogether in the unobtrusive form of narration and description. The distinguishing peculiarity of the present work is, that all the processes of the historian's mind are suppressed, and the results alone given. By this method he has added to the interest of the history, but deprived himself of all that reputation which half-bred minds confer upon the show of judgment and argumentation. His narrative reads as simply and clearly as if it had cost no labor of thought and investigation. Many of its delighted readers will be but little impressed with the force of the mind whence it proceeded, and pronounce it almost as easy to write as to peruse. It may not, therefore, be out of place to attempt here an analysis of the narrative process, and indicate the various powers it calls into action. Such a course may have some effect in checking the presumptuous underestimate which undeveloped geniuses ever put upon finished works, which have been so artistically organized as to seem artless.

If we form an idea of the materials from which Mr. Prescott's history was constructed, and place them in opposition to the work itself, we cannot fail to see a great space between the two, through which the historian's mind must have passed in successive steps. In contemporary histories, biographies, chronicles, state papers, etc., principally in a MS. form, he was compelled to search for his facts. In the examination of these, contradictory statements were to be reconciled — falsehood, error, prejudice, credulity, and all the many forms of misrepresentation, were to be detected — and order and connection were to be educed from the midst of confusion. The industry, the research, the analysis of character, the long trains of minute reasoning, the sagacity which instinctively rejects the smoothest and most plausible lie, — in short, all those intellectual powers which are exercised in a judicial scrutiny of evidence, and which, when exhibited to the reader, convey so high an opinion of a historian's mental capacity, — Mr. Prescott is content to banish from his page. After subjecting his authorities to this alembic process, and sifting out the truth they contained, the facts thus mastered were to be vividly realized in their original life, and placed in their right relations, so that the principles they embodied or illustrated could be distinctly apprehended by the reader, without being expressed to him in propositions. Here, also, was a long and delicate process, which Mr. Prescott suppresses, in which the historian, at once surveying the whole field of events, and understanding their individual import, sees both the intentions of the actors and the operations of general laws, brings effects into distinct connection with causes, and from the loose links of occurrences rivets the chain of events. After his facts had thus been connected so as to form an organic whole, after the history had taken its shape in his own mind, he had still the additional task of embodying it in a form of expression which would convey it to other minds exactly as it animated his own.

We do not suppose there can be any controversy as to his success in this last and most important process. It would be difficult to name a history which excels that of the Conquest of Peru in the art of making the forms and colors of things shine through the expression. The style is a running stream, which mirrors objects so fully and distinctly that we are hardly conscious of the medium through which they are seen. Such a diction impresses us only by what it conveys. On reading the book for the first time, we could easily recollect its events, and retained clear conceptions of its characters; but we should have been puzzled to answer a question regarding the structure of its style. We hardly noticed a paragraph in which words took the place of things, or in which anything was said merely for the sake of saying it well. Yet we found, on an after examination, sentences bending beneath the weight of matter, instances of terse, keen, tingling expression, of verbal felicities, of animated and picturesque description, and an absence of that baldness and poverty of language which usually characterizes what is called a simple style. The diction is neither stilted nor mean; it neither courts nor discards ornament; but moves on with a beautiful and dignified ease, yielding gracefully to the demands of different objects as they rise, and with all its genuine simplicity and fine abandonment to the things it describes, is still always the style of a historian, not of a story-teller. To preserve thus a certain inherent dignity of manner, without a sacrifice of sweetness, melody, raciness, and "polished want of polish," — to maintain constantly a distinction between the historian and the chronicler, the narrator and the gossip, — to glide so fearlessly along the dizzy edges of familiar narration without ever slipping into bathos or flippancy, — is a triumph which few have succeeded in achieving, and which Mr. Prescott himself has only fully reached in the "Conquest of Peru." In considering his remarkable felicity in narration, it is not singular that he has reduced to this shape a great deal of matter which might have been expressed in a different and more ambitious form.

In this incomplete analysis, we think we have indicated that good narration is not a single power, but a combination of many powers; that it not only implies sensibility, imagination, and command of language, but also often includes the results of the most toilsome drudgery of investigation, and the most stringent exercise of the understanding. In passing from the form to the subject of the present work, the first feeling of the reader is that of regret that so much power should be lavished on such a theme; and surely, if Mr. Prescott's narrative had ceased with the mere conquest of Peru, we should think the matter unworthy of his pen. We hardly can bring to mind another instance of such an audacious violation of all principle, moral and political, as the invasion and theft of Peru by the Spaniards. The enterprise was dignified by none of those high thoughts and great passions which often lend a kind of moral interest to actions which justice and humanity must still condemn. It was essentially a buccaneering expedition, whose naked object was plunder and murder, without any pretence of bigotry or superstition to modify its depravity; and it was conducted by a herd of vagabonds and profligates, who broke into a country as a band of burglars would break into a dwelling. The black flag of the pirate waves over the whole immortal gang whose courageous avarice subverted the empire of the Incas. Their fame is the fame of infamy. They would occupy no place in the memories of men, if their rascality had not sounded depths of wickedness beyond the common experience of men. But, considered as a piratical expedition, their enterprise was successful. They glutted their cruelty and rapacity to the full, committing more murders, producing more misery, and obtaining more money, than any other band of robbers that ever organized for plunder. They proved themselves master workmen in the ignoble art of ruining nations, and were eminently successful in sowing the seeds of ineradicable hatred against the whole Spanish race in the hearts of the people they oppressed. They were the enemies, not merely of the Peruvians, but of human society itself, — violators of order, of justice, of humanity, of every principle which binds communities together. If the historian had left the subject with the triumph of these valorous outcasts and reprobates, he might have had much to interest and instruct the reader, in exhibiting the meeting of two dissimilar races; in detailing wild and stirring deeds of adventure performed amid scenery the most striking and sublime; and in representing the worst passions of the human heart in unbridled exercise, restrained neither by humanity as a sentiment, nor by humanity as a policy, as they swept in a storm of fire and blood over the doomed empire of Peru. But such a limitation of the subject, rich though it would be in description and characterization, would leave a painful sense of moral confusion on the mind, and would lack historical and artistical completeness. Mr. Prescott has therefore done well in devoting but half of his work to the conquest, and in proceeding on to narrate the bloody feuds of the conquerors, and the final settlement of the country under Gasca. This extension of the subject, by which we see the fearful retribution which followed guilt, and the natural operation of those eternal laws which it violated, though it occasions a greater diversity of persons and events, really furnishes the requisite unity of the work. In this respect we do not know but the subject, as treated by Mr. Prescott, has more true historical unity than the Conquest of Mexico; for, though it has less unity of story, it has a wider variety of incidents and characters included under a stricter unity of law.

The History of the Conquest of Peru is introduced by a long and luminous dissertation on Peruvian civilization, which contains all the facts which are known regarding the institutions and modes of existence of the people. This presents a clear view of the national life of the Peruvians, comprehending their religion, government, science, letters, mechanical arts, and industrial energy. There is much in this dissertation to startle our imaginations and unsettle our theories. We are accustomed to consider governments as taking their character from the character of their people, — as being growths, not manufactures. Even in most despotisms the tyrant seems but the nation individualized. In this respect there is little difference between Austria and the United States, Turkey and France. In Peru, however, we have the spectacle of the most humane and perfect of despotisms, having its source in the government, and working down into the masses, moulding their character into new forms, and effecting a radical change in their nature. We perceive savages reduced to obedient and unquestioning subjects, under a theocracy which had as complete possession of their souls as of their persons. But the strangest mystery of all is, that the Inca despots appear to have regulated their acts by fundamental principles, and to have shown none of those insane caprices which are characteristic of absolute sovereigns. Adored as gods, and implicitly obeyed as governors, they still seem to have made the physical well-being of their people and the development of the resources of their empire the objects of their government, instead of gratifying their self-will at the expense of both. Property and money, beggary and idleness, were alike unknown in Peru. The state looked out that every person labored, and that every person was comfortable. It treated its subjects as a kind master treats his domestic animals. Their wills and understandings were not recognized as having an existence, in regard to matters of government; but they were not oppressed. The Incas seem to have been the wisest despots the world has seen, in forbearing to exercise capricious power, and in making the happiness of their people the policy of their administration. Into this land, thus governed, the Spaniards brought war, poverty, misery, pestilence, famine, and the thing they called their religion. Their object from the beginning was to wring from the wretched inhabitants all they possessed, and to doom them to a slavery which differed from a massacre only in its prolonged suffering. They had not even the wisdom of the pagan masters they supplanted; and, in the folly of their tyranny, dried up the very sources of wealth. Their policy was one of blunders as well as crimes. They might have considered the natives as oxen and horses, but their stupidity consisted in exterminating them by over labor. It is curious that in all the arts of government, which it is equally the interest of despots and democrats to practise, and in which the greatest power is reconciled with the greatest beneficence, the Incas were immeasurably superior to the Spaniards. It might be said that the conquest was the victory of a superior over an inferior race, and that the natural consequences were tyranny and rapacity. But we have not this poor excuse for Spanish Christianity and Spanish civilization; for, in the case of Peru, the conquerors ruined a country which had been subdued previously by the Incas, and in which the superior race had used their power to civilize the savages they conquered, and to improve their condition. In every light in which we can view the subject, we must be compelled to award the Incas wisdom and beneficence superior to the Spaniards, and to acknowledge they approached nearer to the idea of Christian civilization.

Foremost among the forcible characters with whom Mr. Prescott's history deals are Pizzaro and Gasca, the representative of rapine and the representative of law. Pizarro is one of those marked individuals, branded with the hot iron of universal reprobation, about whom there can be but little difference of opinion. He seems to have been sent into the world, or, at least, to have been sent into Peru, in order to render depravity despicable; and it is but justice to say that he appeared to feel the dignity of his great mission, and doggedly bent himself to its performance. He had in large measure all those qualities which awaken admiration for the world's butchers, — a clear head, a hard heart, force of will, constancy of purpose, daring, dauntless courage, complete surrender of his mind to one object, — but they were all developed in connection with such unutterable baseness, fraud, hypocrisy, and cruelty, that he seems the very genius of infamy impersonated. The mind instinctively spurns him as a cold, calculating, vulgar villain, without any generous enthusiasm, without any lofty purposes, performing the most enormous crimes from no mixed motives, and in his combination of great capacity with cruelty, treachery, and meanness, never appearing in a more noble shape than as a sort of monstrous compound, made up of Alva, Arnold, and Scapin. There is no danger that such a character will be attractive to the imagination, or that his ignoble depravity will win for him, out of the jail and the pirate-ship, any other sentiment than contempt or abhorrence. He had not even that honor which is said to obtain among thieves, and as a trickster and liar occupies a peculiar pinnacle of infamy among his comrades as well as adversaries. He felt within himself a superiority to all scruples of shame or conscience, and knew that he could outwit the worst and wickedest of his gang at their own weapons. Some portion of his courage and daring may have sprung from the inward conviction that he could be placed in no exigency from which he could not extricate himself by crime. He obtained an empire by being capable of an act of treachery beyond the conceptions of any of its inhabitants, and then attempted to cheat his accomplice out of his portion of the spoils by a refinement of perfidy of which that old ruffian had never dreamed. He was ever sounding new depths of baseness, and originating unheard-of schemes of rapine; and his companions and followers must have continually felt, with deep humility, how insignificant were their most strenuous efforts downward, compared with the giant leaps of the trickster Hercules at their head. During the whole narrative of his exploits and adventures, we anxiously look for some event in which his great energies will appear connected with some moderation in wickedness; but we are continually disappointed. When he marches with less than two hundred men right into the heart of an empire, we expect some new development of the science of war or diplomacy, some brilliant achievement of arms or policy. But it all ends in the old story of massacre and pillage, supported by the old plea of necessity and prudence. We continually feel that all he does would be infinitely clever in a buccaneer, a highwayman, or an incendiary, but it awakens none of the associations connected with a conqueror. Essentially a vulgar villain, he has incurred not merely the condemnation of the good for his depravities, but is visited with the secret hate of energetic wickedness everywhere, for so rudely tearing aside the decent drapery of sin, and depriving vice of all its dignity. He has made murder and robbery on a great scale an everlasting jeer to levity, and an everlasting stigma to benevolence.

With all this, it is doubtful if, in the quality of courage, a braver man than Pizarro ever lived. He did not know fear. Famine, fatigue, pestilence, had no convincing arguments for him. He feared neither nature, man, nor God, but pushed doggedly on in his course of practical atheism, breasting the elements, slaying his fellowmen, unconcerned about the future. His courage, therefore, great as it was, has its disgraceful side; through this, his highest quality, the insensibility and lowness of his character glare like an imp from the pit. Could we occasionally refer his crimes to weakness, impulse, or bigotry; could we sometimes see his force of will struggling with the phantoms of conscience, or the dread monitions of religion; if from that mass of bad passions festering at his heart any signs of a soul had ever flashed; if, in short, he had sometimes, for variety sake, performed a noble or refrained from a wicked action; we might modify a little the contemptuous horror with which we view his courageous baseness. But, as it is, he stands out there in history, naked and shivering under the pitiless pelting of a storm of execration, not as a warrior and conqueror, but as a trickster, traitor, liar, thief, incendiary, murderer; — an embodiment of the Newgate Calendar, sneaking under the titles of marquess and conquistador. There is, however, one incident connected with his death which evidences some sensibility. It cannot be said of him that he died and made no sign. After defending himself, with his accustomed valor, against his assassins, he was overpowered by numbers, and received several terrible wounds. "Jesu!" he exclaimed, in that dying moment; and, "tracing a cross with his finger on the bloody floor, he bent down his head to kiss it, when a stroke, more friendly than the rest, put an end to his existence." There is something sublime in this flashing forth of the religious sentiment, in the moment of death, from a nature which seemed destitute even of religious bigotry and superstition; and something horrible in the contemplation of the only religious act of a long life of turbulence and sin being balked by the very hand which slew his body. That dark spirit passed to its last account with its hoarded lusts thick upon it.

In strong contrast with Pizarro and the other Spaniards, and the only honest man in Mr. Prescott's volumes, is Pedro de la Gasca; and the most attractive portion of the work is devoted to him. He was a peaceful ecclesiastic, sent out by the Spanish government to recover Peru, after the previous viceroy, Blasco Nuñez, had been deposed and slain, in an insurrection against the royal authority, headed by Gonzalo Pizarro. The country was entirely in the latter's hands, and the people were with him. Gasca entered the country without any military force; proclaimed pardon for all past offences; announced the revocation of the ordinances which had provoked the rebellion; by inimitable coolness, sagacity, and energy, succeeded in winning over some of the most important of Gonzalo's captains; and, in a comparatively short time, entirely ruined the insurgents, and reinstated the royal authority in every part of Peru. The whole work, both in its conception and direction, was exclusively his own. The only thing that Spain gave him was absolute authority, and he conquered Peru by the simple force and wisdom of his single mind. Such a conquest was a grander exercise of genius than ever Cortés or Pizarro displayed; and we think that, next to Columbus, Gasca takes the first rank among the great Spaniards connected with the discovery and colonization of America. His genius would be contested by some, because he was one of those rare men who possess great powers in such perfect harmony with great virtues, that the might of their nature is only seen in the effects they produce. To the vulgar eye, their unobtrusive excellence often passes for commonplace. All repose unbounded reliance in their integrity and intelligence, and they generally succeed in everything they undertake, but their sagacious virtue is rarely honored with the name of genius. They are called men of moderation, of common sense, — men who originate nothing, but can apply everything; and in general estimation they bear about the same relation to narrower and intenser natures which light bears to lightning. Now, it seems to us that force and insight are the characteristics, and influence the measure, of genius; and where we see great results produced by a sagacious proportioning of means to ends, we infer the genius of their author. Gasca's course, indeed, strikes us more by its intelligence than its moral elevation. A man of the most stainless integrity, he had still to crush a rebellion, and restore a country to its allegiance to the Spanish crown, by means which would be operative among a collection of depraved soldiers and petty tyrants. Superior himself to vanity, ambition, avarice, fear, and treachery, he saw perfectly into the characters of those with whom he was to deal, understood the nature of the complaints which had led to the rebellion, and understood also the feeling of lingering loyalty which still dwelt in the fears or the sentiments of the rebels. He first gave them no excuse for continuing adverse to the crown, by abolishing the ordinances which had caused their resistance; and then proffered to the followers of Gonzalo those inducements which he knew would be operative in the minds of knaves. If anything were wanting to complete our contempt of the Spaniards in Peru, we have it in the detestable treachery of the men who deserted and betrayed Gonzalo, after having been sworn to his interests and enriched by his bounty.

Gasca knew more than all the captains and intriguers in Peru put together; and by virtue of this knowledge he gained the mastery of all. The only man who could have prevented by his intelligence the destruction of the rebels was Gonzalo's Mephistophelian lieutenant, Carbajal; and his advice, which was submission, Gonzalo would not follow. It is curious to contemplate Gasca among the profligate soldiers of Peru, if it were only to observe the instinctive homage which vice pays to virtue. His qualities, like diamonds, derived their value from their rarity. There were enough courageous stabbers and reckless intriguers in the country; there was no lack of gold, and silver, and merchandise; but truth and honesty were scarce and inestimable. The usual laws which regulate supply and demand began to operate. Among a set of liars, and perjurers, and traitors, and murderers, a true, faithful, loyal, and just man, was at once a phenomenon and a priceless treasure. At the same time, he comprehended all Peru in his capacious mind, and he ruled it because he knew all its inhabitants better than they knew themselves. Virtuous himself, all the resources and tricks of vice were more visible to his eye than if he had mastered them by experience. No plotter, who had passed all his life in intrigue, was so sure in his judgment of rascality, so certain in the means he took to circumvent it. He was one of those wise men who read things in their principles, and he therefore never made mistakes. He saw, as in prophetic vision, the remotest results of all his acts; and accordingly, when he had commenced a course of policy, he never wavered, never experienced a doubt of his success, because he knew what must happen from the nature of things. This insight into the principles of events, this settled faith based on the clearest intelligence, is the crowning glory of the genius of action. Gasca, in Peru, evinced a capacity for government which the complex affairs of a European empire would not have exhausted.

In order to do full justice to Mr. Prescott's work, we should present to our readers some extracts illustrating its excellences of narration and description; but this our limits will not permit. The mind of the author yields itself with a beautiful readiness to the inspiration of his subject, and he leads the reader along with him through every scene of beauty and grandeur in which the stirring adventures he narrates are placed. We would refer particularly to the description of the passage of the Andes, as an evidence of the accuracy with which pictures of scenery may be impressed on the historian's imagination, and, through him, upon the reader's, without the original objects ever having been present to the eye of either. The account of the massacre at Caxamalca is also exceedingly vivid and true, and is probably one of the most splendid passages in Mr. Prescott's works. After this bloody, treacherous, and cowardly murder, Pizarro addressed his troops before they retired for the night. When he had ascertained that not a man was wounded, "he bade them offer up thanksgivings to Providence for so great a miracle — without its care they could never have prevailed so easily over the host of their enemies; and he trusted their lives had been reserved for still greater things." No invective, though steeped in fire and gall, is calculated to excite so much detestation as this simple statement of the murderer's blasphemous hypocrisy. It is one of those monstrosities of canting guilt, " on which a fiend might make an epigram."

It is curious to observe, in the tangled web of intrigue, treachery, and murder, which meets us in the history of the conquest, how the moral laws which were violated by the conquerors avenged themselves. Murder generated murder, and misery brought forth misery. First, Atahualpa was murdered by a legal farce got up by Almagro and Pizarro; then Almagro was murdered in the same way by Pizarro; Pizarro, in his turn, was assassinated by the followers of Almagro's son, Diego; and the latter fell in battle with the Spanish authorities, under Vaca de Castro. Hernando Pizarro passed the largest portion of his life in a Spanish prison; Juan, the best of the brothers, was killed by the Peruvians; and Gonzalo, a man of some generosity and openness of mind, and of a chivalrous temper, after having arrived by rebellion to the supreme command in Peru, was betrayed by his followers, and executed as a traitor. In these various feuds, most of the original gang of pirates who conquered the country either fell in battle or were executed on the scaffold; their stolen property passed into the possession of others; and even the few who did not die a violent death were under the control of two masters — gambling and licentiousness — which gave them poverty and disease for wages. As their crimes brought no good to themselves, so, also, they laid Peru under a curse from which she has not yet recovered. The seeds of a new empire can never be sown by the outcasts of an old one; and those who look upon a country with the eyes of a pickpocket will soon ruin everything in it which nature will allow human folly and wickedness to destroy. The history of the conquest of Peru, as presented in the vivid pages of Mr. Prescott, is capable of conveying many lessons on the retribution which follows conquest and rapine, which late events in our own history show that we have incompletely learned. It would seem that every man of common intelligence and common patriotism would rather see the power of his country palsied, than made the instrument of crime. Such a misuse of strength never has been and never can be successful. The poisoned chalice will inevitably be returned to our own lips, for the world is ruled by divine, not demoniacal agencies. Look at the subject in what light we may, from the view of religion or the view of common sense, we must still admit that we cannot balk or elude those eternal laws of the universe, which deny lasting power to the energies of robbery and the schemes of rapine. The laws of God, in their slow, silent, and terrible operation, will still move tranquilly on, turning all our glory to shame, all our strength to weakness; though we, in the mad exultation of our guilt, turn night into day with our bonfires, and rend the skies with our huzzas.

SHAKSPEARE'S CRITICS.*

THOSE who consider the science of criticism as nothing more than a collection of arbitrary rules, and the art of criticism but their dextrous or declamatory application, rejoice in a system of admirable simplicity and barren results. It has the advantage of judging everything and accounting for nothing, thus gratifying the pride of intellect without enjoining any intellectual exertion. By a steady adherence to its doctrines, a dunce may exalt himself to a pinnacle of judgment, from which the first authors of the world appear as splendid madmen, whose enormous writhings and contortions, as they occasionally blunder into grace and grandeur of motion, show an undisciplined strength, which would, if subjected to rule, produce great effects. A Bond-street exquisite complacently surveying a thunder-scarred Titan through an opera-glass, is but a type of a Grub-street critic measuring a Milton or a Shakspeare with his three-foot rule.

But the golden period of this kind of criticism, when mediocrity sat cross-legged on the body of genius, and

* Shakspeare's Plays, with his Life. Illustrated with many hundred Wood-cuts, executed by H. W. Hewet, after designs by Kenny Meadows, Harvey, and others. Edited by Gulian C. Verplanck, LL.D., with Critical Introductions, Notes, etc., Original and Selected. New York: Harper & Brothers. 3 vols. 8vo.

Lectures on Shakspeare. By H. N. Hudson. New York: Baker & Scribner. 2 vols. 12mo. — *North American Review, July*, 1848.

sagely delivered its oracular nonentities, has happily passed away. The fat bishop of the elder time who discovered that the Paradise Lost was a licentious and blasphemous poem, and the lean authorling who first informed the world that Shakspeare was an inspired idiot, have both departed into the void inane. The period has gone by when France could dismiss Shakspeare from the company of Corneille and Racine as a clever barbarian, or England herself rate him as a sort of miraculous monstrosity, — neither so elegant as Waller, nor so correct as Mr. Pope. The old antithesis between genius and judgment, taste and creative power, which has sparkled and rung in so many knowing sentences, has now lost most of its point, and is enjoyed only as a gem from the antique. It is no longer the fashion for beauty to be tested by elegance, or truth by mechanical correctness, or nature by convention, or art by artifice. Mr. Prettyman, with his conceited lisp, and Sir Artegal's Talus, with his iron flail, have both been banished from the gardens of the Hesperides.

This substitution of a philosophy of criticism for an anarchy of dogmas is especially seen in the recent editions of Shakspeare. Fifty years ago, he was compared, in reference to his commentators, to Actæon hunted to death by his own dogs. But the present generation has witnessed a marked change in the spirit and principles of the criticism by which he has been tried. Could all those Sir Francis Wrongheads of the last century, who undertook to patronize Shakspeare as a wild, unregulated genius, and kindly volunteered their praise on the score of his great faults being balanced by great beauties, suddenly start up in the present age, we may well imagine with what a stare of blank amazement they would observe his elevation to the throne of art. It might reasonably be supposed that old John Dennis and Mr. Rymer would retire in disgust to their tombs, rather than accept the boon of life in a generation devoted to so Egyptian an adoration of deformities. The difference between an old critic picking flaws in Shakspeare's expression of passion, and a modern critic raving about the artistic significance of Shakspeare's puns, indicates the extremes of criticism through which the "myriad-minded" has passed. At present there appears to be no danger that his intellectual supremacy will be questioned. The antiquary who ventures to stammer a little in the old jargon is quietly dropped by good society; the sciolist who blurts out a blunt objection is vehemently hissed into non-existence. Schlegel's prediction, that Shakspeare's fame for centuries to come would "continue to gather strength, like an Alpine avalanche, at every moment of its progress," seems to be in the process of verification; for with every new edition and criticism the giant dilates into larger and larger dimensions. He has invaded France; he has conquered Germany. The principalities and powers of literature find no safety but in the acknowledgment of his supremacy. To the old republic of letters he comes as the intellectual Cæsar, who is to establish a universal dominion. The different orders of the literary state, far from opposing his pretensions, are engaged in hymning his divinity. Here and there some lean Cassius mutters treason against the god, complains that he bestrides the world like a Colossus, and leaves other poets little to do but peep about for dishonorable graves; but all peevish exceptions are drowned in the universal shout which lifts his name to the skies.

> "Nothing can cover his high fame but heaven ;
> No pyramids set off his memories
> But the eternal substance of his greatness."

This idolatry of Shakspeare is partly the cause and partly the effect of a new school of criticism, which assumes to judge works of art after a new code of principles. The mistake which the old order of critics made consisted in overlooking the doctrine of vital powers. They judged the form of Shakspeare's works by certain external rules, before they had interpreted the inward life which shaped the form. Shakspeare's genius was always felt as supreme above others, because its reality and force could not be resisted; but the criticism which should have made it understood as well as felt, which should have accounted for its effects, pursued exactly the opposite course. Instead of attempting to translate it to the understanding by evolving its principles, it placed it in antagonism to certain notions in the understanding, which were unfounded in the nature of things. Because genius has its own laws, it is not therefore to be considered lawless; yet such was the judgment passed upon Shakspeare's genius by men who, substituting dogmatism for analysis, did not possess the first requisite of a critic, that of understanding the thing criticized. The consequence was, an absurd opposition between judgment and feeling, taste and genius. Men were compelled to admire what they were taught to condemn. We perceive the effect of this even in a man of such comprehensive sympathies as Dryden. Nothing can be more contemptible than Dryden's criticism on Shakspeare's art; yet when he abandoned his rules, and trusted to his own conceptions of excellence, — when he ceased to judge as a critic and spoke as a poet, — nothing can excel the warmth or the accuracy of his rhapsodies. Eliminate from his celebrated passage on Shakspeare every term which may be called critical, and there is nothing in English literature, from Ben Jonson to Coleridge, which contains so true a representation of Shakspeare's mind.

Now, the critical revolution which has taken place in the present century does not pretend so much to increase our sympathy with Shakspeare as to increase our knowledge of him; and accordingly we perceive its influence not merely in the opinions of men of imagination and sensibility, but in those of critics chiefly distinguished for sense and understanding. The revolution, being one of principles, has affected the judgments of writers who bear, in mind and character, the same relative position to the present period which the old critics bore to their time. It would be unjust to compare Schlegel and Coleridge with Johnson and Malone, as indicating a change in the general scope and spirit of literary judgments; but if we compare Johnson with Hallam, we are still conscious of a great and essential difference, — a difference not so much in the faculties employed as in the principles by which they are guided. This is so true, that the meaning of judgment and taste, so far as the results obtained by their exercise are concerned, has completely altered. When Dr. Johnson said of Cymbeline, that to notice its defects and improbabilities in detail were "to waste criticism on unresisting imbecility," he proved himself a person of great judgment, according to the principles of the eighteenth century; but a man who hazarded such an opinion now would be set down, we will not say as an ignoramus, but as one whose taste was under the dominion of individual caprice, and whose judgment was wholly deficient in correctness.

The two works named at the head of the present article, Mr. Verplanck's edition of Shakspeare, and Mr. Hudson's Lectures, are a fair indication of the progress which criticism has made within a century. Neither could have been produced fifty years ago, for the materials were wanting. Mr. Verplanck had the wide field of English antiquarian, verbal, and æsthetical criticism open to him, and he has swept over the whole domain. He has especially availed himself of the researches of various commentators, without, however, adopting their insufferable prolixity of statement. His edition, though it has the character of a *rifacimento*, still combines a greater number of positive merits, and is calculated for a wider variety of readers, than any with which we are acquainted; but it is so in virtue of the judgment the editor has evinced in selecting the peculiar excellences of many editions, and in avoiding the peculiar faults of each. He had at his command a singularly rich collection of materials, embodying the results of a century of research, and containing the separate items of a good edition floating about in an ocean of words. There was, therefore, a constant strain upon his judgment and taste in the mere task of selection and compression. Antiquarians and commentators are apt unconsciously to rate their discoveries and illustrations as of more value than the things to which they refer; and Shakspeare especially has been victimized by a class of lynx-eyed dogmatists, always quarrelling among themselves, and each claiming for the morsels of useful knowledge he has contributed a ludicrous importance.

Mr. Verplanck has shown much strength and catholicity of mind, in not being embarrassed by the varying opinions of this army of acute triflers, at the same time that he has largely availed himself of their labors. In the notes to each play; in tracing out the sources, historical and romantic, of the plots; in the bibliographical discussion as to the order in which the plays were printed, he blends his own learning very gracefully with what he has condensed from others. The text appears to be the portion of the work on which he has expended the greatest care, and is the result of a most cautious comparison, word by word, of the original quarto editions of the various plays with the original folio published by Heminge and Condell, and of both with the editions of Malone, Collier, and Knight. Though, from the nature of the case, the text of no one editor can be so perfect as to settle all disputes regarding particular passages, we think it must be conceded to Mr. Verplanck that he has executed this difficult and delicate task with a great deal of acuteness and sagacity, and displayed a much clearer insight into the spirit and form of Shakspeare's style than a large majority of those who have undertaken the drudgery of its arrangement.

But it is as a critic, rather than as an editor, that Mr. Verplanck claims our attention here. His introductions to the plays are really additions to the higher Shakspearian criticism, not so much for any peculiar felicity in the analysis of character, as in the view, partly bibliographical, partly philosophical, which he takes of the gradual development of Shakspeare's mind and the different stages of its growth. It is the first connected attempt to trace out Shakspeare's intellectual history and character, gathering, to use Mr. Verplanck's own words, "from various, and sometimes slight and circumstantial, or collateral, points of testimony, the order and succession of his works, assigning, so far as possible, each one to its probable epoch, noting the variations or differences of style and of versification between them, and in some cases (as in Romeo and Juliet, Henry Fifth, and Hamlet) the alterations and improvements of the same play by the author himself, in the progress of his taste and experience; thus following out, through each successive change, the luxuriant growth of his poetic faculty and his comic power, and finally, the still nobler expansion of the moral wisdom, the majestic contemplation, the terrible energy, the matchless fusion of the impassioned with the philosophical, that distinguished the matured mind of the author of Hamlet, of Lear, and of Macbeth." In this portion of his labors, Mr. Verplanck has shown a solidity and independence of judgment, and a power of clearly appreciating almost every opinion from which he dissents, which give to his own views the fairness and weight of judicial decisions. His defects as a critic are principally those which come from the absence in part of sensitive sympathies, and of the power of sharp, minute, exhaustive analysis. He is of the school of Hallam, a school in which judgment and generalization rule with such despotic control, that the heart and imagination hardly have fair play, and strongly marked individualities too often subside into correct generalities.

Before hazarding any remarks on Mr. Hudson's striking Lectures, it may not be out of place to refer to a few of the philosophical critics who have preceded him, in order that his station among them may be calculated with some degree of accuracy. After a careful perusal of his work, we have been forced to the conclusion, that, in spite of its faults, there is no single critical production on Shakspeare which equals it in completeness and force of thought in the examination of individual characters. It is a work which no person could have written without devoting himself with rare constancy to one object, and without availing himself to some extent of the labors of his predecessors in the same department of thought. The materials for a critical view of Shakspeare are widely scattered. Almost every eminent poet and critic of Germany and England has, within the last half-century, recorded his impressions of the world's master mind; and perhaps in the stray observations of Goethe we have glances into the nature of Shakspeare's genius as profound and accurate as ever were won by the intensest toil of inspection. Hallam, Carlyle, Campbell, and many others, have presented striking criticisms on the plays, or thrown out valuable suggestions respecting the characters, in works not exclusively devoted to Shakspeare. Hazlitt, Mrs. Jameson, and Ulrici, have produced separate volumes on the subject. Of the professed critics, however, Schlegel and Coleridge, as they are first in point of time, appear to us first in respect to excellence. They were, to a great extent, the originators of the school of philosophical criticism, and we find in them a systematic statement of its principles, in their application to all forms of imaginative literature.

The history of the variations of criticism with regard to Shakspeare would involve a consideration of all critical theories, from those founded on individual impressions to those based on an observation of the essential laws of mental growth and production. These two extremes of criticism, as different as subject and object, are often confounded, — a work of art as it affects a particular mind being commonly a convertible phrase for a work of art as it is in itself. The middle ground between the two has most obtained among those who are called men of culture. This consists in testing the value of all works of art by their conformity to certain rules generalized from the productions of a particular school, — as if the romantic drama, as seen in Shakspeare, should be judged by the principles of the classic drama, as seen in Sophocles. It is evident, we think, that if criticism be a science, if it assume to convey any real knowledge, it deals not with individual impressions or arbitrary rules, but with laws; and its progress will be determined by its success in employing a right method to discover the laws of the objects to which it refers. As the philosopher is content to investigate and establish the laws of the human mind and the phenomena of nature, leaving to the sceptic or the idealist the luxury of denying their existence or supplying better from his own resources, so the critic is bound to pursue a similar method with regard to a work of art, and to interpret, if he can, its inward meaning and significance. This, at least, is the process in all other sciences. If a plant, insect, fish, or other animal, is to undergo a scientific examination, a *savan* is not welcomed with a shower of honorary degrees because he has felicitously ridiculed its external form, or shown its want of agreement with some other natural object, but because he has investigated its inward mechanism, indicated its purpose, and shown that its form is physiognomical of its peculiar life. Now, we think that Hamlet and Lear are as worthy of this tolerant treatment as a bird or a fish; at least, we are confident that no scientific knowledge of either can be obtained in any other way. Because the principle implies that a true creation of the intellect has thus an independent existence and merit of its own, and is to be judged by its own laws, or its own fitness to serve the purposes of its creation, it does not thence follow, that its relative merit, as compared with other works of art, is altogether put beyond the jurisdiction of criticism. Because a rose may be considered a finer flower than a violet, we are not bound to test the beauty of one by its agreement with the other. At least, in regard to the productions of the intellect, there can be no accurate classification, no settlement of their position in the sliding-scale of excellence or greatness, without understanding the spirit and life of each.

Now, the great merit of SCHLEGEL consisted in discarding from his system all quibbles respecting superficial differences in the form of works of genius, and looking directly at the inward life which animated and shaped the form. His view of Shakspeare, which did so much to revolutionize the tone of English criticism, is contained in his Lectures on Dramatic Art and Literature, delivered in Vienna, in the spring of 1808. Had he written nothing else, this work would be sufficient to place him among the greatest critics of the world. It not only develops a system of principles of uncommon reach and depth, but contains a review of the dramatists and dramatic literature of Greece, Rome, France, Italy, England, Spain, and Germany, grappling sturdily with all the vexed questions of dramatic art which start up in each stage of the inquiry. Almost for the first time, we find, in his work, a critic who profoundly appreciates at once the drama of Greece, England, and Spain, and does it in virtue of following out the central principle of a comprehensive critical system. Sweeping over the whole field of dramatic literature, he detects, in the variety of its kinds, in its metempsychosis through various forms, the true character of each period of its development, and considers the genius of each period in relation to the materials it assimilated and the purposes it served. He is an ardent and intelligent admirer of Æschylus and Sophocles, and for that very reason contemns all attempts to reproduce them in other ages. As he really understands the great Greek dramatists, he sees the excellence of Shakspeare and Calderon in their departure from the Greek models. Starting with a distinct idea of the difference between mechanical regularity and organic form, he is at once a remorseless critic of mediocrity and an interpretative critic of genius; for, by demanding that a work of art, however modest its pretensions, shall be an organic whole with a central principle of life, he discards from his sympathies the productions of the most accomplished artisans of letters, and the most ingenious combinations of inanimate parts. His work is the first attempt at viewing the dramatic literature of the world under the light of a principle broad enough to include every variety of intellectual excellence, and overlooking nothing informed with a living soul.

Had the author been entirely free from individual bias, and had he possessed also the faculty of contracting his vision with as much facility as he dilated it, his work would hardly have left much for later critics to perform; but we perceive, here and there, the effect upon his mind of the literary controversies in which he had been engaged, and some of his individual judgments are contrary to the catholicity of his principles. Besides, as his comprehensiveness was not accompanied by corresponding acuteness, he not unfrequently becomes the dupe of his own refinements, especially in criticizing the details of a work of art; for we imagine a truly acute man is not so likely to be deceived in a criticism of particulars, as a comprehensive one is, who affects subtilty in order to bring the details of a thing into harmony with his general conception. In Schlegel's celebrated view of Shakspeare's mind and art, we perceive the influence of this defect. Nothing can be more lucid than his exposition of the general character and scope of Shakspeare's genius, and of the principles by which it should be judged; but, when he comes to review the particular plays, his very determination to find excellence in everything often leads to his missing the greatest excellence. He is so occupied in tracing out the main design of the piece, and exhibiting the pervading unity through all the variety of parts, that he comparatively overlooks the characterization. Now, the fundamental idea, the ultimate principle, the living root, of one of Shakspeare's plays, can be reached only by an intense conception or exhaustive analysis of the characters,—for these give to the main design its peculiar Shakspearian coloring and significance; and to exhibit the dependence of the parts on the main design, without fully appreciating the parts, results in reducing the whole to something little above commonplace. Every attempt to follow a purely synthetic process in an exposition of Shakspeare's plays has been a failure, because it requires a mind capable of reproducing Shakspeare's own conceptions, and grasping with one effort of imagination a Shakspearian whole. To exhibit a tragedy like that of Hamlet as it grew up in the creator's mind, indicating the exact period when the different characters necessarily branched off from the trunk in obedience to the law at its root, would seem to require a genius such as has not yet taken criticism for a vocation. Goethe seems to have had some inward idea of the secret of Shakspeare's processes, but the scattered observations in which he hinted his knowledge are but stammering expressions of his conception.

The leading merit of Schlegel, as we have already said, is rather in breadth of view than in any surpassing felicity of individual criticism; and in regard to Shakspeare, we think him inferior to Coleridge in strong and vivid conception, and in the power of flashing a great impression of a character or incident upon the mind, through modes of expression which only a poet can command. With all his wilfulness and vagaries, Coleridge possessed, as a critic, not only grand glimpses of the inmost spirit of a work of art, but a remarkable faculty of intellectual analysis; and as he had made Shakspeare and his creations the subject of profound and contemplative study, he was eminently calculated for the office of his interpreter, both to the understanding and the imagination of his countrymen. But he lacked the talent of writing clearly in prose. A series of conceptions as they stood in his mind never found adequate expression on his page. He has sentences of wonderful beauty, distinctness, and force, embodying separate thoughts of the greatest originality and depth; but there is little connection or orderly arrangement of matter in his prose works. He offends against the first principle of his own critical code, being essentially a writer of parts, not of wholes,—of fragments, not of systems. In respect to principles, he is probably the first critic of the century; in respect to criticisms, he occupies a much lower rank. His fragments on Shakspeare are of great value, but their value consists chiefly in their suggestiveness, in the bright hints they have afforded to those who have had the sagacity to plant them in their own minds, and allowed them to germinate.

HAZLITT'S work on the Characters of Shakspeare's Plays is a medley of great and small matters, ranging from criticism to vituperation, from the exhibition of Shakspeare to the exhibition of himself. Hazlitt's sense of his own individuality was so strong, that he could not altogether forget it in the contemplation of the most objective of poets; and though his volume bears on every page the marks of his acute and penetrating intellect, and is animated by bursts of his captivating but distempered eloquence, the general impression it leaves on the mind is unsatisfactory. It is supposed that many of the finest observations in his work were gathered in conversations with Coleridge.

MRS. JAMESON'S volume on the Female Characters is a most eloquent and passionate representation of Shakspeare's women, and in many respects is an important contribution to critical literature. Its defects are so covered up in the brilliancy and buoyancy of its style, that they are likely to escape notice. In the beautiful tumult of bright words, and the uniform glare of the representation, we are apt to overlook the lack of close and searching examination. Fine and true as are many of her remarks, and valuable as is much of the information she dares to give, she still is too apt to blend her own individuality with the individualities she is describing, and to think she is comprehending Shakspeare when Shakspeare is simply comprehending her. We feel it difficult to say thus much in abatement of the praise cheerfully awarded to one of the most fascinating books in the language, but we hardly think that any judicious admirer of Mrs. Jameson can suppose that Shakspeare's heroines could pass through the medium of her mind without a modification of their essential character.

But exceeding all books on the great dramatist in bulk and pretension is Ulrici's big octavo on Shakspeare's Dramatic Art. This is German in the worst sense of the word, being so strange a conglomeration of sense and fanaticism, of sagacity and dulness, that it is impossible to call it either excellent or execrable. It is learned, ingenious, acute, often eloquent, often profound, gives evidence of careful research and deep thought, and is worthy to be read by every man who can muster courage to read it; but it hardly conveys any impression of Shakspeare at all. The author regards his system first, himself second, and his nominal subject last. He takes as high ground for Shakspeare's genius as can possibly be assumed, and then impresses on his whole works the peculiar form of his own dominant dogma. Shakspeare, according to him, consciously or unconsciously, wrote in perfect harmony with the truth of things, and the "ground-idea" of every one of his plays is a theological doctrine. When he comes to develop this general principle, we find that he is not taking Shakspeare as an object of critical investigation, but as an illustration of his own philosophical and theological opinions; and the "thousand-souled" Shakspeare, the "oceanic mind," dwindles down into a mere auxiliary of the "one-idea'd" Ulrici. The characters are not analyzed, and are viewed only in reference to the axiomatic moral they are said to convey. The great "ground-idea" of the book may be said to consist in the assumption that Shakspeare wrote his plays to illustrate the five points of Calvinism. We do not say that these points cannot be found in Shakspeare, for almost every subjective mind finds there exactly what it brings; but it is somewhat ridiculous for a person to suppose that he has measured the genius of the world's master dramatist, when he has merely given the measure of himself. Ulrici's ingenuity and learning are sufficient to enable him to make out a plausible case; but he appears to us as far from Shakspeare in spirit as old Rymer himself.

Ulrici is an indication of the extravagances to which the principles of an interpretative criticism may seem to lead, when they are employed as a mere cover under which to smuggle individual impressions. In the Lectures of Mr. Hudson, we perceive that a right application of the same principles may result in a positive addition to knowledge. Although the American critic has his own eccentricities of opinion and expression, and displays occasionally a disposition to fight his own battles under Shakspeare's banner, he still contrives generally to maintain a marked line of distinction between his own impressions and the laws of the objects he investigates. His work, apart from its independent merits of composition and criticism, stands in intimate relation to the productions of his predecessors, especially to those of Schlegel and Coleridge. Possessing in a considerable degree the power of learning from other minds without becoming their vassal, Mr. Hudson's Lectures are the result of a study both of Shakspeare and his critics. By thus embodying in his own work the most valuable portion of former Shakspearian criticism, he is enabled to advance beyond it. The leading characteristic of the philosophical critics, that of excessive generalization, which led them comparatively to neglect the analysis of Shakspeare's characters, he has unconsciously avoided, from the instinctive antipathy of his mind to all generalities not vitally connected with objects. Though his passionate dislike of abstractions deprives his Lectures of that appearance of comprehensiveness which comes from a suppression, rather than an inclusion, of details, and though it is sometimes felt as a real defect, still it is that quality of his mind which has enabled him to succeed in the most neglected department of Shakspearian criticism, that of evolving the elements and laws of the individual characters, and indicating their application to practical life.

Before, however, we attempt a consideration of Mr. Hudson's positive merits as a thinker and critic, we must notice some obvious peculiarities of his character and style. These can hardly be allowed to elude criticism on the ground of their genuineness, for we are by no means inclined to give the critic the advantage of being judged in accordance with the philosophical principles he may apply to poets. The first impression which a reader obtains of Mr. Hudson is undoubtedly that of a powerful but somewhat perverse writer, gifted with more than an ordinary degree of combativeness, and battling for opinions with all the energy of a man engaged in a personal conflict. Possessing a strong and sturdy understanding, quick and deep sympathies, an affluent fancy, and a biting wit, with a large command of the most vigorous and apposite language, and a perfect fearlessness as to whom or what he hits, he stalks into the company of decorous critics and prim essayists with his Shakspearian thesis in his hand, and, on the slightest intimation of a desire for controversy, incontinently rains down on his opponents a storm of propositions, arguments and epigrams, from which they are glad to escape by a precipitate flight. Nothing can be more unphilosophical than Mr. Hudson's manner, and it is in strange contrast with the polite sneer, and somewhat prim and reserved contempt, with which Schlegel dismisses an opponent, or the exclamatory regret with which Coleridge mourns the narrowness of a critic's creed. Alike in narrative, in the exposition of principles, in the analysis of characters, in side thrusts at popular foibles and delusions, Mr. Hudson's style is characterized by intensity and intellectual fierceness. His only mode of conquering an adversary is to overthrow him, and when he has him down he ends the matter by pommelling him to death. He enters the lists as Shakspeare's champion; and woe to the unlucky wight, no matter how accredited his reputation as an author, who has at any time dropped incautious expressions raising a doubt of Shakspeare's supremacy. Thus, Mr. Hume's unfortunate remark respecting the Elizabethan age, as regards the correctness and taste of its literature, affords the occasion of a furious attack on that acutest of metaphysicians, in which every weak point in his mind is pricked and pierced with the most remorseless certainty of aim, until he expires at last in an agony of epigrams. Some miserable heretics against the true critical faith, whose stupidity and insignificance preserve them from being roasted in the slow fires of wit, but who have been lifted into some celebrity by the enormity of their crimes in attempting to improve Shakspeare down to popular taste, are loaded with nicknames and pelted with scornful epithets. Nahum Tate, one of these plebeian butchers of the poet's plots and style, is hooted at as a "wooden-headed man," and his improved Lear is kicked from sentence to sentence down a truculent paragraph, until at last our sympathies plead for poor Nahum on the ground of the wrong implied in cruelty to animals. This feeling, that meddling with Shakspeare's plays is literally sacrilege, and objecting to them is audacious heresy, indicates how thorough is our author's worship of his subject, and how intensely he has realized it to his mind as a living reality.

The style of Mr. Hudson is a fair image of his intellect and character, admitting considerable variety of expression, but stamped throughout with strongly marked and peculiar traits. It is the vehicle, not merely of analysis and reflection, but of wit, satire, scorn, passion, and fancy. Often, indeed, the former qualities find their raciest expression under the latter, and the reader is favored with a chain of logical deduction the links of which are epigrams, or with a theory impaled on a scalpel festooned with imagery. It would be difficult to describe the style, for it varies with the writer's moods and the subjects treated, and is restrained neither by self-imposed nor rhetorical rules. Now bristling with antithesis, now flashing with satire, — at one time melting into softness and sweetness of diction, at another bringing out the thought with a jerk in a perfect verbal spasm, — now sharp, crisp, biting, scornfully defiant, each short sentence exploding into sparkles, and then again rolling on in a grand succession of harmonious periods, — it always has the merit of clearness and precision, and in all its alternations, from scientific terms which approach the obscure to homely phrases which fall plump into the inelegant, there is little chance of missing the meaning. It is a style full of the energy of life, but a life which is sometimes galvanized into spasmodic strength.

The author's command of language is despotic, and like all despots he not unfrequently exercises his power capriciously. This is shown principally in extravagance of statement and in repetition of thought. The first is, to a great extent, the result of his greatest merit, for extravagance in expression comes as often from intense as from feeble conception, resulting in one case from the boiling over of the mind in vehement language, in the excitement produced by proximity to a great object which awakens all its powers, and in the other being merely an attempt to make words perform the office both of thinking and expression. Mr. Hudson, except, perhaps, in his analysis of Shakspeare's female characters, does not give to his subjects that remoteness which admits of their calm contemplation, but writes close to the vital truth of the thing he describes, with that tingling of the blood which such an immediate contact with the soul of passion and the life of thought produces and prolongs. To dive into the depths of Hamlet's mind, or to follow step by step the progress of crime in the heart and imagination of Macbeth, or to pass resolutely into that awful region of passion whose terrible gusts rend the frames of Othello and Lear, is not a thing to be done or recorded with an even pulse and a cool brain. We accordingly think that, in such instances as these, Mr. Hudson's extravagance of expression, though not always strictly accurate as to thought, is eminently true to feeling, and will be more successful in stamping on the reader's mind a living impression of the characters than if he had weighed his words with more scrupulous care. But he has an exaggeration of statement of another kind, which consists in lifting persons into the perfection of principles, and of confounding possibilities with realities. Thus, in the view of Shakspeare's mind, in many respects a masterly specimen of thought and composition, he makes Shakspeare to be what he really only approached, and seems to forget that, after all which can be said of him as a great man, with large powers harmoniously combined, he was still a man, and not humanity. This extravagance we know is simply the extravagance of epigram, aiming to suggest the truth more vividly by exaggerating it; but an analyst so close, fierce, and subtile, as Mr. Hudson, with his felicity and pride in limitations, has hardly a right to expect that his readers or critics will allow him to claim exemption from the very letter of the law.

The other fault of Mr. Hudson, that of repetition, is common to him with almost all lecturers. He has less of it than Cousin and Villemain, in whose discourses the leading ideas are made to perform an amount of labor, in the mere changing of dress and attitude, which at last wears and wastes them away. The repetition we observe in Mr. Hudson results from an occasional fanaticism of acuteness, which is sceptical of the ability of a proposition to convey a complete idea, and is eager to express all its elements. Though he embodies the most refined distinctions of analysis with uncommon skill and verbal certainty, he lingers occasionally too long on one subtilty, presents it in a variety of attitudes through a succession of brilliant sentences, and, indeed, indulges his power of condensed expression at the expense of real condensation of thought. Thus, an acute or profound observation is often first stated in language whose meaning ignorance itself cannot miss, then embodied in an image, then again forced into an antithetic or epigrammatic form, and afterwards, perhaps, slyly made to perform the office of sting to a gibe, until, in the end, it is hammered out of the head in the very attempt to hammer it in. This characteristic is more especially observable in the earlier lectures, in which, being compelled to present the profoundest principles of philosophical criticism in a popular form, his eagerness to make them readily apprehended leads him to push them into every minor avenue to the mind, as well as to send them on the direct road to the understanding.

We have one more cause of quarrel with Mr. Hudson before we proceed to the positive merits of his book. It is so rare to have a critic before our court of literary justice, that when we do, it is proper to make him feel how "sharper than a serpent's tooth" is the bite of criticism to an author. Our present objection refers to the explosions of Mr. Hudson's individuality in the guerilla warfare which he wages against the reformers and transcendentalists of our enlightened age. This bush-fighting along the main road of the text, though it lends raciness to the style, and will doubtless delight many who have no appreciation of his great merits as a thinker and critic, is often carried to the extreme limits of a reviewer's forbearance. Many of his remarks are unquestionably acute and just, and as far as they ridicule strutting pretension, presumptuous imbecility, and complacent ignorance,—as far as they unmask the "moral bullies and virtuous braggadocios" who are engaged in beating up a little conscience into a great deal of ethical and political froth, or probe sharply those small coteries of elegant souls, where

"Self-inspection sucks his little thumb,"—

we have little to say in objection, except that his digressions somewhat break the unity of his discourse; but he himself is sometimes forced by his contempt or indignation to the opposite extreme, and to class, in appearance at least, the principles of civil and religious liberty under the general head of conceit and spiritual pride, and to exalt conformity to church and state into the perfection of wisdom and piety. This seems to us "more excellent foolery than the other;" and though we would not directly charge it upon Mr. Hudson, there are rash and peevish expressions in his book, which might be forced to bear such a construction.

We have thus noticed at some length Mr. Hudson's peculiarities of manner, not because they affect the integrity of his interpretation of objects, or seriously detract from the intrinsic value of his work, but because they are calculated to raise false issues regarding its merits, apart from the shock they sometimes give to good taste. Admitting everything which can be said against it on these points, it has still solid excellences of thought and style which require a different treatment. We shall, therefore, now attempt to indicate its leading characteristics as a work of philosophical criticism.

Mr. Hudson has thrown the whole strength of his mind into the analysis of the plays, especially the characters. In this respect, Schlegel, Coleridge and Hazlitt, are imperfect and meagre in comparison with him, though for his own success he is considerably indebted to their previous labors. He has practically established one important fact in regard to Shakspeare's characters, that each is not only an individual, but a whole class individualized; and that, as the ideal or common head of a class, it is not only admirable as a character, but indicates the tendencies of a large body of men. So intense is the individuality of each character, that it is only when a powerful analysis has resolved it into its elements that we perceive the vast amount of thought and observation it embodies. This analysis, applied to all his characters, conveys a living idea of the amazing force, clearness, and grasp of Shakspeare's mind, in its relative comprehension of the actual and possible of human nature, and, better than all vague panegyric, demonstrates his unapproachable greatness. For the first time in the history of the intellect, we find in him a mind whose creative vitality is commensurate with its comprehension; reaching down into the heart of things with as much facility as it stretches over and around them; seizing, at once, the elements of human nature, and generalizing the world of men, interpreting the latter by light derived from the former, and by the harmonious action of his powers of conception, combination, and observation, enabled to express mankind in men, and womankind in women. When to this we add the capacity of combining the elements of humanity into new and strange forms of being, which are neither natural nor unnatural, but supernatural, we have an object for contemplation which criticism cannot exhaust, and which it has hardly begun to conceive. The wonder is, not that Shakspeare could have created so many characters, but that he could have comprehended a world in so few; that he was so rare a combination of the poet and philosopher as to grasp truth in the concrete, and embody the most gigantic generalizations of the intellect in living forms. Were his characters merely individuals, or merely personified ideas, they would not contain within themselves a fraction of their present applicability to life. As it is, he has occupied almost every department of thought. Goethe has testified that he found it difficult to avoid an imitation or repetition of Shakspeare, when he strove most conscientiously to express himself or his own creations.

In this analytic portion of his labors, Mr. Hudson has opened and worked many rich veins of thought, and indicated practically what is meant by Shakspeare's opulence and breadth of mind. If, however, he had merely analyzed the characters, and exhibited their wealth of suggestiveness, he would have performed but one important portion of a critic's duty. He has not only done this, but has forcibly conceived the characters as individuals, and happily blends their personal traits with their general significance, in reproducing them to the imagination and understanding. Shakspeare's plays constitute a kind of world in themselves, and no person of deep and delicate sympathies can dwell in it long without giving a positive existence to its men and women, and referring to Hamlet and Falstaff and Cordelia as though they were the companions of his eye as well as mind. This is especially true of Mr. Hudson. He appears as the lover or enemy of many characters whom Shakspeare is content to represent; and considers what they are and what they do as subjects of approval or condemnation, as much as if they were veritable personages in actual life. This intense realization is, perhaps, the greatest charm of his book, though at the same time it is one of the disturbing forces in his style, and the occasion of many a gust of intellectual wrath. It gives a certain heartiness to his most abstract discussions of principles, and through its influence the peculiar Shakspearian quality of each character rarely escapes his imagination when it eludes his analysis. Indeed, in this interchange of the synthetic and analytic processes of criticism, his various powers appear in all their force and refinement, for he commonly contrives to leave a concrete impression of a character upon the mind after he has subjected its elements to the minutest scrutiny. The result of his examination of each play is a view of its plot and design through the characters, and he thus lifts it into a Shakspearian region of thought, action, and being. The mistake of the German critics, as we have remarked, consists in bringing down the play into a comparatively commonplace region of existence, by overlooking the modification which everything receives from Shakspeare's own individuality, and from not adequately perceiving that it is the characters which lend greatness to the action and plan of the piece.

In exhibiting the mutual dependence of the characters, and their connection with the drama in which they appear, Mr. Hudson is very successful. He clearly understands that individuals in Shakspeare, as in life, are developed by mutual contact and collision; and accordingly he views each person in his relations, and interprets his character in the light cast upon it from all parts of the play. For instance, in the masterly analysis of Iago, he sometimes discards the little demon's own self-communings as furnishing evidence of his motives, on the ground of his being a measureless liar; and indicates, in many instances, the sureness and subtilty of Shakspeare's knowledge of human nature, in making his deceivers thus practise deception upon themselves, and lie even in soliloquies. In this portion of his labors, Mr. Hudson displays a delicacy of thought, a capacity to follow the minutest and most complex operations of the mind, and occasionally a microscopic nicety of vision, which would not discredit the most accomplished metaphysician.

It would be difficult to decide whether our critic has been more successful in delineating Skakspeare's men or women. Certainly no reader, who judged of the scope of his powers by their exercise in controversy, or in grappling sturdily with some knotty difficulty which had to be removed by main strength, would give him credit for the delicacy and clearness of his perception of moral beauty, and the refinements of the affections. The exquisite felicity with which he touches without profanely handling the most ideal of Shakspeare's heroines, and his constant sense of a certain sacredness attaching to the sex, are in strange contrast, not only to his rough-and-tumble mode of upsetting a critical dunce, but to his close and fierce exposition of an Iago and a Goneril. His delineations of Rosalind, Beatrice, Viola, Perdita, Juliet, Cordelia, Desdemona, Hermione, not to mention others, are conceived with great subtilty of sentiment and imagination, and have an indefinable charm caught from an intense sympathy with their natures. These ideal creations of the great poet, more truly and vitally natural than most of the women of actual life, he has contrived to reproduce whole upon his page, in the clear sweetness and beautiful dignity of their characters, and has been especially successful in setting forth their innate, unconscious purity of soul, shining through the most equivocal circumstances, and lending a glory to the simplest acts and expressions. It would be vain to look elsewhere for so complete a demonstration of Shakspeare's unrivalled success in exhibiting womankind in women, or a more thorough exposure of the fallacy that Beaumont and Fletcher excelled him in female characters. No extracts would convey a full impression of the felicity with which Mr. Hudson has entered into the spirit of

Shakspeare's heroines; and we can quote but one specimen in justification of our praise. The following is a portion of his remarks on Perdita: —

"The second part of Winter's Tale introduces us to very different scenes and persons from those which make up the first. The lost princess, and heir-apparent of Bohemia, two of the noblest and loveliest beings that ever fancy conceived, occupy the centre of the picture, while around them are clustered rustic shepherds and shepherdesses, amid their pastimes and pursuits, the whole being enlivened by the tricks and humors of a merry pedler and pickpocket. The most romantic beauty and the most comic drollery are here blended together. For simple purity and sweetness, the scene which unfolds the loves and characters of the prince and princess is not surpassed by anything in Shakspeare, and of course is not approached by anything out of him. All that is enchanting in romance, lovely in innocence, elevated in feeling, sacred in faith, is here brought together, bathed in the colors of heaven. The poetry is the very innocence of love, embodied in the fragrance of flowers. Clad in immortal freshness, this scene is one of those things which we always welcome as we do the return of spring, and over which our feelings may renew their youth forever: in brief, so long as nature breathes, and flowers bloom, and hearts love, they will do it in the spirit of what is here expressed.

"Perdita is a fine illustration of native intelligence as distinguished from artificial acquirements, and of inborn dignity bursting through all the disadvantages of the humblest station. Schlegel somewhere says, 'Shakspeare is particularly fond of showing the superiority of the innate over the acquired;' but he has nowhere done it more beautifully or more powerfully than in this unfledged angel.

'The prettiest low-born lass that ever
Ran on the green-sward, nothing she does or seems
But smacks of something greater than herself.'

Just as much a queen as if she were brought up at court, and just as much a shepherdess as if she were born a shepherd's daughter, the graces of the princely and the simplicities of the pastoral character seem striving which shall express her loveliest. She is not a poetical being; she is poetry itself; and everything lends or borrows beauty at her touch. A playmate of the flowers, when we see them together, we can hardly tell whether they take more inspiration from her, or she takes more from them; and while she becomes the sweetest of poets in making nosegays, the nosegays in her hands become the richest of crowns. Courted by the prince in disguise at one of their rustic festivals, herself the mistress of the feast, she transforms the place into a paradise." — Vol. I., pp. 331, 332.

There is too wide a variety of subjects included in Mr. Hudson's volumes to allow us room for a special criticism on his treatment of each. His lectures on As You Like It, The Tempest, Midsummer Night's Dream, Cymbeline, and Romeo and Juliet, afford perpetual stimulants both to attention and controversy. In these he has given powerful, and for the most part accurate, delineations of Prospero, Shylock, Jaques, Romeo, Mercutio, and Caliban, not to mention Ariel, the Nurse, and Bottom. His sketches of Malvolio as "self-love-sick," — of Jaques as a refined epicure of sentimental emotion, "an utterly useless, yet perfectly harmless man, seeking wisdom by abjuring its first principle," — of Parolles, "that prince of braggarts, that valiant word-gun, that pronoun of a man, a marvellous compound of wit, volubility, impudence, rascality, and poltroonery," as a "bugbear of pretension and shadow in man's clothing," — of Master Slender, as a "most potent piece of imbecility, an indescribable and irresistible nihility, who is obliged to be *sui generis* from a lack of force of character to imitate or resemble anybody else," — of Caliban, as "a strange, uncouth, malignant, yet marvellously lifelike confusion of natures, part man, part demon, part brute, whom Prospero by his wonderful art and science has educated into a sort of poet," — are all admirably done and faithful to the subject; but we can only allude to them. In the sharp analysis and genial reproduction of the comic characters, Mr. Hudson shows that he is as capable of understanding the philosophy of the ludicrous as of sympathizing with its mirth.

But the finest portion of his work is that devoted to the four great tragedies, Macbeth, Lear, Hamlet, and Othello. These bear evident marks of much elaboration in thought and diction, and rank, in our opinion, with the best specimens of philosophical criticism in English or German literature. The vigor and brilliancy of the style, and the verbal felicities and *Hudsonisms* with which it is variegated, are likely to dazzle away attention, in some degree, from the real weight and importance of the matter. It would be absurd to say that they are altogether original, for complete originality on subjects which have engaged the attention of so many powerful intellects would be another name for extravagance and paradox; but they are original in the sense of containing the deeply meditated opinions of one mind, who, while he has freely sought light from other minds, has evidently adopted no opinions which he has not scrupulously examined. Some views which are prominent in other writers he has included in his own, by altering their relations and limiting their application; but he has not hesitated to reject many which are well accredited. The wonderful characters of these dramas he appears to have profoundly studied, especially in regard to the practical wisdom which may be evolved from them by close study; and his elucidation of their moral and mental constitution is always able, even when it leaves room for controversy. No one critic has excelled him in the forcible presentation to the understanding and imagination of such a gallery of characters as Macbeth, Lady Macbeth, Hamlet, Polonius, Ophelia, Lear; Cordelia, Othello, Iago, and Desdemona.

Mr. Hudson's general idea of Hamlet, Shakspeare's enigma in character, is that of "conscious plenitude of intellect, united with exceeding fulness and fineness of sensibility, and guided by a predominant sentiment of moral rectitude;" and he attempts to show, with great force and ingenuity, that Hamlet is withheld from action, not from the lack of will, but by the strife in his mind between incompatible duties; filial piety prompting him to obey the commands of the ghost, conscience forbidding him to commit regicide and murder; and the result is, that the greatness of his nature can be expressed only in thought. It might be objected to this, that will is a relative term, and even admitting that Hamlet possessed more will than many who act with decision and rapidity, the fact that his other powers were larger in proportion justifies the common belief, that he was deficient in energy of purpose. Mr. Hudson says that he always acts with decision, where his moral nature is not divided between incompatible duties; but this might be said with as much truth of the most inefficient person, it being the characteristic of a healthy mind that the will is in such harmony with the conscience and the intellect that there can be no strife between duties, but there must be a resolute choice of one course of action as on the whole the wisest and best. The truth is, Hamlet is so complex a creation, and includes within the general unity of his character such a variety of elements, that it is almost impossible to start any theory regarding him which shall adequately translate our feeling of his individuality into an intellectual form; and Mr. Hudson himself is compelled to admit that there is a mystery about him which "baffles the utmost efforts of criticism," and to present his own view with more indecision and less positiveness than is usual with him.

It would be easy to prove that the play of Hamlet, considered as a work of art, is not so great as two or three of the other tragedies; but the feelings of men will always pronounce in favor of its containing the greatest of Shakspeare's characters. Considered in respect to its universality, Lear, Macbeth, and Othello, are but great specialities in comparison; more distinctly apprehended, it is true, and addressing with more potency the strongest passions and affections, but rather invigorating us with a grand impression of human powers and capacities, than prompting those "thoughts which wander through eternity," or touching that inward sense of our inefficiency as moral beings, which is the mournful fascination of Hamlet. The reading or representation of the other plays produces a rush and glow of the blood, a feeling of power and greatness as connected with the energies of guilt and the struggles of passion, a wonderful sense of what man is able to effect both in obeying and conquering conscience. The impression left by Hamlet is that of profound melancholy.

Many of the various elements in Hamlet's character Mr. Hudson has distinctly exhibited, and acutely reconciled some of its apparent inconsistencies; and, as a whole, we think his essay will bear comparison with the best which have been written on this exhaustless subject. The other characters of the play, especially Ophelia and Polonius, are admirably discriminated.

The lecture on Macbeth is the ablest in the volume for sustained vigor of thought and style. Its leading excellence consists in that absorption of the writer's mind in his subject which lends to his essay a portion of the grandeur of the play itself, while it prevents him from indulging in any freaks of digression. The general view taken of Macbeth and Lady Macbeth we think is as original as it is true, and it is sustained with much power. Imagination, considered both as a faculty of the mind and as an element of character, is most profoundly analyzed; and in a passage of which we can give but a small part, it is applied to the settlement of various disputes regarding the degree and kind of guilt which should attach respectively to these partners in crime.

"A strong and excitable imagination, set on fire of conscience, naturally fascinates and spell-binds the other faculties, and thus gives an objective force and effect to its own internal workings. Under this guilt-begotten hallucination, the subject loses present dangers in horrible imaginings, and comes to be tormented with his own involuntary creations. Thus conscience inflicts its retributions, not directly in the form of remorse, but indirectly through imaginary terrors which again reäct on the conscience, as fire is kept burning by the current of air which itself generates. In such a mind the workings of conscience may be prospective and preventive; the very conception of crime starting up a swarm of terrific visions to withhold the subject from perpetration. Arrangement is thus made in our nature for a process of compensation, in that the same faculty which invests crime with unreal attractions also calls up unreal terrors to deter from its commission. A predominance of this faculty everywhere marks the character and conduct of Macbeth. Hence his apparent freedom from compunctious visitings, even when he is in reality most subject to them. He seems conscienceless from the very form in which his conscience works; seems flying from outward dangers, while conscious guilt is the very source of his apprehensions. It is probably from oversight of this that some have pronounced him a mere cautious, timid, remorseless villain, restrained from crime only by a shrinking, selfish apprehensiveness. Undoubtedly there is much in his conduct that appears to sustain this view: he does indeed seem dead to the guilt, and morbidly alive to the dangers of his situation; free from remorses of conscience, and filled with terrors of imagination; unchecked by moral feelings, and oppressed by selfish fears: but whence his wonderful and uncontrollable irritability of imagination? How comes his mind so prolific of horrible imaginings, but that his imagination itself is set on fire of hell? The truth is, he seems remorseless only because in his mind the agonies of remorse project and translate themselves into the spectres of a conscience-stricken imagination.

"In Lady Macbeth, on the contrary, the workings of conscience can only be retrospective and retributive: she is too unimaginative either to be allured to crime by imaginary splendors, or withheld from it by imaginary terrors. Without an organ to project and embody its workings in outward visions, her conscience can only prey upon itself in the tortures of remorse. Accordingly, she knows no compunctious visitings before the deed, nor any suspension or alleviation of them after it. Thus, from her want or weakness of imagination, she becomes the victim of a silent but most dreadful retribution. Conscience being left to its own resources, she may indeed possess its workings in secret, but she can never for a moment repress them; nay, she cannot reveal them if she would, and she dare not if she could; the fires burn not outwards into spectres to sear her eyeballs and frighten her out of her self-possession, but concentrate themselves into hotter fury within her. This is a form of anguish to which Heaven has apparently denied the relief or the mitigation of utterance. The agonies of an imbosomed hell cannot be told, they can only be felt; or, at most, the awful secret can be but dimly shadowed forth, in the sighings of the furnace when all is asleep but the unquenchable fire, or in the burning asunder of the cords that unite the soul to its earthly dwelling-place. With such amazing depth and power of insight does Shakspeare detect and unfold the secret workings of the human mind!" — Vol. II., pp. 165—167.

The Weird Sisters Mr. Hudson has painted in all their moral hideousness and grotesque grandeur.

"The Weird Sisters, indeed, and all that belongs to them, are but poetical impersonations of evil influences: they are the imaginative, irresponsible agents or instruments of the devil; capable of inspiring guilt, but not of incurring it; in and through whom all the powers of their chief seem bent up to the accomplishment of a given purpose. But with all their essential wickedness, there is nothing gross or vulgar or sensual about them. They are the very purity of sin incarnate; the vestal virgins, so to speak, of hell; radiant with a sort of inverted holiness; fearful anomalies in body and soul, in whom everything seems reversed; whose elevation is downwards; whose duty is sin; whose religion is wickedness; and the law of whose being is violation of law! Unlike the Furies of Æschylus, they are petrific, not to the senses, but to the thoughts. At first, indeed, on merely looking *at* them, we can hardly keep from laughing, so uncouth and grotesque is their appearance: but afterwards, on looking *into* them, we find them terrible beyond description; and the more we look into them, the more terrible do they become; the blood almost curdling in our veins, as, dancing and singing their infernal glees over embryo murders, they unfold to our thoughts the cold, passionless, inexhaustible malignity and deformity of their nature." — Vol II., p. 148.

The essay on Lear is full of admirable matter, showing, however, a struggle with the difficulties of the subject. In some respects it is the most powerful and the most characteristic of Mr. Hudson's Lectures. Lear himself is analyzed at considerable length, and the amazing grandeur of the character, as it develops itself under the pressure of unnatural wrong, and the might and variety of passions which are let loose throughout the drama, are set forth with great distinctness and a firm clutch of the subject in all its parts. Edmund is finely dissected and well discriminated from Iago and Richard. Kent and Edgar are clearly portrayed in their connection with the general design of the play. The description of Cordelia we have referred to before; but her heavenly beauty is not more fully shown than the selfishness and "hell-born tact" of her sisters. "There is a smooth, glib rhetoric," says Mr. Hudson, "in their professions, unsweetened with the least infusion of feeling, and a dry, hard, icy alertness of thought and speech in what afterwards comes from them, which is almost terrific, and which burns an impression into our minds from its very coldness;" and further on he does full justice to the "wantonness and intrepidity of their malice." The Fool has ever been a stumbling-block to critics of the play; but Mr. Hudson, instead of denying his right to be in it at all, has wisely attempted to show Shakspeare's object in placing him there. We extract the concluding paragraph of his view of the character.

"I know not, therefore, how I can better describe the Fool, than as the soul of pathos in a sort of comic masquerade; one in whom fun and frolic are sublimed and idealized into tragic beauty; with the garments of mourning showing through and softened by the lawn of playfulness. In his 'laboring to outjest Lear's heart-struck injuries,' we see that his wits are set a-dancing by grief; that his jests are secreted from the depths of a heart struggling with pity and sorrow, as foam enwreathes the face of deeply troubled waters. So have I seen the lip quiver and the cheek dimple into a smile, to relieve the eye of a burden it was reeling under, yet ashamed to let fall. There is all along a shrinking, velvet-footed delicacy of step in the Fool's antics, as if, awed by the holiness of the ground, they had put the shoes from off their feet; and he seems bringing diversion to our thoughts, that he may the better steal a sense of woe into our hearts; as grief sometimes puts on a face of mirth, and then gets betrayed by its very disguise. It is truly hard to tell whether the inspired antics which glitter and sparkle from the surface of his mind be in more impressive contrast with the dark, tragic scenes into which they are thrown, like rockets into a midnight tempest, or with the undercurrent of deep, tragic thoughtfulness out of which they falteringly issue and play." — Vol. II., pp. 273, 274.

We have little space left to remark on Mr. Hudson's criticism of the tragedy of Othello. Iago, Othello, and Desdemona, characters well fitted to test the strength and delicacy of his powers of analysis and interpretation, he has treated very differently from most of Shakspeare's critics. Iago he considers as acting, not from revenge, but from a certain intellectual pride and "lust of the brain;" in regard to his own assignment of the motives for his deeds, our critic agrees with Coleridge in calling it "the motive-hunting of a motiveless malignity." This character is Mr. Hudson's masterpiece of intellectual anatomy. Iago is the perfection of demoniacal cleverness, and it is pleasant to see the wonderful inward mechanism of his unmatched malignity of nature thus exhibited in all its subtilty and complexity of arrangement and movement. Othello is represented as the exact opposite of Iago, even in respect to jealousy, which, being a mean and despicable passion, is more appropriate to our honest Ancient than to the noble Moor. Mr. Hudson thinks that Othello acted neither from jealousy nor revenge, but from a sense of justice, in destroying Desdemona; that he killed her, not from suspicion, but from evidence of her guilt; and the fact that this evidence was the manufacture of Iago's diabolical ingenuity does not alter the motives of his conduct. There can be little doubt that this view is substantially the true one. Othello gives evidence, not only in his character taken by itself, but in various portions of the play, that jealousy and revenge can have no place in his open and ingenuous mind; and in the last scene he particularly discriminates between murdering Desdemona and sacrificing her. But we think that the critic does not sufficiently consider, in his eloquent admiration of Othello's character, that though the intention of the latter is to punish crime, he has a wild way of doing it, and that the frightful tempests of passion which sweep over his mind, and hurry him into the commission of the deed, are characteristic not so much of a just man as of a noble barbarian, who mistakes the object of justice from the very fact that justice with him is a passion rather than a principle. We do not believe, as Mr. Hudson seems to do, that Shakspeare intended Othello as a model of manhood, but as an instance of the weakness of a noble nature, in being the victim of hot and treacherous impulses, when those impulses pointed in the direction of honor. The fact that he does not act from jealousy, revenge, or any mean motive, but from passions noble and generous when properly restrained, does not vindicate his manhood from the reproach of folly in giving himself up to the excesses of his sensibility. Mr. Hudson praises the objectiveness of Othello's mind, and if we consider the Moor only in his calm moments, the praise is deserved; but no person, who has ever felt the stir of a fierce impulse when he has thought himself wronged or insulted, need be told that passion not only blinds the best intellect, but draws the conscience itself into its boiling depths; not only impels to act without a clear view of the case, but for the time sanctifies the impulse as right and just. Every true and great man, therefore, distrusts what his passions teach, and no person can be a model of manhood whose nature is their victim.

The most beautiful portion of the lecture is that devoted to the representation of Othello and Desdemona, in respect to their fitness for each other; and a triumphant answer is given to the many objections to the match on the score of color and character. Mr. Hudson calls it "the chaste union of magnanimity and meekness." In his delineation of Desdemona, he develops the exceeding beauty of this most delicate and exquisite of Shakspeare's women, with uncommon refinement of sentiment and certainty of minute analysis,—at the same time a little injuring the effect by snapping his epigrammatic torpedoes in the faces of the champions of woman's rights. This delineation is an illustration of the flexibility with which the writer adapts his style to the tone and character of his subject, and of his singular felicity in exhibiting the pathos of gentleness, and the beauty of deep, strong and quiet affection.

Mr. Hudson, in these lectures on Shakspeare, has made the analysis of every character the occasion of observations on a wide variety of subjects which its nature suggests. He has thus given his philosophy of life, in relation to the practical operation of the passions and beliefs of men; and we think he has been especially successful in treating that important branch of ethics which refers to the passage of virtues into vices, through their connection with pride, vanity, or extravagant enthusiasm. As a large portion of the world's goodness is, like King Richard's frame, but half made up, and offends from its inharmonious and partial character where it is most impressive by its separate qualities, the field open to the ethical analyst is unbounded;

and as we have rather ungently touched on some of Mr. Hudson's digressions, it is but just to observe that he has evinced throughout a disposition to disconnect virtue from cant, fanaticism, and conceit; that he has detected with a sure eye, and whipped with an honest ardor, the excellence which is self-conscious, and the purity which is proudly malignant; and that he has exhibited, with a fine union of sagacity and eloquence, the beauty of that humble goodness which seeks to elude the eye, which "vaunteth not itself and is not puffed up." In a period like the present, when conscience rushes to the rostrum and explodes in fifth-rate heroics, and every "puny whipster" of morality mistakes his appetite for notoriety for a call from the seventh heaven to rail at every person wiser and better than himself, such lessons in ethics may not be without their effect, recommended as they are by a vigor and wit as inexhaustible as the folly and fanaticism on which they are exercised. We trust that the present volumes will not be the last in which the author's keen intellect and sturdy character will find adequate expression. He has not, as yet, touched the historical plays of Shakspeare, a sphere of investigation and interpretation where he may win additional honors. In choosing the world's great poet as the text for his inquiries into human nature, he has a subject which, however it may exhaust the resources of criticism, is in itself exhaustless. The present work we consider an evidence rather than the measure of his capacity; and when we next meet him on the open field of literature, we trust to find some extravagances retrenched and some peculiarities suppressed, which now to some extent injure his style, and encumber the movement of his mind.

RICHARD BRINSLEY SHERIDAN.*

THE elegant edition of Sheridan's dramatic works, published by Moxon, betrays one strange blunder, in including the entertainment of The Camp, a feeble farce written by Sheridan's friend Tickell, and altogether unworthy of preservation in any form. The biography furnished by Leigh Hunt possesses little merit beyond an occasional luckiness of phrase and an occasional felicity of criticism. It is written with more than his usual languid jauntiness of style, and with less than his usual sweetness of fancy. Indeed, that cant of good feeling and conceit of heartiness, which, expressed in a certain sparkling flatness of style, constitute so much of the intellectual capital of Hunt's sentimental old age, are as out of place, in a consideration of the sharp, shining wit, the elaborate diction, and polished artifice of Sheridan's writings, as in the narration of the brilliant depravities and good-natured good-for-nothingness of Sheridan's character. Like all Hunt's essays, however, it is exceedingly amusing, even in its vivacious presumption and

* The Dramatic Works of Richard Brinsley Sheridan. With a Biographical and Critical Sketch. By Leigh Hunt. London: Edward Moxon. 8vo. pp. 153.

Speeches of the Right Honorable Richard Brinsley Sheridan. Edited by a Constitutional Friend. London: Henry G. Bohn. 3 vols. 8vo. — *North American Review, January*, 1848.

genial pertness; but a man like Sheridan, the dramatist, the orator, the politician, the boon companion,

> "The pride of the palace, the bower, and the hall,"

deserved a less supercilious consideration. Hunt's sketch conveys a far more vivid impression of himself than of his subject.

The prominent qualities of Sheridan's character were ambition and indolence, the love of distinction and the love of pleasure; and the method by which he contrived to gratify both may be said to constitute his biography. From the volatility of his mind and conduct, it would be a misuse of language to say that he had good principles or bad principles. He had no principles at all. His life was a life of expedients and appearances, in which he developed a shrewdness and capacity, made up of talent and mystification, of ability and trickery, which were found equal to almost all emergencies. He most assuredly possessed neither great intellect nor great passions. There was nothing commanding in his mind, nothing deep and earnest in his heart. A good-humored selfishness and a graceful heartlessness were his best substitutes for virtue. His conduct, when not determined by sensuality, was determined by vanity, the sensuality of the intellect; and in both he followed external direction. Yet, such as he was, the son of an actor, indolent, immoral, unlearned, a libertine and a drunkard, without fortune and without connections, he achieved high social, literary, and parliamentary distinction. His life was one long career of notoriety and sensuality. At the age of twenty-six he had written some of the most sparkling comedies in the English language. From that period he became a politician, and eventually was ranked with

Burke, Fox, and Pitt, among the most accomplished orators in the House of Commons. No other man with such moral habits, joined to such slender acquirements, ever raised himself to such an elevation by pure force of tact and talent. It might be said that Fox was as dissipated; but then Sheridan, unlike Fox, had not been educated for a legislator; and more than all, he had none of Fox's power of impassioned argumentation, none of his greatness and generosity of soul. Burke, like Sheridan, attained a prominent position in the most aristocratic of parties, without the advantages of birth and connections; but then he had the advantage of being the greatest statesman of his country, and Sheridan could make no pretensions to Burke's force of character and amplitude of comprehension, to his industry, his learning, or to that fiery and flexible imagination which penetrated all with life. It must be allowed that Sheridan approached neither of these men in solid reputation; but as his ambition was but one side of his love of pleasure, the notoriety which immediately succeeded his efforts was all he desired. His vanity fed and his senses gratified, there was little left for ambition to seek, or pleasure to crave. All that there is in immediate fame to intoxicate the possessor, all that there is in fame which can be *enjoyed*, he obtained with the smallest possible scorning of delights, and the smallest possible living of laborious days.

Sheridan was essentially a man of wit. By this we do not mean that he was merely a witty man, but that wit was as much the predominant element in his character as it was the largest power of his mind. From his habit of looking at life and its duties through the medium of epigram, he lost all sincerity of thought and earnestness of passion. From his power of detecting what was inconsistent, foolish, and bad in the appearances of things, he gradually came to estimate appearances more than realities, and to do everything himself for effect. His intellect became an ingenious machine for the manufacture of what would tell on the occasion, without regard to truth or falsehood. The consequence was a wonderful power of contrivance, of shrewdness, of *finesse*, of brilliant insincerity, without any vitality of thought and principle, without any intellectual character. His moral sense, also, gradually wore away under a habit of sensual indulgence, and a habit of overlooking moral consequences in ludicrous relations. His conscience could give him no pang which a jest could not heal. Vice, therefore, appeared to his mind as pleasantry as well as pleasure, and wit "pandered will." For instance, he was notoriously unfaithful to his marriage vow. To no man could adultery wear a more jocose aspect. "In marriage," he says, "if you possess anything good, it makes you eager to get everything else good of the same sort." He made no scruple of cheating his creditors, but to his mind dishonesty was merely a practical joke. It was the same with everything else. Crime appeared to him as a kind of mischievous fun, and Belial always reeled into his meditations hand in hand with Momus. Blasphemy, intemperance, adultery, sloth, licentiousness, trickery, — they were mere jests. No man ever violated all the common duties of life with such easy good-nature and absence of malignant passions. He became unmoral rather than immoral.

In considering Sheridan's career, we continually meet this wit as a disposition of character as well as a power of mind. It gives a lightness and airiness to the many rascalities and insincerities of his life. No man's vices have been more leniently treated, because their very relation provokes a smile. He fascinates posterity as he fascinated his contemporaries. Falsehood, heartlessness, sensuality, insincerity, all those qualities which bring contempt on other men, in him wear an attractive aspect; and in consideration of his being such a "good fellow," the common rules by which we judge of character have been waived in his case by general consent.

It would be impossible to set forth the talents of this remarkable adept in mystification and Regius Professor of appearances, without some sketch of his life. He was the son of Thomas Sheridan, the actor and elocutionist, and was born in Dublin, in the month of September, 1751. His father was a man of no mean capacity, but spoiled by an obstinate conceit of his powers, which made his talents pass with others for less than they were worth. His mother, whom Dr. Parr pronounced quite celestial, was the writer of two or three plays, the novel of Sidney Biddulph, and the Tale of Nourjahad. Her nature was much finer than her husband's, a fact she contrived to conceal almost as much from herself as from him. Richard early displayed an indisposition to learn; and rather than relinquish the sports for the studies of boyhood, he endured with heroical resignation the stigma fastened upon him by his father, of being an "impenetrable dunce." In 1762, he was sent to Harrow, then under the direction of Dr. Robert Sumner, and having for one of its under-masters no less distinguished a person than Dr. Parr. Neither of these eminent scholars could overcome, either by command or persuasion, his indolence and indifference, though their exertions were prompted by the conviction that his mind was naturally of no common order. The fact that some of his aristocratical school-fellows taunted him with being "a player's son," however much it might sting his sensitive vanity, could not rouse in him the spirit of emulation. He preferred to make both masters and pupils his friends by his good-humor and engaging manners, and was soon the most popular person in the school. The boys emulously prompted him in the recitations of his class; and his brilliant mischievousness as often amused as provoked the masters. He seems to have escaped the discipline of the rod even under such a believer in the birch as Dr. Parr. That good-natured audacity and that fascinating address, which captivated so many in his subsequent career, and rarely forsook him in the wreck of character and fortune, were partially developed in his youth. But he was not happy at school. He was constantly in that state of wretchedness which results from the struggle of vanity with indolence, — for years always behind his companions, and trusting to momentary expedients to escape the consequences of idleness.

At Harrow he remained until his seventeenth year, and left it with but a distant acquaintance with any branch of knowledge, imperfectly versed even in grammar and spelling, but still with some dexterity in English verse, and some knowledge of polite literature. We should judge that Pope and Wycherley had been his favorite authors, not merely because his rhymes were modelled on the one and his plays betray the influence of the other, but because he always pretended to dislike Pope and to be ignorant of Wycherley. He never seems thoroughly to have mastered the mystery of spelling. At the age of twenty he spelt thing, *think*, whether, *wether*, which, *wich*, where, *were*, and appeared to take a malignant delight in interfering with the domestic felicity of double *m*'s and *s*'s. At Harrow he was not considered vicious by Dr. Parr, who charged his subsequent irregularities upon his being thrown upon the world without a profession. At the period of his leaving school he was strikingly handsome, with that fire and brilliancy in his eyes which afterwards added so much to the effect of his oratory.

He was not sent to the university, either from his father's inability to bear the expense, or from a despair of its effect in making him a student. The elder Sheridan took him home, and undertook to complete his education under his own eye; but Richard proved as indocile a pupil there as at school, and carelessly followed his own tastes. At Harrow he had formed a friendship with a vivacious school-fellow, named Halhed, who was afterwards a judge in India, and in connection with him had translated into English verse some of the poems of Theocritus. Halhed went to Oxford, but kept up a correspondence with Sheridan at Bath. They projected various works, among which was a farce entitled Jupiter, a volume of loose stories to be called Crazy Tales, and a translation of Aristænetus. The latter was completed, though Sheridan's portion was long delayed by his indolence, and the incessant references he was compelled to make to his dictionary. It was published in 1771, but failed to bring either the fame or profit which the juvenile book-makers had anticipated. The book in itself is worthless, both in the original and translation; but the latter is curious as indicating the light and libertine tone of thought, and the command of florid commonplaces of diction, which Sheridan had acquired at the age of nineteen. Neither in its morality nor composition does it give any promise of future excellence in life or letters.

But the peculiar character of his mind, and the style in which he was eventually to excel, are well displayed in a small ironical essay, written about the year 1770, and devoted to a mock assignment of reasons why the Duke of Grafton should not lose his head. The meanness, fickleness, unpunctuality, and licentiousness, of the noble duke, are quite felicitously caricatured. The position is gravely taken, that his Grace's crimes are not of such a nature as "to entitle his head to a place on Temple Bar;" and to the charge of giddiness and neglect of public duty the author triumphantly opposes some undoubted facts.

"I think," he observes, "I could bring several instances which would seem to promise the greatest steadiness and resolution. I have known him to make the Council wait, on the business of the whole nation, when he had an appointment to Newmarket. Surely this is an instance of the greatest honor; — and if we see him so punctual in private appointments, must we not conclude he is infinitely more so in greater matters? Nay, when Wilkes came over, is it not notorious that the Lord Mayor went to his Grace on that evening, proposing a scheme, which, by securing this fire-brand, might have put an end to all the troubles he has caused? But his Grace did not see him; — no, he was a man of too much honor; — he had *promised* that evening to attend Nancy Parsons to Ranelagh, and he would not disappoint her, but made three thousand people witnesses of his punctuality."

We perceive here that covert, sharp edge of ingenious wit, which was silently fashioning Sheridan's mind and character.

During the first few years after leaving school, Sheridan seems to have lived in his father's family, without any definite purpose in life, and only varying the monotony of gayety and idleness with occasional experiments in composition. In 1771, he published a poem called Clio's Protest, or the Picture Varnished, in which the principal beauties of Bath are celebrated in some four hundred rather loose-jointed octosyllabic lines. There is one couplet, however, which has become classic: —

"You write with ease to show your breeding,
But easy writing's curst hard reading."

In this poem, also, there are eight lines which altogether exceed any other poetical attempts of Sheridan, where the least pretension is made to sentiment.

"Marked you her cheek of rosy hue?
Marked you her eye of sparkling blue?
That eye in liquid circles moving;
That cheek abashed at man's approving;
The one Love's arrows darting round;
The other blushing at the wound:
Did she not speak, did she not move,
Now Pallas, now the Queen of Love?"

At Bath, Sheridan fell in love with Miss Linley, a fascinating young singer of sixteen, whose beauty and accomplishments had turned the heads of the whole town. In his management of the affair he displayed as much *finesse* as passion. Among a crowd of suitors, he seems to have been the only one who had touched her heart, and the only one whose intentions were concealed. His brother, Charles Francis Sheridan, and his friend Halhed, were among his rivals, yet both were ignorant of his passion, and both made him their confidant. The father of Miss Linley seems to have looked upon her from an exclusively business point of view, and would, of course, naturally oppose her engagement to a penniless idler like Sheridan. His project of her life was simply this: money was to be made by her profession as a vocalist, and her singing was to lead the way to a profitable marriage. Indeed, he had already engaged her hand to an honest-hearted elderly gentleman by the name of Long; but she escaped from the engagement just before the period set for the marriage, by secretly representing to him the impossibility of his ever gaining her affections. He magnanimously broke off the alliance, without betraying the reason; and when Mr. Linley threatened a prosecution, generously settled £3000 upon her to satisfy the father's demands. Romance has hardly a nobler instance of disinterestedness, and certainly Miss Linley never possessed, in lover or husband, so true and unselfish a friend.

Then followed her elopement, and the scandal about Captain Mathews. This portion of domestic history is still involved in perplexing contradictions. As far as we can glean the facts, they are these: Miss Linley had become disgusted with her profession, partly from the intrigues of Sheridan to push his suit, partly from her being pestered with the dishonorable advances of a married libertine by the name of Mathews. It has been asserted that the latter had touched her heart, as well as awakened her fears, and also that Sheridan assisted or prompted his addresses, probably as a refined stratagem to force her into a position which would make his services necessary to her peace and honor. In that tumult of mind springing from the conflict of various fears and passions, she formed the romantic determination, advised or supported by Sheridan, of eloping to France, and entering a convent. He offered to be her protector in the journey, was accepted, and the design was at once carried into effect. On arriving at London, he raised the necessary funds for the expedition from an old brandy merchant, a friend of his father, by representing that he was running away to France with an heiress. At Calais, according to the most trustworthy accounts, he persuaded her that her character was so compromised by her elopement, that its salvation depended on an immediate marriage with him. They were accordingly secretly united, in March, 1772. Mr. Linley overtook them at Calais, but not before the ceremony had been performed; and after some explanation of the affair from Sheridan, in which the private marriage does not appear to have been mentioned, took his daughter back to England. Sheridan also returned, to brave an exasperated father, and to fight a couple of duels with Captain Mathews, in the last of which he was seriously wounded. But with all his fine-spun intrigues and their unpleasant results, there did not appear to be any hope of his being able to claim his wife. The elder Sheridan and Mr. Linley were both opposed to the union, and both seemingly ignorant that a marriage had occurred. Every precaution was employed to keep the lovers apart. Mr. Thomas Sheridan made his son take an oath never "to marry" Miss Linley. Mr. Linley cautiously watched his daughter. A year's war of cunning and contrivance ensued, in which Sheridan was of course victorious. Among other expedients to see her, he at one time disguised himself as a hackney-coachman, and drove her home from the concert-room. They were finally married, according to the English fashion, in April, 1773, — having fairly outwitted their parents in all their schemes, and at last obtained their consent or connivance to the union. The elder Sheridan, however, discarded his son, and was not reconciled to him for years.

During this excited period of his life, Sheridan did not sacrifice his characteristic indolence and habit of procrastination. A shamefully libellous account of his second duel with Captain Mathews was published in a Bath paper. Indignant at this impudent lie, he resolved to answer it immediately, but first told his friend Woodfall to publish it in his paper, in order that the public might see the charge and the refutation. Woodfall followed his directions, circulated the scandal through his columns, but never could induce Sheridan to write the promised exposure of the calumny. This is in perfect character, — to hazard his life in two duels, and then bear the imputation of cowardice rather than take the trouble of writing a letter!

The circumstances which attended his courtship and marriage gave him great notoriety. His own talents and fascinating manners, together with the musical and personal accomplishments of his wife, naturally brought him into much society. For nearly two years, he subsisted, after his own mysterious fashion, with no known income except the interest on the £3000 settled by Mr. Long on Mrs. Sheridan. Though he was entered as a student in the Temple, neither his intellectual nor social tastes would admit of a serious study of the law. But during this period he wrote the exhilarating comedy of The Rivals, which was produced at Covent Garden in January, 1775. It failed on the first night, from the stupidity or indifference of the actor who performed Sir Lucius O'Trigger. Another having been substituted in this part, the play was very successful, and has been popular ever since. It placed Sheridan, at the age of twenty-three, at the head of living dramatists. Nothing so brilliant had been brought out on the English stage since Farquhar; and while its wit and hilarity suggested the old school of comic dramatists, it was open to no objection on the score of decency.

The design of Sheridan in The Rivals was not dramatic excellence, but stage effect. In seeing it performed, we overlook, in the glitter and point of the dialogue, the absence of the higher requisites of comedy. The plot is without progress and development. The characters are overcharged into caricatures, and can hardly be said to be conceived, much less sustained. Each has some oddity stuck upon him, which hardly rises to a peculiarity of character, and the keeping of this oddity is carelessly sacrificed at every temptation from a lucky witticism. The comic personages seem engaged in an emulous struggle to outshine each other. What they are is lost sight of in what they say. Sparkling sentences are bountifully lavished upon all. Fag and David are nearly as pungent as their masters. The scene in the fourth act, where Acres communicates to David his challenge to Beverley, is little more than a brilliant string of epigrams and repartees, in which the country clown plays the dazzling fence of his wit with all the skill of Sheridan himself. When Acres says that no gentleman will lose his honor, David is ready with the brisk retort, that it then "would be but civil in honor never to risk the loss of a gentleman." Acres swears, "odd crowns and laurels," that he will not disgrace his ancestors by refusing to fight. David assures him, in an acute *non sequitur*, that the surest way of not disgracing his ancestors is to keep as long as he can out of their company. "Look'ee now, master, to go to them in such haste — with an ounce of lead in your brains — I should think might as well be let alone. Our ancestors are a very good sort of folks, but they are the last people I should choose to have a visiting acquaintance with." No dramatist whose conception of character was strong would fall into such shining inconsistencies.

The truth is, in this, as in Sheridan's other comedies, we tacitly overlook the keeping of character in the blaze of the wit. Everybody laughs at Mrs. Malaprop's mistakes in the use of words, as he would laugh at similar mistakes in an acquaintance who was exercising his ingenuity instead of exposing his ignorance. They are too felicitously infelicitous to be natural. Her remark to Lydia, that she is "as headstrong as an allegory on the banks of the Nile," — her scorn of "algebra, simony, fluxions, paradoxes, and such inflammatory branches of learning," — her quotation from Hamlet, in which the royal Dane is gifted with the "front of Job himself," — her fear of going into "hydrostatic fits," — her pride in the use of "her oracular tongue and a nice derangement of epitaphs," — are characteristics, not of a mind flippantly stupid, but curiously acute. In the scene where Lydia Languish tells her maid to conceal her novels at the approach of company, the sentimentalist is lost in the witty rake; "Lord Ainsworth" being ordered to be thrust under the sofa, and "The Innocent Adultery" to be put into "The Whole Duty of Man."

Sir Anthony Absolute is the best character of the piece, and is made up of the elder Sheridan and Smollet's Matthew Bramble. Doubtless Sheridan had many a conversation with his father, of which the first scene between Sir Anthony and Captain Absolute is but a ludicrously heightened description. The scenes, also, where the doctrine and discipline of duelling are discussed, and in which Acres and Sir Lucius shine with so much splendor, the author may have obtained in the course of his difficulties with Captain Mathews. Falkland is a satire on a state of mind which Sheridan himself experienced during his courtship of Miss Linley. The fine talk of Falkland and Julia is as unintentionally ludicrous as any comic portion of the play. We can easily imagine how the author himself might have made Puff ridicule it. Indeed, Sheridan's attempts at serious imagery rarely reached beyond capitalizing the names of abstract qualities, or running out commonplace similes into flimsy and feeble allegories. His sentiment, also, is never fresh, generous, and natural, but almost always as tasteless in expression as hollow in meaning. The merit of The Rivals is in its fun and farce; and the serious portions, lugged in to make it appear more like a regular comedy, are worse than the attempts of Holcroft, Morton and Reynolds, in the same style.

The farce of St. Patrick's Day, which Sheridan brought out a few months after The Rivals, though written in evident haste, bears, in a few passages, marks of that elaborate and fanciful wit in which the chief strength of his mind consisted. In the second scene of the first act, the dialogue between Lauretta and her mother, on the relative merits of militia and regular officers, is keen and sparkling. "Give me," says Lauretta, "the bold, upright youth, who makes love to-day, and has his head shot off to-morrow. Dear! to think how the sweet fellows sleep on the ground and fight in silk stockings and lace ruffles." To this animated burst of girlish admiration, Mrs. Bridget contemptuously replies: — "To want a husband that may wed you to-day and be sent the Lord knows where before night; then in a twelvemonth, perhaps, to come home like a Colossus, with one leg at New York and the other at Chelsea Hospital!" This is one of the most startlingly ludicrous fancies in Sheridan's works.

The success of The Rivals seems to have inspired Sheridan with industry as well as ambition, for during the summer of this year he wrote the delightful opera of The Duenna. It was produced at Covent Garden, in November, 1775, and had the unprecedented run of seventy-five nights, exceeding even the success of The Beggar's Opera by twelve nights.

The diction of The Duenna, and the management of its character and incident, evince a marked improvement upon The Rivals. The wit, though not so intellectual as that of The School for Scandal, is so happily combined with heedless animal spirits, as often to produce the effect of humor. It glitters and plays like heat-lightning through the whole dialogue. Epigram, repartee, and jest, sparkle on the lips of every character. The power of permeating everything with wit and glee, — love, rage, cunning, avarice, religion, — is displayed to perfection. It touches lightly, but keenly, on that point in every subject which admits of ludicrous treatment, and overlooks or blinks the rest. The best of the songs are but epigrams of sentiment. There is a spirit of joyous mischievousness and intrigue pervading the piece, which gives a delicious excitement to the brain. Little Isaac, the cunning, overreaching, and overreached Jew, is the very embodiment of gleeful craft, — "roguish, perhaps, but keen, devilish keen." The scene in which he woos the Duenna, and that which succeeds with Don

Jerome, are among the most exquisite in the play. The sentiment of the piece is all subordinated to its fun and mischief. The scene in the Priory with the jolly monks is the very theology of mirth. Father Augustine tells his brothers of some sinner who has left them a hundred ducats to be remembered in their masses. Father Paul orders the money to be paid to the wine-merchant, and adds, "We will remember him in our cups, which will do just as well." When asked if they had finished their devotions, their reply is, "Not by a bottle each."

The wit of The Duenna is so diffused through the dialogue as not readily to admit of quotation. It sparkles over the piece like sunshine on the ripples of running water. There are, however, a few sentences which stand apart in isolated brilliancy, displaying that curious interpenetration of fancy and wit, in which Sheridan afterwards excelled. Such is Isaac's description of the proud beauty, — "the very rustling of her silk has a disdainful sound;" and his answer to Don Ferdinand's furious demand to know whither the absconding lovers have gone: — "I will! I will! but people's memories differ; some have a treacherous memory: now, mine is a cowardly memory, — it takes to its heels at the sight of a drawn sword, it does i' faith; and I could as soon fight as recollect." In the same vein is Don Jerome's observation on the face of the Duenna: — "I thought that dragon's front of thine would cry aloof to the sons of gallantry; steel-traps and spring-guns seemed writ in every wrinkle of it." The description of the same old lady's face, as "parchment on which Time and Deformity have engrossed their titles," was omitted in the published copy; though brilliant, he could afford to lose it. The Duenna's delineation of little Isaac, after that deluded Jew has called her as "old as his mother and as ugly as the devil," reaches the topmost height of contemptuous hyperbole. "Dare such a thing as you," she exclaims, "pretend to talk of beauty? — A walking rondeau! — a body that seems to owe all its consequence to the dropsy! — a pair of eyes like two dead beetles in a wad of brown dough! — a beard like an artichoke, with dry, shrivelled jaws which would disgrace the mummy of a monkey!" But perhaps the most purely intellectual stroke of pleasantry is the allusion to Isaac, — who has forsworn the Jewish faith, and "has not had time to get a new one," — as standing "like a dead wall between church and synagogue, or like the blank leaves between the Old and New Testament."

Mr. Moore has given a few sentences from the manuscript of The Duenna which do not appear in the printed copy. Among these is the following fine soliloquy of Lopez, the servant of Don Ferdinand: —

"A plague on these haughty damsels, say I: — when they play their airs on their whining gallants, they ought to consider that we are the chief sufferers, — we have all their ill humors at second-hand. Donna Louisa's cruelty to my master usually converts itself into blows by the time it gets to me; she can frown me black and blue at any time, and I shall carry the marks of the last box on the ear she gave him to my grave. Nay, if she smiles on any one else, I am the sufferer for it; if she says a civil word to a rival, I am a rogue and a scoundrel; and if she sends him a letter, my back is sure to pay the postage."

Sheridan's brilliant success as a dramatist led to his investments in theatrical property, — a fertile source of pecuniary difficulties to him in after years. In June, 1776, he purchased a portion of Garrick's share in the patent of Drury Lane Theatre. For this property he paid £10,000. How he obtained the money has never been ascertained. Hunt conjectures that it was borrowed from some wealthy nobleman. But the mysterious principles of Sheridan's science of finance, or *finesse*, have never been laid open. He afterwards, in 1778, bought Mr. Lacy's moiety for £45,000, and thus having the control of the theatre, he made his father the manager, — a reconciliation having taken place a short time before. In raising all this money Sheridan must have displayed a power of persuasion and management which would have done honor to a Chancellor of the Exchequer. It is doubtful if even Mr. Pitt, who performed miracles in the way of loans, ever equalled it.

The first fruit of Sheridan's new interest in the drama was A Trip to Scarborough, altered, with but few additions, from Sir John Vanbrugh's Relapse. This was really a service to the cause both of comedy and decency, for the original play, though one of the most richly humorous in the language, and in Lord Foppington, Sir Tunbelly Clumsey, and Miss Hoyden, containing characters which could not well be lost to the stage, was still conceived in so libertine a spirit, and deformed with so audacious a coarseness of expression, that it must soon have passed from the list of acting plays. This comedy shows us at once the superiority of Vanbrugh to Sheridan in humor and dramatic portraiture, and his inferiority in wit and polish. Sheridan could not have delineated with such consistency of purpose that prince of coxcombs, Lord Foppington. As an illustration of the difference between the manner of the two dramatists, we extract a portion of the dialogue between Young Fashion and his brother, on the return of the former to his native country, a penniless adventurer: —

"*Fashion.* Now your people of business are gone, brother, I hope I may obtain a quarter of an hour's audience with you.

"*Lord Fop.* Faith, Tam, I must beg you 'll excuse me at this time, for I have an engagement which I would not break for the salvation of mankind.

"*Fash.* Shall you be back to dinner?

"*Lord Fop.* As Gad shall judge me, I can't tell; for it is passible I may dine with some friends at Donner's.

"*Fash.* Shall I meet you there? For I must needs talk with you.

"*Lord Fop.* That I 'm afraid may n't be quite so praper; for those I commonly eat with are a people of nice conversation; and you know, Tam, your education has been a little at large. But there are other ordinaries in town, very good beef ordinaries, — I suppose, Tam, you can eat beef? — However, dear Tam, I 'm glad to see thee in England, stap my vitals."

This is the perfection of coxcombical heartlessness and egotism, — the sublime of ideal frippery. It is easy to distinguish here between the hearty exaggeration of humor and the hard caricature of wit.

Sheridan reached the height of his dramatic fame in May, 1777, by the production of The School for Scandal, a comedy which still occupies the first place on the stage, and which will ever be read with delight for the splendor, condensation, and fertility of its wit, the felicitous contrivance of some scenes and situations, the general brilliancy of its matter, and the tingling truth of its satirical strokes. As a representation of men as they appear, and manners as they are, it has the highest merit. The hypocrisies of life were never more skilfully probed, or its follies exposed to an ordeal of more polished scorn. It was triumphantly successful from the first, and during its long run exceeded most other attractions of town life. Probably no comedy ever cost its author more toil, or was the slow result of more experiments in diction and scenic effect. It was commenced before The Rivals. With his usual sagacity, Sheridan contrived that it should appear, in a great measure, as the hasty product of an indolent genius, spurred into activity by the pressure of business engagements. Mr. Moore, in his life of the author, has introduced us into the workshop of the literary mechanician, shown us the scattered limbs of the characters, the disjointed sentences of the dialogue, and the little grains of diamond dust as they first sparkled into substantial being. Every portion was elaborated with the nicest care, — not to purchase elegance by dilution, but to fix the volatile essence of thought in the smallest compass of expression, to sharpen the edge of satire to the finest point, to give scorn its keenest sting. Beginning with weakness and verbiage, he did not end until he had reduced his matter to the consistency as well as glitter of the most polished steel.

The last contribution of Sheridan to dramatic literature was the farce of The Critic, produced in 1779; we say the last, for his adaptations of Pizarro and The Stranger, twenty years after, were contributions neither to literature nor the stage. The Critic excels everything of its kind in the English language, for it is to be compared with Buckingham's Rehearsal and Fielding's Midas, not with Beaumont's Knight of the Burning Pestle. The wit always tells, and never tires.

Thus, at the age of twenty-eight, Sheridan, the "impenetrable dunce" of his first schoolmaster, had contrived to enrich English letters with a series of plays which are to English prose what Pope's satires are to English verse. We may now pause to consider the nature and extent of his comic powers, and his claim to be ranked among the masters of comic genius.

Sheridan's defects as a dramatist answer to the defects of his mind and character. Acute in observing external appearances, and well informed in what rakes and men of fashion call life, he was essentially superficial in mind and heart. A man of great wit and fancy, he was singularly deficient in the deeper powers of humor and imagination. All his plays lack organic life. In plot, character, and incident, they are framed by mechanical, not conceived by vital, processes. They evince no genial enjoyment of mirth, no insight into the deeper springs of the ludicrous. The laughter they provoke is the laughter of antipathy, not of sympathy. It is wit detecting external inconsistencies and oddities, not humor representing them in connection with the inward constitution whence they spring. The great triumphs of comic genius have been in comic creations, conceived through the processes of imagination and sympathy, and instinct with the vital life of mirth. Such are the comic characters of Shakspeare, of the elder dramatists generally, of Addison, Goldsmith, Fielding, Sterne, Scott, and Dickens. A writer who grasps character in the concrete gives his creation a living heart and brain. His hold upon the general conception is too firm to allow his fancy to seduce him into inconsistencies for the sake of fine separate thoughts. Everything that the character says is an expression of what the character is. Such a creation impresses the mind as a whole. Its unity is never lost in the variety of its manifestation. This is evident enough in the case of Falstaff, for the living idea of the man impressed on our imaginations gives more mirthful delight than his numberless witticisms. The witticisms, indeed, owe much of their effect to their intimate relation with the character. But the principle is no less true, though less evident, of Mercutio, Beatrice, and the airier creations of mirth generally. We conceive of them all as living beings, whose wit and humor do not begin with their entrance, or cease with their exit from the scene, but overflow in fun, whether we are by to hear or not. Such creations represent the poetry of mirth, and spring from profound and creative minds.

Now, Sheridan's comic personagès display none of this life and genial fun. They seem sent upon the stage simply to utter brilliant things, and their wit goes out with their exit. Everything they say is as good as the original conception of their individuality, and character is therefore lost in the glare of its representation. In truth, Sheridan conceived a character as he conceived a jest. It first flashed upon his mind in an epigrammatic form. In his Memoranda, published by Moore, we find the hints of various dramatic personages embodied in smart sayings. Thus, one is indicated in this significant sentence: — "I shall order my valet to shoot me, the first thing he does in the morning." Another is sketched as "an old woman endeavoring to put herself back into a girl;" another, as a man "who changes sides in all arguments, the moment you agree with him;" and another, as a "pretty woman studying looks, and endeavoring to recollect an ogle, like Lady ——, who has learned to play her eyelids like Venetian blinds." In all these we perceive wit laughing at external peculiarities, and subjecting them to the malicious exaggeration of fancy, but not the dramatist searching for internal qualities, and moulding them into new forms of mirthful being. The character is but one of the many pleasantries it is made to speak. In those instances where Sheridan most nearly produces the effects of humor, it is done by the coöperation of brisk animal spirits with fancy, or by adopting and refining upon the delineations of others.

We would not, in these remarks, be considered as underrating Sheridan's real powers. He is undoubtedly to be placed among the wittiest of writers and speakers. His plays, speeches, and the records of his conversation, sparkle with wit of almost all kinds, from the most familiar to the most recondite. Though seldom genial, it is never malignant; and if it rarely reaches far beneath the surfaces of things, it plays over them with wonderful brilliancy. No English comic writer, who was not also a great poet, ever approached him in fineness and remoteness of ludicrous analogy. In delicacy of allusion, in exquisite lightness and certainty of touch, in concise felicity and airiness of expression, his wit is almost unmatched. It has been asserted that he had not a fertile fancy, and that he gained much of his reputation by the care with which he husbanded his stores. He was doubtless often complimented for his readiness when he least deserved it, and was cunning in the concealment of preparation. But we think he was so entirely a wit as to be choice to daintiness in what he employed, and to aim at perfection in its verbal expression. He would not always trust to a mere flow of animal spirits to fashion the light idea of the minute; for his object was not mere hilarity, but the keen, subtile, piercing strokes of the intellect. We believe he suppressed more sparkling jokes than he ever wrote or uttered; that the fertility of his fancy was great, but that its expression was checked by his taste. There are as many stories of his readiness as of his premeditation. His calling Whitbread's image of the phœnix "a poulterer's description of a phœnix," and his objecting to a tax on mile-stones as unconstitutional, because "they were a race *who could not meet to* remonstrate," are as happy as any of his most elaborated epigrams.

Brilliant as had been the success of Sheridan as a dramatist, he commenced, shortly after the production of The Critic, a still more brilliant career as an orator and politician. His powers of conversation, and his delight in social pleasures, brought him into terms of intimacy with many prominent members of the Whig opposition, who could appreciate both his talents and good-fellowship. Through Lord John Townsend, he became acquainted with Mr. Fox, and they were mutually pleased at their first meeting. Fox declared Sheridan the wittiest man he had ever known. An introduction to Burke soon followed. He soon became one of the most welcome visiters at Devonshire House, "where politics was made to wear its most attractive form, and sat enthroned, like Virtue among the Epicureans, with all the Graces and Pleasures for handmaids." At Brooks's Club-house, where the Whig politicians blended conviviality with business, he soon shone preëminent among the hardest drinkers and wittiest talkers, — the very man to do honor to that

> "liberal Brooks, whose speculative skill
> Is hasty credit and a distant bill;
> Who, nursed in clubs, disdains a vulgar trade,
> Exults to trust, and blushes to be paid."

There his spirits were repressed by no attempt on the part of his associates, noble by birth or genius, to assert the lord or the Right Honorable. The usual style of address was Jack Townsend, Ned Burke, Tom Grenville, Dick Sheridan, and the like. The ease and familiarity of the whigs in their social intercourse, and those signs of the times which indicated their approaching change from opposition to administration, offered stimulants both to Sheridan's love of pleasure and to his ambition. He joined the party, and, with a few exceptions, was faithful to its creed and leaders through life. His brilliancy and adroitness made him an able coadjutor of Burke and Fox in assailing the corruptions of the court, and defending the liberties of the people. He was to be a thorn in the side of toryism.

After performing some minor services to his party, he was sent to the House of Commons as a member for the borough of Stafford, in October, 1780. The nation was suffering under the calamities of the American war, and Lord North's administration was assailed with every weapon of argument and invective, by an opposition strong in popular favor and aristocratic connection, but bitterly hated by the king. Sheridan's first speech was a comparative failure. It was on the subject of a petition complaining of the undue election of himself and his colleague. He launched into an indignant vindication of his constituents. When he had concluded, Mr. Rigby, a member of the tory administration, coolly ridiculed his elaborated rage. Sheridan was not prepared to reply; but Fox came to the rescue of his friend, and informed the right honorable gentleman that, "those ministerial members who chiefly robbed and plundered their constituents might afterwards affect to despise them, yet gentlemen who felt properly the nature of their trust would always treat them and speak of them with respect." In an assembly where such language as this was the commonplace of debate, it was evident that a man, to keep his position, must learn to think quick and strike hard; and Sheridan felt that he had much to learn before he could rank high in his new profession. He asked his friend Woodfall to tell him candidly what he thought of his first attempt, and received the discouraging reply, that speaking did not appear to be in his line, and he had much better have adhered to his former pursuits. "It is in me, however," said Sheridan, after a short pause, "and by ——, it shall come out!" From this moment his training as a debater commenced, and he spared no effort to perfect himself in his art.

He had many personal advantages suitable to an orator, — a powerful frame, a face which, though coarse in some of its features, was capable of great variety of expression, a deep, clear voice, and an eye of piercing brilliancy, which never winked. Beneath all his indolence and sensuality, he possessed a desire for distinction, and an ambition for effect, which inspired him with sufficient industry to master the details of particular questions, and prepare sparkling declamation to delight his audience. He had not that depth of feeling and earnestness of purpose by which the great orator identifies himself with his subject; but he could imitate those qualities admirably. His sly, subtile intellect was always on the watch for occasions for display, and he seized them with exquisite tact. Besides, he had a long training in the House of Commons; and though as a debater he never reached the first rank, from his lack of perfect readiness and his want of familiarity with principles, he still developed in the end a sturdy political courage, and a command of expedients, which enabled him to meet without flinching the fiercest attacks of the treasury bench, and to bear bravely up even against the arrogant scorn of Pitt.

During the first few years of Sheridan's political life, he produced but a small impression; but he was steadily feeling his way into notoriety. Enjoying the friendship of Fox, Burke, and all the prominent whigs, he was insensibly educating himself into a politician. On the overthrow of Lord North's administration, and the formation of the Marquis of Rockingham's, in March, 1782, he was appointed one of the under-secretaries of state. This office he occupied but four months. The death of Lord Rockingham split the whig party into two divisions. One of these, the Rockingham confederacy, led by the Duke of Portland and Mr. Fox, and to which Burke and Sheridan belonged, was the traditional whig party, the heir of the principles of the Revolution, and was supported by the strength of the old whig families. It was essentially aristocratic in its constitution, and derived much of its power from the wealth, stability, and parliamentary influence of the great whig lords. The other was the remnant of Lord Chatham's party, who had combined with the Rockinghams in the opposition to Lord North, and, on the overthrow of the latter, had received a share of the spoils. It was led by Lord Shelburne, father to the present Marquis of Lansdowne, and was more popular in its character than the other division of the whigs. George the Third, who bitterly hated the whig oligarchy, seized the opportunity presented by the death of the Marquis of Rockingham of dealing it a heavy blow. He appointed Lord Shelburne, instead of the Duke of Portland, prime minister. Shelburne, without consulting his colleagues, accepted. Fox, Burke, and the other "old whigs," immediately resigned and went into opposition.

There were thus three parties in the House of Commons, the tory adherents of Lord North making the third. To carry on the government, it was necessary for two of these to unite. After some negotiations between the two divisions of the whigs, which resulted in nothing, Fox formed a coalition with Lord North, and, after a short, sharp struggle, came into power. This was the most imprudent thing, judged by its effects, ever done by the whig party; for by the great body of the nation it was considered a scandalous contempt of public principle, and it fixed an odium on Fox and Burke from which they never wholly recovered. Sheridan, who, from his lack of strong passions and high purposes, often excelled his greater contemporaries in his judgment of the temper of the people, strenuously opposed the coalition. He could not appreciate the objects of Fox and Burke, but he was shrewd enough to discover the inefficiency of their means.

In the new ministry Sheridan was made secretary of the treasury, and gained thereby some knowledge of arithmetic, which he often paraded afterwards in discussing the financial measures of Mr. Pitt. The coalition ministry did not long exist; it was detested both by the king and people. The most ridiculous and atrocious falsehoods were manufactured with regard to the objects of its leaders. Its fate was sealed when Mr. Fox's East India Bill was introduced. This great measure passed the House of Commons by a large majority, but it was defeated by intrigue and treachery when it came to the House of Lords. On the failure of the bill, Fox and his colleagues were instantly dismissed by the king, although they still possessed a majority of votes in the lower house. William Pitt, then just entering upon his political career, was made prime minister, — fought for three months, against a majority of the House of Commons, one of the greatest parliamentary battles on record, — and on the dissolution of parliament, and the election of a new House of Commons, found himself firmly seated in power. The whigs went into long and hopeless opposition.

This was one of the most exciting periods in English political history, but its consideration belongs rather to the biography of Burke and Fox than of Sheridan. One of his most felicitous retorts, however, occurred in an early scene of this hurried drama. While Pitt was serving under Lord Shelburne, Sheridan fired some epigrams into the ministry, which would have shone bright among his happiest dramatic sallies. Pitt, in that vein of arrogant sarcasm for which he was afterwards so much distinguished, informed him, that if such dramatic turns and epigrammatic points were reserved for their proper stage, they would doubtless receive the plaudits of the audience; but the House of Commons was not the proper scene for them. Sheridan, who was morbidly sensitive to any allusion which connected him with the stage, determined to silence such insinuations forever. He felt, he said, flattered and encouraged by the right honorable gentleman's panegyric on his talents, and if he ever engaged again in the compositions to which he alluded, he might be tempted to an act of presumption, — to attempt an improvement on one of Ben Jonson's best characters, — the character of the *Angry Boy* in The Alchemist. Nothing could have been better and bitterer than this retort; and it pleased Sheridan so much, that he made a cast of the whole play, assigning each of the prominent opponents of his party a character in harmony with the whig doctrine regarding his disposition. Lord Shelburne was Subtle; Lord Thurlow, Face; Mr. Dundas, Doll Common; Mr. Rigby, Sir Epicure Mammon; General Conway, Dame Pliant; and His Majesty himself was honored with the part of Surly.

In an extravagantly burlesque sketch of Sheridan, written by his friend Tickell in a copy of The Rivals, there is a finely ludicrous account of the popular clamor against the leaders of the coalition ministry, the humor of which will be appreciated by all who know the political history of the time, and the means used to prejudice both king and people against the connection. It contains also a pertinent allusion to Sheridan's devotion to the bottle, and, through the exaggeration of caricature, enables us to judge of his habits and character at this period.

"He [Sheridan] was a member of the last parliaments that were summoned in England, and signalized himself on many occasions by his wit and eloquence, though he seldom came to the House till the debate was nearly concluded, and never spoke unless he was drunk. He lived on a footing of great intimacy with the famous Fox, who is said to have concerted with him the audacious attempt which he made, about the year 1783, to seize the whole property of the East India Company, amounting at that time to about £12,000,000 sterling, and then to declare himself Lord Protector of the Realm by the title of Carlow Khan. This desperate scheme actually received the consent of the lower house of parliament, the majority of whom were bribed by Fox, or intimidated by his and Sheridan's threats and violence; and it is generally believed that the revolution would have taken place, if the lords of the king's bedchamber had not in a body surrounded the throne, and shown the most determined resolution not to abandon their posts but with their lives. The usurpation being defeated, parliament was dissolved, and loaded with infamy. Sheridan was one of the few members of it who were reëlected; — the burgesses of Stafford, whom he had kept in a constant state of intoxication for three weeks, chose him again to represent them, which he was well qualified to do."

The fact of his reëlection, mentioned in the last sentence of this fine caricature, is the more to be noted, as a hundred and sixty members of the old parliament, favorable to Fox and North, were defeated. These called themselves, with much truth as well as pleasantry, "Fox's Martyrs."

In following Mr. Fox into opposition, Sheridan soon became one of his most efficient supporters. Mr. Pitt's administration found in him a powerful opponent; and he was especially felicitous in ridiculing the pretensions of the tories, and galling them with pointed declamation. Incapable of projecting leading measures, and deficient in those higher qualities of mind which made Burke and Fox great statesmen, he was the most effective of partisans. When pressed to speak on topics which required extensive knowledge, or an appeal to authorities, he would say humorously to his political friends, — "You know I'm an ignoramus, but here I am; instruct me, and I will do my best." As a man of wit, — of wit not only as a power of mind, but as a quality of character, — he detected weak points in argument, or follies in declamation, with an instinctive insight. In the habit of recording in a memorandum-book his most ingenious thoughts as they occurred to him, he had ever at hand some felicities to weave into every speech. A few of his brilliant ideas absolutely haunted him, and he took especial pleasure in varying their application, and making them tell on different occasions. One of these is well known. In his private memoranda he speaks of one "who employs his fancy in his narratives, and keeps his recollections for his wit." This idea was afterwards directed against a composer of music turned wine-merchant, — a man, he said, "who composed his wine and imported his music;" — and was finally shot off, in a seemingly careless parenthesis, in a speech in reply to Dundas, — a right honorable gentleman, ("who depends on his imagination for his facts, and his memory for his wit,") &c. Again, he had a great love of a witty metaphor drawn from the terms of military science. It first appears as a kind of satire on his own reputation for extempore jests. "A true-trained wit," he says, "lays his plans like a general, — foresees the circumstances of the conversation, — surveys the ground and contingencies, — and detaches a question to draw you into the palpable ambuscade of his ready-made joke." In another memorandum he sketches a lady who affects poetry. "I made regular approaches to her by sonnets and rebuses, — a rondeau of circumvallation, — her pride sapped by an elegy, and her reserve surprised by an impromptu; proceeding to storm with Pindarics, she, at last, saved the further effusion of ink by a capitulation." Exquisite as this is, it is even exceeded in the shape in which he presented the general idea in the House of Commons. Among the members of the whig party who had "ratted," and gone over to the administration, was the Duke of Richmond, a man who had been foremost in the extreme radical ranks of his former connections. In the session of 1786, the duke brought forward a plan for the fortification of dock-yards. Sheridan subjected his report to a scorching speech. He complimented the duke for the proofs he had given of his genius as an engineer.

"He had made his report," said Sheridan, "an argument of posts; and conducted his reasoning upon principles of trigonometry as well as logic. There were certain detached data, like advanced works, to keep the enemy at a distance from the main object in debate. Strong provisions covered the flanks of his assertions. His very queries were in casements. No impression, therefore, was to be made on this fortress of sophistry by desultory observations; and it was necessary to sit down before it, and assail it by regular approaches. It was fortunate, however, to observe, that, notwithstanding all the skill employed by the noble and literary engineer, his mode of defence on paper was open to the same objections which had been urged against his other fortifications; that if his adversary got possession of one of his posts, it became strength against him, and the means of subduing the whole line of his argument."

From 1780, the period of his entering parliament, to 1787, Sheridan, though he had spoken often, had made no such exhibition of his powers as to gain the reputation of a great orator. But about this time the genius and moral energy of Burke started a subject, which not only gave full expression to his own great nature, but afforded the orators of his party a rare occasion for the most dazzling displays of eloquence. We refer, of course, to the impeachment of Hastings. In all matters relating to the affairs of India, Burke bore sovereign sway in his party. It was he who projected the unsuccessful India bill, on which the coalition ministry was wrecked. Defeat, however, was not likely to damp the energies of a mind like his, when it had once fastened on an object; and he kept alive among his associates the determination to bring the spoilers of India to a public account for their misdeeds, and to hold them up to hatred and execration as worthy successors of Cortés and Pizarro, in plundering and depopulating the empire they had conquered. Burke was the only man in England in whom the prosecution of Indian delinquency and atrocity was a fixed passion as well as a fixed principle. By his ardor and complete comprehension of the subject, he communicated his enthusiasm to his party, — a party which always appeared best when it had public criminals to brand and public corruptions to expose. In bringing forward in the House of Commons the various charges against Hastings, the charge relating to the spoliation of the Begums was allotted to Sheridan. He was probably well supplied by Burke with materials, and he resolutely determined to give the subject that attention which would enable him to make an effective speech. Of all the men engaged in the prosecution, he was perhaps the most superficial in the feeling with which he regarded the crimes against which he was to declaim. His conscience and passions were not deeply stirred against the criminal. Hunt says, in his light way, that the inspiration of Burke in this matter was a jealous hatred of wrong, the love of right that of Fox, "and the opportunity of making a display at somebody's expense that of Sheridan, without any violent care either for right or wrong." With regard to the latter, at least, the remark is just. We can conceive of nothing more ludicrous than the idea of Sheridan sitting down with his bottle and documents, and, by dint of hard drinking and cautious reading, concocting ingenious epigrams out of the frauds, and framing theatrical thunder against the crimes, of the great oppressor of India.

However, the event was such as to reward all his diligence. His speech was made on February 7, 1787, and occupied five hours and a half in the delivery. All parties agreed in its extravagant praise. Fox said, that all he had ever heard, all that he had ever read, when compared with it, dwindled into nothing, and vanished like vapor before the sun. Burke and Pitt declared it to be unequalled in ancient or modern eloquence. Logan, who had written a defence of Hastings, went that evening to the House with the strongest prepossession against Sheridan and in favor of Hastings. After the former had been speaking an hour, he observed to a friend, — "All this is declamatory assertion, without proof." When he left the House, at the end of the speech, he exclaimed, — "Of all monsters of iniquity, the most enormous is Warren Hastings." Windham, who was no friend to Sheridan, said, twenty years afterwards, that, in spite of some faults of taste, it was the greatest speech within the memory of man. The most significant sign of its effect was the adjournment of the House, on the ground that the members were too much excited to render a fair judgment on the case, — a ground that Burke very happily ridiculed. The practice of cheering at the end of a good speech commenced with this splendid effort of Sheridan.

There can be little doubt that this was, on the whole, the greatest production of Sheridan's mind. There is no report of it deserving the name. Although he had the speech written out, he would never publish it. With his usual sagacity, he judged that the tradition of its effects would give him more fame than the production itself. To account for his success is difficult. A great deal is to be referred to the materials which his subject presented for oratorical display, to his beautiful delivery of particular passages, to the care with which he elaborated the whole, and to the surprise of the House at its superiority over all his previous speeches. He most certainly did not possess that deep feeling of horror and detestation for the crimes of Hastings which animated the breast of Burke. Several years afterwards, when the Prince of Wales introduced him to Hastings, he had the meanness to tell the latter that he had attacked him merely in the way of his vocation as a whig politician, and trusted that it would not be considered as a test of his private feelings. Hastings did not condescend to answer him, but turned scornfully away. If the passion was thus in a great measure simulated, it certainly was not expressed, as far as we can judge from passages here and there in the imperfect printed report, in a style very much above verbiage and fustian. The passages which would have best vindicated the eulogies it received were probably the epigrammatic portions; and these must have been of surpassing brilliancy, not only from the ingenuity of Sheridan's mind, but from the startling contrasts with which the subject itself was replete. Thus, the most felicitous passage which can be gleaned from the printed report is that in which reference is made to the sordid spirit of trade which blended with all the operations of the East India Company as a government, and disgraced even their boldest achievements, which showed the meanness of pedlers and the profligacy of pirates. "Alike," he says, "in the political and military line, could be observed auctioneering ambassadors and trading generals; — and thus we saw a revolution brought about by affidavits; an army employed in executing an arrest; a town besieged on a note of hand; a prince dethroned for the balance of an account. Thus it was they exhibited a government which united the mock majesty of a bloody sceptre and the little traffic of a merchant's counting-house, — wielding a truncheon with one hand, and picking a pocket with the other."

On the 3d of June, 1788, Sheridan, having been appointed one of the managers of the impeachment of Hastings, delivered before the Lords in Westminster Hall another oration on the same charge he had so brilliantly urged in the House of Commons. The fashionable excitement caused by this great state trial is said to have reached its height on the occasion of his speech. Fifty guineas were known to have been paid for a ticket. The oration, including the examination of evidence, occupied four days; and although it did not wring the hearts and overpower the understandings of the audience, like the impassioned and comprehensive orations with which Burke opened the impeachment, it still produced the liveliest sensation. Burke, whose whole soul was in the success of the cause, and who was delighted with everything which helped it forward in popular estimation, was heated with admiration during its delivery. "There," he exclaimed to Fox, while listening to some passages, "there, that is the true style; something between poetry and prose, and better than either." Fox replied, that he thought the mixture was likely to produce poetic prose, or, what was worse, prosaic poetry.

On the fourth day Sheridan strained his powers to the utmost to charm and dazzle his auditory. In referring to one crime of Hastings, he made an allusion to the great historian of the age. Gibbon was present, and in his Memoirs has recorded the pleasure he experienced in receiving such a compliment before all that was great and noble in the nation. "Not in the annals of Tacitus," said Sheridan, "not on the *luminous* page of Gibbon, could be found described such a monstrous act of cruelty and treachery." At the conclusion of the speech, he sunk back in the arms of Burke, as if overcome with fatigue and emotion. One of his prosaic whig friends came up to him and said,—"Why, Sherry, did you compliment that tory, Gibbon, with the epithet *luminous?*" "I meant *vo-luminous*," answered Sheridan, in a hoarse whisper.

It is commonly believed that the speech in Westminster Hall was substantially the same as that delivered in the House of Commons, although, in its diffusion through two days, Fox and many others considered it inferior to his first effort. Burke, however, in his celebrated eulogy on the oration, said, that from poetry up to eloquence, there was not a species of composition of which a complete and perfect specimen might not be culled from it. Now, there is extant a *verbatim* report of the speech; and Mr. Moore, in his Life of Sheridan, has quoted all those passages which even the partiality of a biographer could pronounce excellent. It is scarcely necessary to say, that there is hardly a page in Burke's own works which is not worth the whole of Sheridan's fine writing, as far as eloquence can be estimated from the written composition. Burke's extravagant praise is to be referred partly to the magnanimity of a rival orator, emulous to outdo all others in hearty recognition of another's merits, and partly to his intense enthusiasm for every effective speech delivered on his side of the subject. In him the success of the impeachment swallowed up every desire for personal notoriety or fame in its prosecution, and he naturally exaggerated the merit of all arguments and eloquence which illustrated or enforced his own views. Sheridan cared little for the impeachment, but cared much for the reputation of a brilliant speech. Posterity has dealt fairly with both. Burke has succeeded in fixing an ineradicable brand of guilt on the brow of an able and unprincipled public criminal, whose great capacity and great services seemed to overawe the world's moral judgment, and has consigned him to an immortality of infamy in orations as imperishable as literature. Sheridan has succeeded in gaining the reputation of an infinitely clever and dextrous speaker, the records of whose speeches are read only in a vain attempt to discover by what jugglery of action such ingenious combinations of words ever imposed upon an audience as the genuine language either of reason, imagination, or passion.

As an orator, Sheridan belongs to a peculiar class. He was certainly the most artificial of speakers, when his ambition led him to imitate Fox in impassioned declamation, or Burke in luminous disquisition and imaginative flights. Moore, in a strain of exquisite flattery, celebrates him as one

> "Whose eloquence, brightening whatever it tried,
> Whether reason or fancy, the gay or the grave,
> Was as rapid, as deep, and as brilliant a tide
> As ever bore Freedom aloft on its wave."

Nothing, as Moore well knew, was more incorrect than the impression of spontaneousness which this eulogy conveys. The private memoranda of Sheridan's speeches show the exact place where the "Good God, Mr. Speaker," is to be introduced; and exhibit painfully elaborated "bursts" of passion, into which it was his intention to be "hurried." With regard to imagery, those figures which start up in the mind of the true orator in the excitement of the moment, instinct with the life of the occasion, were in Sheridan's case carefully fashioned out beforehand and bedizened with verbal frippery, cold and lifeless in themselves, but made to tell upon the audience by grace and energy of manner. It has been repeatedly noticed, that in the notes of Burke's speeches nothing is observable but the outline of the argument and the heads of the information; in the notes of Sheridan's, little is seen but images, epigrams, and exclamations.

Sheridan has been often classed with Irish orators, that is, with orators having more feeling and imagination than taste. Irish oratory, it is very certain, is not confined to Hibernians, neither does it comprehend all Irish speakers. Its leading characteristic is sensibility. But this sensibility is good or bad, according to the mental powers by which it is accompanied. In Burke, it appeared in connection with an understanding and an imagination greater than any other orator ever possessed, and second, if second at all, only to Bacon among statesmen. In Grattan, it took the form of fiery patriotism, stimulating every faculty of his intellect, and condensing the expression of thought and fancy by pervading both with earnest passion. In Curran, it quickened into almost morbid action one of the readiest and most fertile, though not comprehensive minds, ever placed in a human brain. In Shiel, it is seen in the rapidity, intensity, and intellectual fierceness, given to the expression of blended argument and fancy. In all of these, sensibility is more or less earnest and genuine, penetrating thought with fire, and thus giving it force to the will as well as persuasion to the understanding. In another class of Irish orators, of which Phillips was once considered the representative, this sensibility is little more than the boiling over of warm blood, without corresponding power of thought or imagination; and it runs into all excesses of verbose declamation and galvanized commonplace. Execrable as it is, however, and doomed to instant damnation in a tempest of hisses as soon as it is printed, it is still not without effect upon uncultivated or excited audiences. This style of oratory is sometimes called imaginative, although its leading absurdities are directly traceable to a want of imagination. It is no more imaginative than Swift's mock reasoning to prove that Partridge was dead is argumentative.

Now, to neither of these classes of Irish orators does Sheridan belong; for genuine sensibility, either in the expression of reason or nonsense, does not enter into the composition of his speeches. He feels neither like Burke nor like Phillips. In serious declamation, he simply attempts an imitation of intense and elevated feeling; and his passion, as artificial and as much made up as the thunder of Drury Lane, finds suitable expression in a diction curiously turgid, in meretricious ornaments, and in a style of imagery plastered upon the argument, instead of growing out of it. If, as a speaker, he had used this florid style without stint, he must have failed. We believe that it did not please his contemporaries much more than it does posterity, and that it was generally held by them to bear about the same relation to the peculiar merits of his speeches, which the fine talk of Falkland and Julia bears to the fun of Acres and the wit of Captain Absolute. What placed him by the side of Burke, Fox, and Windham, as an orator, was not his earnestness of feeling, but his equalling them in the felicity with which they exposed crime, corruption, sophistry, and hypocrisy, to ridicule and contempt. His most successful imitations of Burke consist in the employment of verbal paradoxes and ironical fancies, in which the opinions and statements of an opponent are exaggerated into a kind of gigantic caricature, and then scornfully eulogized. Pretence of all kinds soon collapses, when subjected to this ordeal of wasting ridicule. The bubble bursts at once, and "is resolved into its elemental suds." As far as we can judge of Sheridan's great speech on the Begums, his most effective weapon of attack was a sarcastic mockery of Hastings's assignment of patriotic motives for his crimes, an epigrammatic expression of hatred and scorn for oppression and rapine, and a singular felicity in dragging down the governor of a vast empire to the level of the common herd of profligates and criminals, by connecting his greatest acts with the same motives which influence the pickpocket and the cutthroat. By bringing the large conceptions and beneficent aims which should characterize a ruler of nations into startling contrast with the small personal objects which animate the heroes of Hounslow Heath, he had an opportunity to play the dazzling fence of his wit with the most brilliant effect. Many of his most swollen comparisons and strained metaphors are redeemed from absolute contempt only by the presence of this mocking spirit. That his great strength consisted in this power of viewing everything under its ludicrous relations is seen in the rapidity with which he ever extricated himself from the consequences of failure in his florid flights. Mr. Law, the counsel for Hastings, very successfully ridiculed one of the hectic metaphors of his speech. "It was the first time in his life," replied Sheridan, "he had ever heard of special pleading on a metaphor, or a bill of indictment against a trope. But such was the turn of the learned counsel's mind, that when he attempted to be humorous, no jest could be found, and when serious, no fact was visible." This retort is worth a thousand such tropes as occasioned it.

Up to the impeachment of Hastings, Fox, Burke, and Sheridan, were closely united; but the illness of the king, which soon followed, brought a question before parliament, which, while it seemed to promise the accession of the whigs to power, resulted only in sowing the seeds of distrust among their leaders. George the Third became insane, and it devolved upon the legislature to appoint or recognize a regent. The Prince of Wales, a selfish debauchee and spendthrift, was the person that would naturally be appointed; and the prince, hating his father and hated by him, was a whig. Mr. Pitt and the tories were determined to restrict his prerogative; the whigs struggled to have him endowed with the full powers of majesty. A fierce war of words and principles was the consequence, in which Fox and Burke gave way to unwonted gusts of passion, and Burke, especially, indulged in some unwise allusions to the king's situation. Sheridan, who for a long time had been the companion of the prince in his pleasures, and in some degree his agent in the House of Commons, was suspected by his friends of intriguing for a higher office than his station in the party would warrant. The king's recovery put an end to the debates, and to the hopes of each. A portion of the disappointment which Burke and Fox experienced was transmuted into dislike of each other, each feeling that the violence of the discussion had injured the party, and each placing the blame upon the other.

Both were suspicious of Sheridan, also, and doubted his honorable dealing in the matter.

This slight feud would probably have been soon healed, if the breaking out of the French Revolution had not given an immediate occasion for all the discontent in the party to explode. Burke, from the first, looked upon that portentous event with distrust; Fox and Sheridan hailed it as an omen of good. The debate on the Army Estimates, in 1790, was the first public sign of the schism between the leaders of the whigs. Sheridan, who seems to have foreseen that Fox and Burke must eventually dissolve their connection, took this opportunity, in an animated but indiscreet speech against Burke's views, to hasten the separation; but he only succeeded in bringing Burke's wrath down upon his own head, and a public disavowal of their friendship. The progress of the Revolution, however, soon brought on a final division of the whig party, upon which a majority of its most influential members went over with Burke to the support of the ministry. Fox and Sheridan, not on the most cordial terms themselves, were left to battle, in the House of Commons, both against their old enemies and a powerful body of their old friends.

There is no portion of Sheridan's political life which is more honorable than his services to freedom during the stormy period between 1793 and 1801. It was a time of extreme opinions. The French Revolution had unsettled the largest intellects of the age, and seditious and despotic principles clashed violently against each other. The tories, to preserve order, seemed bent on destroying freedom; and the radicals, enraged at the attacks on freedom, or deluded by the abstract commonplaces of the French school, overlooked order in their struggle against oppression. Fox, Sheridan, Grey, Tierney, Erskine, were the nucleus of a legal opposition to the ministry, and, at the head of a small minority of whigs, defended the free principles of the constitution against the court, the administration, and popular clamor. Sheridan adhered generally to his party, though he contrived to escape some of its glorious unpopularity by giving a hearty support to the government on a few trying occasions. His various speeches during this period display his usual brilliancy, with passages here and there of powerful declamation. It is needless to say that his dissipation and debts were on the increase. His patriotism was not allowed to dull the edge of his sensuality. In his habits of mystification, too, in the preparation of his speeches, he displayed his customary cunning. In 1794, when called upon, as one of the prosecutors of Hastings, to reply to Mr. Law, he spent two or three days in such close application to reading and writing, as to complain to a friend of having motes in his eyes. When he entered Westminster Hall, he was asked by one of his brother-managers for his bag and papers. He answered, that he had none, and must get through with his speech as he best might; — "he would abuse Ned Law, ridicule Plumer's long orations, make the court laugh, please the women, and, in short, go triumphantly through his task." Much to the surprise of the managers, he succeeded admirably.

In 1792, Mrs. Sheridan died. She was a woman of fine mind, warm heart, and uncommon beauty, entering with zeal into her husband's interests, and making his home as happy as the home of a libertine could be, who was gifted with good-nature rather than principle, with affectionate sensations rather than a heart. In 1795,

Sheridan married again. The lady was Miss Ogle, daughter of the Dean of Winchester, and represented as young, accomplished, and thoroughly in love. Sheridan's powers of fascination neither dissipation nor the reputation of a *roué* could weigh down.

During this stormiest period of English politics, Sheridan preserved the same virtue in his speeches, and the same self-indulgence in his conduct, which characterized his whole life. When Pitt resigned, and the Addington ministry was formed, in 1801, he, following the example of a few other whigs, gave that feeble government, with its toothless toryism, a kind of support. But the inflated incapacity of that administration could not fail to draw laughter from him, the prince of laughers. Addington was nicknamed "The Doctor." When one of his measures was suddenly opposed by the Scotch members, usually loyal to ministers, Sheridan set the House of Commons in a roar by addressing the premier from Macbeth, — "Doctor, the thanes fly from thee!" On the return of Pitt to power, Sheridan went again into opposition. Of all his later speeches, his most celebrated is one which he made in 1805, on his motion for repealing the Defence Act. It was written during the debate, at a coffee-house near Westminster Hall, and was full of the fiercest attacks upon the premier. Pitt, commonly so insensible, is said to have writhed under its declamatory sarcasm; and many who were present thought they discerned at times in his countenance an intention to fix a personal quarrel upon his flashing adversary. After the death of Pitt, in 1806, and the formation of the Fox and Grenville ministry, Sheridan was appointed Treasurer of the Navy, an office which he deemed altogether below his deserts, and which indicated that his position in the party had not advanced since 1789. The administration was dissolved shortly after the death of Fox, owing to the determination of Lord Grenville to push the Catholic claims. Sheridan, though an Irishman himself, and with every feeling of nationality arrayed on the side of Catholic emancipation, was still vexed at the ministry for committing itself to the measure, from his selfish fear of losing office. He knew the king would not consent to it, and he had not the high Roman feeling of Lord Grenville, who was indisposed to shape his course according to the path marked by the bigotry of the monarch. "He had heard," Sheridan said, " of people knocking out their brains against a wall; but never before knew of any one building a wall expressly for the purpose."

After his loss of office, Sheridan's efforts in parliament were not frequent. He became engaged in various intrigues regarding the formation of new administrations, in which he lost the confidence of his political friends. His intimacy with the Prince of Wales, and his declining health and reputation, seem equally to have hurried him into dishonorable tricks and insincerities. At last, in 1812, rendered desperate by the loss of his theatrical property, embarrassed in purse, and almost bankrupt in character, he closed a brilliant political life by an act of treachery which will ever stain his name. On the death of Mr. Perceval, great difficulty was experienced in forming an administration. There was a probability of the whigs again coming into power; overtures were made to Lords Grey and Grenville to form a ministry. They would not accept, unless the household were dismissed. Lord Yarmouth, one of this number, requested Sheridan to convey to the two whig lords their intention to resign, rather than be an obstacle to the formation of a ministry. Had Sheridan done this, the political history of England might have been essentially different, and measures of reform might have dated from 1812, instead of 1832. But he betrayed his trust, partly because he was aware that the Prince Regent did not really desire the accession of the whigs, and partly because he disliked the inflexible character of the lords who would have been at the head of affairs. He not only did not communicate the offer of Lord Yarmouth, but, when a rumor of it had transpired, offered to bet five hundred guineas that it was not in contemplation. His treachery was discovered too late to be repaired. Lord Liverpool, "commonplace and loving place," obtained the premiership, and held it during fifteen years of tory rule.

Closely following this shipwreck of character, Sheridan lost his seat in parliament. This was almost equivalent to a loss of his personal liberty, for he was no longer safe from arrest. From this time to his death, he gathered in the harvest of long years of indolence, extravagance, and vice. Disease was secretly wearing away his originally powerful constitution. His face, once so full of intelligence and beauty, had become deformed and bloated with intemperance. His old friends looked coldly upon him. Brilliant powers of conversation and fascinating address no longer characterized the faded wit and shattered debauchee. The Prince Regent, for whom he had so often sacrificed his interest and honor, left him "naked to his enemies." All the mortifications which could result from wounded pride and vanity, and the sense of decaying intellect, thickened upon him. His ruin was swift and sure. His creditors seized upon everything which the pawnbroker had not already taken.

Even Reynolds's portrait of his first wife as Saint Cecilia passed from his possession. In the spring of 1815, he was arrested and carried to a sponging-house, where he was retained two or three days. His life sufficiently shows that his sense of shame was not quick, but he was deeply humiliated at this arrest, feeling it as "a profanation of his person."

And now came the misery of his last scene. He appeared to feel that his life was drawing to a close. To some sharp remonstrances from his wife on his continued irregularities, he replied in an affecting letter. "Never again," he wrote, "let one harsh word pass between us during the period, which may not perhaps be long, that we are in this world together, and life, however clouded to me, is spared to us." His last illness soon followed. Even his dying bed was not free from the incursions of writs and sheriffs. He was arrested, and would have been taken away in his blankets, had not his physician threatened the officer with the consequences of committing murder. At last, on the seventh of July, 1816, in his sixty-fifth year, he died.

Then came the mockery of a splendid burial. Dukes, royal and noble, bishops, marquesses, earls, viscounts, right honorables, emulously swelled the train of his funeral. "France," said a French journalist at the time, "is the place for an author to live in, and England the place for him to die in." In the Poet's Corner of Westminster Abbey, the only spot remaining unoccupied was reserved for the body of him whose death-bed was not safe from the sheriff's writ. Tom Moore, in a fine strain of poetical indignation, published just after Sheridan's death, thus cuttingly refers to the noble lords who "honored" the funeral: —

"How proud they can press to the funeral array
Of him whom they shunned in his sickness and sorrow!
How bailiffs may seize his last blanket to-day,
Whose pall shall be held up by nobles to-morrow!"

The task of lightening the misery of Sheridan's last hours was left to such commoners as Samuel Rogers, Thomas Moore, and good Doctor Bain.

The moral of Sheridan's life lies on the surface, and we shall not risk any commonplaces of ethical horror in commenting upon its hollowness and its sins. The vices for which he was distinguished are generally reprobated, and their position in the scale of wickedness is sufficiently marked; but they are not the darkest kind of vices. We are not of that number who select him from his contemporaries, and expend upon his follies and errors the whole strength of their indignation. Allowing him to have been as bad as his nature would allow, we believe he was a much better man than many of his contemporaries who are commonly praised as virtuous. The man who brings misery upon himself and his family by intemperance and sloth is justly condemned, but he is innocent compared with one who, from bigotry or lust of power, would ruin or injure a nation. George the Third is praised as a good king; but the vices of Sheridan's character were mere peccadilloes compared with the savage vices which raged and ruled in the heart of his Majesty. In a moral estimate which included all grades of sin, Sheridan would compare well even with Lord North, William Pitt, or Spencer Perceval, with all their social and domestic merits. The American war and the war with France originated, or, at least, were continued, in a spirit which approaches nearer to the diabolical than the sensuality of Sheridan; and we feel little disposed to chime in with that morality which passes over all the rats and liberticides, the servile politicians and selfish statesmen, the bad and bigoted spendthrifts of blood and treasure, during a whole generation, to hurl its heaviest anathemas upon one poor, weak, volatile, brilliant, and hard-pressed *roué*.

But while we thus remember that there are natures which have contrived to indulge darker passions than he ever dreamed, without coming under the ban of either historian or moralist, and while we therefore have little sympathy with one class of Sheridan's judges and critics, we do not join in the absurd sentimentality of another class, who strive hard to place his case among the infirmities and calamities of genius. The sources of his errors were not those which have sometimes hurried large and unregulated minds into evil, and there is something ridiculous in placing him by the side of the Otways, the Savages, the Chattertons, the Burnses, and the Byrons. With regard to his calamities, there is hardly another instance in literary history of a man who enjoyed so much fame with such moderate powers, and who was enabled to run so undisturbed a career of sensuality from manhood to within three years of his death. What commonly goes under the name of enjoyment of life he had in full measure, not only without the check which comes from means limited by honest scruples, but almost without the remorse with which conscience usually dashes unhallowed pleasure. And with respect to the desertion of which he complained in the last years of his life, it was, as far as regarded his political connections, the result of his political treachery; and as his personal friendships sprang from the fellowship of vice rather than feeling, he had no right to expect that the rakes and good fellows, his companions of the bottle and the debauch, would be the bankers of his poverty, or the consolers of his dying hours.

HENRY FIELDING.*

There is no word more provokingly equivocal than history. In one sense, it simply indicates a department of literature; in another, the sum and substance of all departments. He who should read all the so-called historians of the world, from Herodotus to Hallam, would, in common phrase, be considered as possessing a knowledge of history; but in respect to the thing itself, he might be more ignorant of many ages and nations than one who had devoted his time to plays and novels. In regard to the history of England, especially, it is curious how small a portion of our realized and available knowledge of the English mind and people is derived from the standard narratives of public events. When, after exhausting the strictly historical department of English literature, we turn to its works of imagination, and from these to the numerous trifles in poetry and romance which every age has poured forth, we discover that we are increasing our historical information, while we are seemingly gratifying only taste, indolence, or whim. Indeed, it is impossible to understand the causes of England's material supremacy in any summary now extant of the persons and events connected with its differ-

* The Works of Henry Fielding, with a Life of the Author. By Thomas Roscoe. London: Henry G. Bohn. 1843. 8vo. pp. 1116. — *North American Review, January*, 1849.

ent stages. That peculiar combination of virtues and vices, of practical sense and stubborn prejudice, which occurs to us when we think of an Englishman, never was obtained from Hume alone. The literature of the country, in the most generous meaning of that word, is therefore a portion of its history, conducting us close to the heart, character, and external costume, the body and soul, of the nation, and enabling us to realize the people as living beings. A drama by Fletcher, a pamphlet by Nash, a satire by Donne, a novel by Mrs. Behn, a comedy by Congreve, not to mention the stores of information in Spenser, Shakspeare, Milton, Dryden, and Pope, may convey more real historical knowledge, and enable us better to understand England in its manners and unwritten institutions, than Holinshed and Carte, than Oldmixon and Burnet. A person whose notions of dignity prevent him from penetrating into such minor avenues of letters will never gain much more than the shell of history. If the object of historical studies be thus to give an idea of a past age, approaching as near as possible in vividness to that which we have of our own, then certainly no student of the eighteenth century should overlook the life and works of Henry Fielding, — dramatist, lawyer, journalist, magistrate, novelist, and man of wit and pleasure about town. Tom Jones and Joseph Andrews may not seem of so much importance as George II. and Sir Robert Walpole; but no one ever followed the adventures of the former without acquiring, unconsciously, a vast amount of information shedding light on the policy of the latter.

Of all the English authors, the most exclusively English, the two into whose very being the life of their age and country passed most completely, are Ben Jonson and Henry Fielding; and no person can be pronounced ignorant of England who has studied their works, and obtained a living conception of their personal characters. Our present concern is with Fielding, who, somewhat deficient in that positiveness and dogmatism of the English character which appear so grandly in old Ben, and in heedless animal spirits suggesting the Irishman rather than the Englishman, still in mind and disposition represents that basis of sensuality, humor, coarse and strong morality, that practical grasp of things in the concrete, and that thorough-going belief in the senses, which characterize the genuine Saxon. Scott, indeed, thinks that Fielding can hardly be relished and understood by persons not habitually conversant with old English life. Doubtless, this is true to a certain extent; but we can name no novelist who so felicitously exhibits human nature through its modification of English nature, or conveys so vivid an idea of both, in modes so universally appreciable.

The period in which Fielding lived and wrote presented a society richly diversified in character and manners, and affording to the novelist exhaustless materials of humor and observation. It had already, in Pope, Swift, Young, Arbuthnot, and others, found its satirists, men who made its crimes and follies the butt of their aggressive wit; but it had not as yet been mirrored on the page of a deep and genial humorist, combining the requisite insight with the requisite toleration to represent it in its peculiar life and costume. The profligacy and levity which disgraced the higher classes had been partially reflected in the comedies of Congreve; and Vanbrugh, with a stronger grasp of character, had brought up Sir Tunbelly Clumsey and Sir Francis Wronghead from the country, to introduce them to the Lord Foppingtons and Sir John Brutes of the town; but the man who should exhibit church and state, town and country, in characters at once national, local, and individual, and be able to present pictures by which after ages might recognize the form and spirit of the time, was yet to appear. Fielding not only possessed the jovial temperament and mental power to perform this truthfully, but the vicissitudes of his life brought him face to face with every order of English society. Born of a noble family, but thrown at an early age into the world to make his own living, he knew almost every form of poverty and distress, and obtained his knowledge of mankind by the scientific process of observation and experience. He knew equally well the mansion of the aristocrat and the garret of the author, the palace and the sponging-house, the court and St. Giles, Westminster Hall and Wapping, the cathedral and the Methodist meeting, the manor-house and the country inn. To dine with the Duke of Roxburgh or his Grace of Bedford in the West End, to sup with Savage or Boyce in a cellar, — to converse with Lord Chesterfield at Pulteney's, and with a country coachman at an ale-house in Dorsetshire, — to hear some member of the great whig connection expatiate on the blessings of the Hanover succession, and to hear some old Jacobite squire roar out a song to Charlie over the water, after the fifth bottle, — to know all varieties of fortune, and consequently all varieties of company, and intensely to enjoy everything short of misery itself, — was the common experience of the great delineator of English character and manners. No other author of his time had his experience of life; and his experience would have converted almost any other author into a spitfire satirist, or moody misanthrope. Towwouse, Squire Western, Parsons Adams, Barnabas, and Trulliber, Dr. Harrison, Colonel Bath, Square, Thwackum, Bliful, Allworthy, Partridge, Fanny, Sophia Western, Mrs. Slipslop, Lady Bellaston, — almost every form which selfishness, baseness, levity, licentiousness, clerical worldliness, political corruption, as well as honesty, innocence, and truth, assumed in the men and women of his age, — Fielding knew with a certainty and accuracy almost approaching the perfection of science. And he surveyed the whole with a kind of inimitable absence of spleen and egotism, more wonderful than his knowledge. His works represent greater varieties of rascality and hard-heartedness than those of almost any other writer; yet he never leaves the impression that human nature is to be given over as beyond redemption, or that the world is effete.

Fielding was born April 22, 1707. He was the son of Edmund Fielding, an officer who served with some distinction under Marlborough, and who eventually was promoted to the rank of lieutenant-general. By his father's side, Henry was connected with the noble families of Kingston and Denbigh, and through the latter with the renowned house of Hapsburg, from which Austria has drawn her emperors. Gibbon, in that burst of enthusiasm for literary fame in which he exhorts the noble Spensers, enriched by the trophies of Marlborough, to consider still "the Fairy Queen as the most precious jewel in their coronet," also finely alludes to Fielding's noble descent. "Far different," he says, "have been the fortunes of the English and German divisions of the family of Hapsburg; the former, the knights and sheriffs of Leicestershire, have slowly risen to the dignity of a peerage; the latter, the emperors of Germany and kings of Spain, have threatened the liberty of the Old and invaded the treasures of the New World. The successors of Charles V. may disdain their brethren of England; but the romance of Tom Jones, that exquisite picture of human manners, will outlive the palace of the Escurial and the imperial eagle of Austria." This confident prophecy seems in the present year to be in the course of fulfilment.

Fielding received the rudiments of education from the Rev. Mr. Oliver, a coarse, avaricious, and narrow-minded priest, whom he afterwards immortalized in the character of Parson Trulliber. From the hands of this clerical bear he was removed, when he arrived at a suitable age, to Eton, where he distinguished himself for his quickness of parts, and laid the foundation of that classical knowledge which he always loved, and which he was so fond of parading even in his novels. At this school he formed the acquaintance of many boys who afterwards became eminent, and among others of Lord Lyttelton, Mr. Fox, and Mr. Pitt. It was his father's intention to make him a lawyer, and accordingly he was sent from Eton to Leyden, in his eighteenth year, to study the civil law. How he conducted himself abroad we are not informed; but launched, as he was, into life in the heyday of youth, and with a constitution which could bear any excesses into which his irresistible animal spirits might impel him, we have always thought that his knowledge of law was principally obtained in experiencing the consequences of its violation. His biographers are careful to inform us that he studied hard with the celebrated Professor Vitriarius, and some of them mournfully regret that his father could not sustain the *expense* of carrying him through a course of study so auspiciously commenced, and which was winning him the approbation of the learned Thebans of Leyden. The probability is, that Fielding's expenses were considerably larger than properly belong to a simple devotee of knowledge, and that General Fielding had to support the *bon vivant* as well as the scholar. At any rate, his father's remittances failed after he had enjoyed the inestimable companionship of Professor Vitriarius for a period short of three years, and he was compelled to return to England. It cannot be doubted that he returned with some knowledge of the world and of the classics, with a keen sense of the pleasurable, and a disposition to gratify it in the elegant recreations suitable to a rake and a blood; but of his civil law we hear no more.

General Fielding was married four times, and had a large and constantly increasing family, which in respect to number was compared to King Priam's; and accordingly, on Fielding's arrival in England, he found his good-natured father perfectly willing that he should be his own master, and willing also to settle on him £200 a year, — an allowance, however, which was never paid. Thus, at the age of twenty, Fielding was cast upon the world of London, with nobody to assist or check him, and with five particularly ravenous senses to provide with objects of necessity or indulgence. He immediately renewed his acquaintance with many of his schoolboy friends, and plunged resolutely into the dissipation of the time. With a handsome person, a constitution of iron, a fund of spirits which glorified the hour and disregarded the future, with brilliant conversational powers and irresistible *bonhommie* of manner, he soon became popular, and ranked among his associates all the good fellows of the day, from the noble profligate to the needy author. But this kind of life requires money, and Fielding probably soon found that there is a limit to the patience of unpaid landladies and the liberality of fashionable friends, and that he must choose an occupation. It is needless to say that Professor Vitriarius and the civil law were forgotten, and that his thoughts were at once turned to the stage, as presenting the best means of solving the problem, how a young adventurer, whose wit and sprightliness were the talk of London society, could gratify an insatiable love of pleasure without heaping up a portentous mountain of debts. At the early age of twenty, therefore, he became a playwright, having no alternative, as he expressed it, but to be a hackney writer or a hackney coachman.

His first comedy, Love in Several Masques, was produced in 1707. Though it succeeded The Provoked Husband, which had attracted large audiences for twenty-eight nights, it still met with a moderate share of success. Wilks, Cibber, Mrs. Booth, and Mrs. Oldfield, did all that good acting could do in promoting the author's interest. When published, the play was dedicated, in an elegant preface, to Lady Mary Wortley Montague, who was a connection of Fielding's. The author may be considered to have started fair in his dramatic career, with nothing to prevent his reaching the most profitable summits of theatrical excellence, provided his genius was calculated for the drama. Congreve, at about the same age, had, under somewhat similar circumstances, laid the foundations of his fortune in The Old Bachelor. But Love in Several Masques indicates none of Congreve's original merit. It is a well-written imitation of the latter's style, bearing about the same relation to its model which Hayley bears to Pope, or the Right Honorable John Wilson Croker to Scott. In character, plot, and diction, it is but a repetition of the established theatrical commonplaces of that period. In the throng of affected similes and ingenious comparisons, which the author forces into his dialogue to make it seem brilliant, we look in vain for one touch of Fielding's peculiar genius, as afterwards evinced in his novels. The play simply exhibits fashionable life after the approved fashion. The beau is "everything of the woman but the sex, and nothing of the man beside it;" the lord considers "beauty as the qualification of a mistress, fortune, of a wife," "virtue so scarce as not to be worth looking after, and beauty so common as not worth the keeping;" and the brisk town wit of the play, with the usual cant of his function, swears that a charming woman, divested of her fortune, is like "Beau Grin out of his embroidery, or my Lady Wrinkle out of her paint." The dialogue is smart and glib rather than witty, with a continual effort after brilliancy. The only thing which distinguishes the play from the hundred forgotten productions of its school is an occasional touch of humanity or hearty sentiment, proving that the best-humored and most joyous man in Great Britain could not altogether forget his nature, even when cramped in the most artificial of styles. There is something amusing in the moral tone of the prologue, whether we consider the freedom of the particular comedy it introduces, or the coarseness of the plays which succeeded it. It expresses, in rather indifferent verse, the ethical object which at that time every fifth-rate professor of ribaldry and licentiousness affected to have in view, however scandalous might be his language and *dramatis personæ*: —

"No private character these scenes expose;
Our bard at vice, not at the vicious, throws.
* * * * *
Humor still free from an indecent flame,
Which, should it raise your mirth, must raise your shame.
Indecency 's the bane to ridicule,
And only charms the libertine or fool.
Nought shall offend the fair one's ears to-day,
Which they might blush to hear, or blush to say."

Fielding was now fairly entered upon his occupation of man of letters, and during the ensuing ten years produced eighteen comedies and farces. The Temple Beau, which succeeded Love in Several Masques, was brought out in 1729. The introductory scene, between Lady Lucy Pedant and Lady Gravely, is a good specimen of malignant genteel raillery; and the scene in which Sir Harry Wilding breaks into his son's chambers in the Temple, and discovers the peculiar kind of law which his darling student is practising, is finely ludicrous; but the play is generally uninteresting and devoid of originality. With these two comedies, Fielding seems to have bid adieu to the school of Congreve, and resolved to try a kind of writing which less tasked his fancy, and which he could despatch in more haste. Tom Thumb, a grand caricature of the popular tragedies of the day, including those of Dryden, and aiming to produce laughter by the broadest gushes of drollery, appeared in 1730, and still keeps the stage. In a similar, though even coarser style, is the Covent Garden Tragedy, produced in 1732. The Coffee-House Politician, which Arthur Murphy gravely praises, could have been written only when the author was drunk. The fumes of gin and tobacco, we think, can be detected in most of his plays after he had been two years at work, there being a sort of brazen vulgarity about them which continually suggests the pot-house. The year 1732 seems to have been the most industrious period of his dramatic life. The Mock Doctor, and The Miser, from Molière, The Debauchees, and The Covent Garden Tragedy, were all produced in this year. The wretchedness of the profession he had chosen is perhaps sufficiently indicated in the character of the entertainments he provided for the public; but in the dedication of The Universal Gallant, in 1734, to the Duke of Marlborough, he indicates another evil. This comedy was condemned with particular emphasis; and he complains bitterly that there were some young gentlemen about town who "made a jest of damning plays." He speaks of the cruelty of this kind of wit, especially as exercised upon a person like himself, depending on his labors for his bread; and he adds, that "he must be an inhuman creature, who would, out of sport and wantonness, prevent a man from getting a livelihood in an inoffensive way, and make a jest of starving him and his family."

About this time, he seems to have conceived the idea of being a manager himself, the ill success of his plays probably rendering the great theatres indisposed to receive his productions. Accordingly, in 1735, he assembled a company of discarded actors, under the name of the Great Mogul's Company of Comedians, to perform his own dramas at the small theatre in the Haymarket. Though this project hardly met with any more success than his other contrivances for a living, failure does not appear to have damped his miraculous spirits, or to have impaired the elastic vigor of his mind. At this theatre, we believe, he brought out his two political satires, Pasquin, in 1736, and The Historical Register, in 1737, which, in themselves of no great importance, were the cause of the celebrated measure of Walpole to restrain the licentiousness of the stage, by giving discretionary power to the Lord Chamberlain to refuse a license for any play which did not meet his approbation.

This measure created at the time a great deal of clamor among the dramatists, and has been the cause of a great deal of cant among them since. During its passage through parliament, Lord Chesterfield delivered a powerful speech against it. It seems to us that the merits of the bill must be considered apart from the motives of the framers, in order to form a correct judgment upon it. That some check was needed, there can be no doubt. The evil which the bill assumed to remedy was one which strikes at the very root of society. To outrage morality and decency in public places of amusement, to have a legalized system of entertainments whose only tendency was to make drunkards, blasphemers, and libertines, might be very justly considered as demanding the interference of the civil power, even by those who would give the largest liberty to the publication of irreligious and immoral opinions. Fielding himself, in 1729, indicated the necessity of some regulation of the stage, when, in mourning over the degradation of authorship, he exclaimed,—"Be profane, be immodest, be scurrilous; and if you would ride in a coach, deserve to ride in a cart." In truth, the obligation of every ruler to enforce decency, if he cannot enforce morality, called for some measure to check the profligate stupidity and comic irreligion which every broken-down Grub-street hack might indite over his morning gin, to feed a vulgar appetite for brutal merriment.

But important as this measure eventually proved in

purifying the stage, nothing can be more ludicrous than to praise Sir Robert Walpole, as Coxe, his biographer, gravely professes to do, for his agency in the reform. He was undoubtedly a man not destitute of virtues, and when we consider that he was a hunted politician, it must be acknowledged he was singularly free from cruel and malignant passions; but it would be absurd to allege a regard for decency as the motive of any of his acts. He had always been accustomed to the English theatre as it had been left by Charles II., — the theatre of Wycherley, Vanbrugh, Congreve, and Farquhar, — and doubtless considered libertinism as a prominent element in every brilliant play. Besides, he was himself utterly destitute of delicacy and refinement. His talk, it is well known, was confined to two subjects, politics and women; and he conversed about the latter in a style to shock even the gentlemen of a generation famous for its preference of plain noun substantives to cautious circumlocutions. His summer revelries at Houghton made him the nuisance of the neighborhood; and if indecency and profanity, inspired by "potations pottle deep," were heard anywhere with peculiar emphasis and shameless vociferation, it was at the board of England's prime minister. The truth is, he cared nothing about the license of the stage until it attacked his darling power. Fielding might have violated every morality and decency of civilized life, without being much disturbed by Sir Robert; but in Pasquin and The Historical Register, he exhibited and exposed the political corruption of the day; and Walpole then found it was high time to put a stop to the demoralization of the drama.

But if Walpole's motive was not a hatred of licentiousness, neither was Fielding's motive a hatred of political corruption. He had a grudge against the prime minister. In 1730, he had solicited his patronage, which Walpole, with his usual contempt for literary men, had refused. In 1731, he dedicated The Modern Husband to him, exhorting him to protect the Muses, reminding him that heroes and statesmen had ever been the patrons of poets, and adjuring him to add to his many noble and patriotic qualities the glory of being the protector of literature. The flattery and the advice Walpole seems equally to have disregarded. Accordingly, Fielding became a patriot, as the word was understood at that day;—that is, he joined those politicians who were indignant at the corruption which they could not themselves wield, or in whose fruits they could not participate. Walpole bought all the patriots he feared, and defied or ridiculed the rest. He never patronized literary merit; but if he discovered a writer able to do the dirty work of political pamphleteering without any scruples whatever,—a man whose mind presented the harmonious combination of tact, impudence, shamelessness, and talent for influencing the mob,—he was ready to give such a person the full enjoyment of the luxuries of the secret-service fund. Thus, he paid £10,000, at different periods, to that "intermediate link between man and the baboon," the profligate Arnall. As far as Fielding's political opinions were concerned, he seems to have viewed Sir Robert with great admiration. In his latest work, he speaks of him as "one of the best of men and of ministers."

We have seen that, during the ten years that Fielding was a dramatist, he averaged about two plays a year. The composition of these occupied but a comparatively small portion of his time. He would sometimes contract to write a farce or comedy in the evening, pass a good portion of the night convivially, and bring in a whole scene the next morning, written on the paper in which his darling tobacco was wrapped. His plays never met with any brilliant success, and failed to provide for his wants. He said himself that he left off writing for the stage at the period when he should have begun. There are some indications of his genius scattered over his comedies, though but little evidence is given of dramatic art. As a playwright, he never reached the success which was afterwards obtained by such men as Holcroft, Morton, and Reynolds.

There are few memorials extant of his mode of life during these ten years of contrivances and failures. That he plunged heedlessly into dissipation, and led the life of a man of wit and pleasure about town, there can be no doubt. As an author, he was distinguished from his brother hacks by having the social position of a gentleman. He repeatedly received pecuniary assistance from Lyttelton and other friends, who were delighted with his vivacity and good fellowship. Lyttelton said that, in conversation, he had more wit and humor than all the celebrities of Queen Anne's day put together. But though thus assisted by the patronage of rich and titled acquaintances, Fielding must have participated more or less in the vices, miseries, and humiliations, of the literary drudge of the time, — the hireling of managers and booksellers, the vagabond by practice and author by profession. The appreciation which the government had of literary men is perhaps best indicated in the remark of George I. to Lord Hervey, who had some sins of verse lying heavy on his soul: — "Do not write poetry, — 'tis beneath your rank;. leave that to little Mr. Pope; — 'tis his trade." A man who, in that day, adopted authorship as a means of livelihood, was immediately associated with one of the most curious bodies of men of which we have any record;—the clan of Grub-street hacks, so remorselessly gibbeted by Pope. During the reigns of George I. and George II., it was very difficult for a man of genius to escape this most miserable of social grades. As soon as he fell into the clutches of a bookseller, he had passed through that gate over which was written, "Let those who enter here leave Hope behind." He had joined that lean and squalid band of *littèrateurs*,

> "Who must, like lawyers, either starve or plead,
> And follow, right or wrong, where guineas lead";—

men on whose brows was blazoned the sign, "Mind to be let;" who were slaves to every stupid, ignorant, and unprincipled publisher, engaged in supplying a demand for frivolity, scurrility, indecency, and sedition; and who, with the tastes of scholars and the wages of draymen, ended at last in being the most dissolute and the most wretched of day-laborers. To be the tenant, at best, of an attic or a cellar; to be hunted by enraged unpaid tradesmen; to wait for weeks in the antechamber of a lord to exchange a dedication for a guinea; to have all the spirit of a man extinguished by the necessity of creeping and cringing before a vulgar taskmaster; to know want and need in all their bitterest forms; to pass at evening from the back-room of a Curll, an Osborne, or a Mist, with a worn-out brain and a jaded body, and rush to purchase a few hours' pleasure in a low debauch; to exercise more ingenuity in dodging bailiffs and bilking landladies than in writing poems or pamphlets;—this was the existence of many an enthusiast who came up to London filled with aspirations after fame, and expecting the fortune of Pope or Swift. Squalor and beggary were the commonplaces of an author's life. "Could I have guessed," says the aggrieved Mrs. Moneywood to Lackless, "that I had a poet in my house? Could I have looked for a poet under lace clothes?" And the good lady goes on to mourn that her floor is all spoiled with ink, her windows with verses, and her door almost beaten down with duns.

But connected with these scholars and men of talent there were all varieties of quacks, pretenders, panders, and buffoons. Authorship was the last refuge of the outcasts of society,—of liars, libellers, and vagabonds,—of penny, half-penny, and two-penny blasphemers and reprobates, —of men who, having tried every other petty contrivance of knavery to filch a livelihood, at last, on the smallest possible capital of grammar and sense, descended to the trade of writing. Any one who will condescend to glance over the minor literature of the period between 1720 and 1770, for the purpose of catching the general character of its composition, will be surprised at the extreme lowness of its moral and intellectual tone. Its stupidity is absolutely amazing, amid all its efforts to be bright by the grace of ribaldry and scurrility; and it becomes difficult at times to consider such lifeless slang and imbecile indecency as the product of the human mind. Scattered over Fielding's various works are allusions to this gang of *littérateurs*, who degraded authorship even below the level to which poverty and improvidence had reduced it, by offering to do the work of scholars and men of ability for a smaller pittance than the miserable one they already received. Such was the ignorant charlatan that Booth, in the novel of Amelia, meets in the sponging-house, collecting subscriptions for a translation of Ovid, of whose language he is as ignorant as a South-Sea islander. The scenes, in The Author's Farce, between Bookweight and his hacks, Dash, Quibble, Blotpage, and Scarecrow, are probably almost literal transcripts of the truth. We extract a specimen, as it tells the story better than any words of ours could do.*

* *Book.* Fie upon it, gentlemen! what, not at your pens? Do you consider, Mr. Quibble, that it is a fortnight since your Letter to a Friend in the Country was published? Is it not high time for an Answer to come out? At this rate, before your Answer is printed, your Letter will be forgot. I love to keep a controversy up warm. I have had authors who have writ a pamphlet in the morning, answered it in the afternoon, and answered that again at night.

Quib. Sir, I will be as expeditious as possible; but it is harder to write on this side the question, because it is the wrong side.

Book. Not a jot. So far on the contrary, that I have known some authors choose it as the properest to show their genius. Well, Mr. Dash, have you done that murder yet?

Dash. Yes, sir, the murder is done; I am only about a few moral reflections to place before it.

Book. Very well: then let me have the ghost finished by this day se'nnight.

Dash. What sort of a ghost would you have this, sir? the last was a pale one.

Book. Then let this be a bloody one. Mr. Quibble, you may lay by that life which you are about, for I hear the person is recovered, and write me out proposals for delivering five sheets of Mr. Bailey's English Dictionary every week, till the whole be finished. If you do not know the form, you may copy the proposals for printing Bayle's Dictionary in the same manner. The same words will do for both.

Enter INDEX.

Ho, Mr. Index, what news with you?

Index. I have brought my bill, sir.

Book. What 's here? For fitting the motto of Risum teneatis Amici to a dozen pamphlets, at sixpence for each, six shillings; for Omnia vincit Amor et nos cedamus Amori, sixpence; for Difficile est Satyram non scribere, sixpence. Hum! hum! hum! — sum total for thirty-six Latin mottoes, eighteen shillings; ditto English, one shilling and ninepence; ditto Greek, four — four shillings. These Greek mottoes are excessively dear.

Ind. If you have them cheaper at either of the universities, I will give you mine for nothing.

When we consider the wretchedness and knavery which were associated in the public mind with the profession of literature, it is not wonderful that such men as Ford, in the reign of Charles I., and Congreve and Hor-

Book. You shall have your money immediately; and pray remember that I must have two Latin seditious mottoes, and one Greek moral motto, for pamphlets, by to-morrow morning.

Quib. I want two Latin sentences, sir, — one for page the fourth in the praise of loyalty, and another for page the tenth in praise of liberty and property.

Dash. The ghost would become a motto very well, if you would bestow one on him.

Book. Let me have them all.

Ind. Sir, I shall provide them. Be pleased to look on that, sir, and print me five hundred proposals and as many receipts.

Book. "Proposals for printing by subscription a New Translation of Cicero Of the Nature of the Gods, and his Tusculan Questions, by Jeremy Index, Esq." I am sorry you have undertaken this, for it prevents a design of mine.

Ind. Indeed, sir, it does not; for you see all of the book that I ever intend to publish. It is only a handsome way of asking one's friends for a guinea.

Book. Then you have not translated a word of it, perhaps.

Ind. Not a single syllable.

Book. Well, you shall have your proposals forthwith: but I desire you would be a little more reasonable in your bills for the future, or I shall deal with you no longer; for I have a certain fellow of a college, who offers to furnish me with second-hand mottoes out of the Spectator for twopence each.

Ind. Sir, I only desire to live by my goods; and I hope you will be pleased to allow some difference between a neat fresh piece, piping hot out of the classics, and old, threadbare, worn-out stuff, that has passed through every pedant's mouth, and been as common at the universities as their drabs.

SCENE V. — BOOKWEIGHT, DASH, QUIBBLE, BLOTPAGE, SCARECROW.

Scare. Sir, I have brought you a libel against the ministry.

Book. Sir, I shall not take anything against them; for I have two in the press already. [*Aside.*

Scare. Then, sir, I have an Apology in defence of them.

Book. That I shall not meddle with neither; they don't sell so well.

Scare. I have a translation of Virgil's Æneid, with notes on it, if we can agree about the price.

Book. Why, what price would you have?

Scare. You shall read it first; otherwise, how will you know the value?

Book. No, no, sir, I never deal that way, — a poem is a poem, and a pamphlet a pamphlet, with me. Look ye, sir, I don't like your title-page: how-

ace Walpole at a later period, men of fine powers, but also of little vanities, should have shrunk from the accusation of authorship, and desired to be considered in their mortal capacity, as gentlemen, rather than in their immortal, as writers. By the inevitable law of association, a man rises or falls in public estimation exactly according to the condition and conduct of the class to which he belongs; and as a class, English authors have not been considered respectable until a comparatively late period. This is, of course, a satire on English society, rather than on its literary men; but ludicrous as the statement may sound, we believe it is accurate. At any rate, Fielding was relieved from the drudgery of his own tasks, the companionship of dissolute associates, and all those corrupt influences which attached to the writer of his time, by an important event, which he and his best friends were inclined to deem his salvation. This was

ever, to oblige a young beginner, I don't care if I do print it at my own expense.

Scare. But pray, sir, at whose expense shall I eat?

Book. At whose? Why, at mine, sir, at mine. I am as great a friend to learning as the Dutch are to trade: no one can want bread with me who will earn it; therefore, sir, if you please to take your seat at my table, here will be everything necessary provided for you: good milk porridge, very often twice a day, which is good wholesome food and proper for students; a translator, too, is what I want at present, my last being in Newgate for shoplifting. The rogue had a trick of translating out of the shops as well as the languages.

Scare. But I am afraid I am not qualified for a translator, for I understand no language but my own.

Book. What, and translate Virgil?

Scare. Alas! I translated him out of Dryden.

Book. Lay by your hat, sir, — lay by your hat, and take your seat immediately. Not qualified! — thou art as well versed in thy trade as if thou hadst labored in my garret these ten years. Let me tell you, friend, you will have more occasion for invention than learning here. You will be obliged to translate books out of all languages, especially French, that were never printed in any language whatsoever.

his marriage, in 1736, to a beautiful, amiable, and accomplished young lady, by the name of Cradock, who, in addition to her other virtues, possessed a fortune of £1500. Fielding's mother, dying about this time, left him a small estate in Dorsetshire, worth £200 a year. He accordingly forswore Bacchus and Momus, the midnight debauch and the green-room, and went with his wife to his estate in the country, with the determination of reforming his life, and devoting his time to study, literature, and domestic pursuits. But he had no sooner arrived at his new home than his natural improvidence, extravagance, and vanity, led him into a style of expense suitable only to a rich country squire. Living among his superiors in fortune, he became emulous at once to rival them in his mode of living. He was by no means an aristocrat. The Earl of Denbigh once asked him the reason of their spelling the family name differently, the earl's branch placing the *e* before the *i*, and Fielding's branch the *i* before the *e*. "I can't tell, my lord," was the philosophic reply, "except it be that my branch of the family first learned how to spell." But now that he was a landholder and country gentleman, Fielding seems to have had his nobility roused; for was it not intolerable that a man of the family of Denbigh and Hapsburg should be excelled in ostentation by the Squire Westerns and Sir Tunbelly Clumseys of his neighborhood? Instead, therefore, of devoting himself to composition, he dashed into the hilarities and hospitalities of English country-life; kept his coach, his dogs, his horses, his servants in yellow liveries, his open house, and free table; and in less than three years he was a beggar, with a constitution shattered by sensual indulgence, and a wife and family dependent on him for support. To these years, however, we owe his knowledge of rural life and character, and to his ruin the novels in which it was embodied. As soon as he found himself incapable of continuing his country life, he at once escaped from the censures and reproaches of his friends and acquaintances, — who, having assisted in his downfall, of course bitterly assailed his improvidence, — and went directly to London, with the intention of studying law. He entered himself as a student in the Temple; alternately studied hard and drank hard; and, after the usual term of probation, was called to the bar. But he was unsuccessful as a lawyer, partly owing to the distrust of attorneys, who hesitated about giving important cases to a wit and a believer in the bottle, and partly to the wild habits of dissipation which still clung to him, and prevented him from giving his serious and undivided attention to any subject. Even his attendance on his profession, desultory as it was, was soon interrupted by fits of the gout, which now began their remorseless work on his tough and solid frame. He gave up law in disgust, and returned to his original occupation of man of letters. He poured forth in rapid succession a series of fugitive pieces, to provide for the wants of the hour. He thought also of resuming his connection with the stage, and wrote his farce of Miss Lucy in Town for that purpose; but the Lord Chamberlain discerned in it an intention to hold up a man of quality to ridicule, and refused his license. We believe, also, that he produced at this time his farce of Eurydice. Its fate is sufficiently indicated on its title-page, being published, not, in the usual phrase, "as it was acted," but "as it was d—mn'd, at the Theatre Royal, Drury Lane."

But the time was approaching when his genius could

find some fit expression of the power and richness it had attained through his manifold experience of life. We owe his novel of Joseph Andrews to a lucky accident. In 1740, Richardson published Pamela. Before this period, prose fiction had hardly occurred to any writer of eminence as affording an opportunity for the acquisition of fame or money. Nonsense, stupidity, and obscenity, or, at best, such moderately clever and immoderately licentious fictions as those of Mrs. Behn and Mrs. Manley, monopolized romance. Novels were below plays and newspapers in respect to literary rank. Indeed, Richardson himself did not contemplate writing a story when he commenced Pamela. A bookseller, who had learned his talent for epistolary composition, induced him to prepare a book of letters for the benefit and instruction of those who found the task of conducting a tender or friendly correspondence to be, what Fuseli's fop found the reading of Milton, "an exceedingly tough business." He commenced his work with this humble purpose; but soon adopted the idea of giving to it the interest of a story, and in three months produced Pamela.

The success of this novel was of that peculiar kind so flattering to an author who starts an original school of composition. The book became the talk of the town, and ran through five editions the first year of its publication. Everybody, high and low, read and commented upon it. At Ranelagh Gardens, the ladies held it up to each other in triumph as they passed. Pope said it contained more good morality than twenty volumes of sermons. Dr. Sherlock, not daunted by some highly drawn scenes, innocently enough indelicate, recommended it from the pulpit. One significant sign of its popularity was its changing the pronunciation of the name itself, which in Pope is accented on the second syllable, and in Richardson on the first, — the public being willing to introduce discord into a line of the former, rather than spoil the harmony of a few verses which the latter had inserted in the novel. Richardson, at the age of fifty, found himself in some measure the centre of attraction, and his exacting and importunate vanity was fed daily with incense of private and public praise. A clique of female puffers and toadies was especially generous and indiscriminate in panegyric, and did everything in the power of foolish women to make him morbidly sensitive to blame or ridicule levelled at himself and his heroine. Fielding watched the fever, and, in a spirit of good-natured mischievousness, resolved to parody the novel, in a mock heroic style, as Cervantes had parodied the romances of chivalry in Don Quixote, and as Scarron had parodied the romances of gallantry in the *Roman Comique*. To a man of his quick sense of the ridiculous, and knowledge of life and character, the glaring faults of Pamela were instinctively evident. The moral pedantry, the conceit of virtue, the exaggerated importance attributed to the conventional distinctions of society, the absence of nature and truth, and the "do-me-good" air of the work, struck his humorous fancy at once. He saw that, in spite of its passages of simplicity and pathos, and the power of mind it evinced, it was still essentially a deception, — that its boasted morality was practically false, and its sentiment mawkish. Pamela thus had the honor to provoke the production of Joseph Andrews, the beauty and exquisite humor of which have immortalized not only itself, but the work it condescended to make the butt of its sunny merriment.

"The History of the Adventures of Joseph Andrews, and his Friend, Mr. Abraham Adams," was published in 1742. It revealed at once that wealth of invention, humor, and character, in Fielding's large and joyous mind, which had heretofore found no adequate expression. If we compare this novel with Tom Jones, we must pronounce it inferior in story, in variety of character, and in the range of its comprehension of life; but it seems to us superior even to that, in glad and exuberant feeling, in sensuous beauty, in warm and overflowing benevolence of spirit, and in the combination of the shrewdest practical observation with the most delicious abandonment to pleasurable impulses. The author seems himself to take the most intense enjoyment in the scenes he describes. He realizes them so thoroughly to his own consciousness, that he communicates the glow of their gladness to the reader. The inartistical arrangement and beautiful waywardness of the narrative; its quick growth from a mere caricature of Pamela to an independent work; the readiness with which the author's mind yields to every temptation to revel in rural scenes of adventure and enjoyment; the unmatched irony of his allusions to the novel he professes so much to admire; the heaped and overrunning measure of delight he continually pours forth from an exhaustless fund of good-natured creativeness; and, especially, the broad and deep gushes of humor, instinct with the very spirit of fun, coming from a heart as beneficent as it is mirthful, and flooding all banks and bounds of conventional propriety with overpowering merriment; make this work one of the happiest, as well as the most natural and most poetical, that ever came from the comic genius of England. But the marvel of the book consists in the union of vast worldly knowledge with childlike enthusiasm, — in the description of the faults and follies of men without the intrusion of an atom of gall or bitterness, and in enveloping the coarsest and most indisputably natural persons and events in a rich atmosphere of romance. It is an exact reflection of life, but a reflection similar to that we sometimes perceive in a still, deep river, which mirrors the trees and shrubs on its banks, and converts everything into beauty without altering its form or hue.

In Joseph Andrews we have the best exponent of Fielding's nature, with its goodness as an instinct and lack of goodness as a principle. No one can read it without feeling that in the author's heart were the germs of a philanthropy as warm and all-embracing as ever animated a human breast; but from the absence of high moral and religious aspiration, it seems to expend itself simply in the desire to make the whole world comfortable. Not a shade of moroseness, intolerance, or malignity, darkens the sunny and breezy tract which clips in his mind. After fifteen years' experience of the selfishness of the world, and with a frame shattered by indulgence in its vices, we find him in Joseph Andrews radically sound in heart and brain, without a trace of misanthropy in his composition, cheerful, cosy, chirping, with a man's large and wide knowledge united to a boy's hopeful and gleeful spirit. If we consider his mind in respect either to its scope or its healthiness, we do not see how we can avoid placing it above that of any English poet, novelist, or humorist, of his century. In strength, depth, and massiveness of mind, Swift might be deemed his equal; but Swift's perceptions were so distorted by his malignities, that he is neither so trustworthy nor so genial as Fielding. Pope, with all his brilliancy, and epigrammatic morality, and analogies from the surfaces of things, appears little in comparison, the moment he snaps and snarls out his spiteful wit and rancorous pride. Addison and Goldsmith, with their deep and delicate humor, and mastery of the refinements of character, have not Fielding's range and fruitfulness; nor, perhaps, his occasional astonishing subtilty of insight into the unconscious operations of the mind. Thus, the huntsman, in Joseph Andrews, grumbles as he draws off his dogs from Joseph and Parson Adams, because his master is in the custom of thus encouraging the creatures to hunt Christians, making them follow *vermin* instead of sticking to a hare,— this being, in the opinion of the servant, the sure way to spoil them. Smollett has occasional touches of pathos and power beyond Fielding; but, not to mention his grossness, his scurrility, and his cynicism, his portraits are caricatures, compared with those which appear in Tom Jones, Amelia, and the novel we have at present under consideration. Richardson, with his intense concentrativeness and hold upon the minutest threads of his subject, his dogged habit of accretion, his matter-of-fact accumulation of uninteresting details, presents so strong a contrast to Fielding's fresh, springing, elastic vigor, and habit of flashing a character or a feeling upon the imagination in a sentence, that comparison is out of the question.

It seems difficult to reconcile Fielding's mind with his temperament. In his life, we find him the most heedless of good fellows, delivering himself up to every impulse of sensibility, tossed and tumbled about on every wave of desire, unguided by the experience he gathers from his follies, and repenting of one excess only to rush immediately afterwards into some other. The fact, that he was in conduct so confirmed a "rowdy," and seemingly as reckless and feather-brained as Tom Fashion, or Sir Harry Wildair, makes us disposed to underrate his intellect. Yet the moment we forget his habit of deifying the moment, and calmly consider his mind, we are amazed at its weight and range, — its sure, steady, deep, and refined perception of the motives of action, — its keen vision, before which cant and hypocrisy instinctively unveil, in the very despair of eluding detection, — its humor, so sly, so shrewd, so profound, so broad, so introversive, penetrating beyond the reach of analysis to the inmost springs of life, — and its just and discriminating views of those things which are commonly overlaid with prejudice and passion.

But passing from these remarks to the work which occasioned them, it is certain that, if Joseph Andrews is the most delightful of Fielding's novels, the first book of Joseph Andrews is the most delightful portion of the whole. The strain of irony in which he alludes in the commencement to Richardson is exceeded only by his stroke at Colley Cibber, who had lately published his gossiping apology for his life. Cibber had called Fielding a "broken wit;" and the latter, in alluding to the former's autobiography, mockingly praises its design. "How artfully, by insinuating that he escaped being promoted to the highest stations in church and state, doth he teach us a contempt of worldly grandeur! How strongly doth he inculcate an absolute submission to our superiors! Lastly, how completely doth he arm us against so uneasy, so wretched, a passion as the fear of shame! how clearly doth he expose the emptiness and vanity of that phantom, reputation!" The account of

Joseph's youth, which follows, — of his position as foot-boy to Lady Booby, and his promotion thence to the post of footman, — of the unfortunate passion which her ladyship experiences for him, and his rejection of her unworthy advances, — of the letter which he writes to his sister, the divine Pamela, describing his temptation, and his being turned away by Lady Potiphar Booby from his place, on account of his heroic virtue, — is steeped through and through with mirth.

The scenes which succeed are even better. Joseph, on his return home, is waylaid at night by robbers, pounded almost to death, and thrown naked into a ditch. A stage-coach passes, and the postilion, hearing a groan, offers to stop. But the coachman tells him to go on, that the stage is confounded late, and that they have no time to look after dead men. A lady, however, interferes, but as soon as she finds the condition that poor Joseph is in, her modesty impels her to desire that he may be left where he is, it being better that he should freeze to death than that her delicacy should be wounded. Every passenger in the coach develops some form of selfishness, — and the coachman, after it is concluded to take Joseph in, swears that it shall not be done unless somebody pays a shilling for the remaining four miles he is to ride. After this point is settled, nobody will lend him a great coat to wrap himself in; the coachman, who has two, refuses, lest they should be made bloody; and the poor fellow must inevitably have perished, were it not that the postilion, whom Fielding is careful to inform us in a parenthesis was transported shortly after for robbing a hen-roost, strips off his own coat, and swearing a great oath, (for which the passengers rebuke him,) exclaims "that he would rather ride in his shirt all his life than suffer a fellow-creature to lie in so miserable a condition."

The scenes which succeed, at the ale-house of Mr. and Mrs. Towwouse, beggar description. Betty, the maid, runs to the surgeon, and he, understanding that some gentleman is hurt, hastily dresses himself; but on being informed that the wounded man is only a poor foot-passenger, gravely rebukes Betty for calling him at unseasonable hours, slips off his clothes again, and quietly returns to bed and to sleep. Mrs. Towwouse, with her pursed lips, her harsh, loud voice, her sharp, red-pointed nose, the two bones which stood at "the upper end of that skin which composed her cheeks, almost hiding a pair of small red eyes," and her poor pin-hearted and hen-pecked husband, now make their appearance. This beautiful shrew, on being informed that her husband had lent poor Joseph one of his shirts, goes off into one of her fits of connubial rage. "But," says Towwouse, meekly, "this is a poor wretch." "Yes," returns his spouse, with unanswerable logic, "I know it is a poor wretch; but what the —— have we to do with poor wretches? The law makes us provide for too many already. We shall have thirty or forty poor wretches in red coats shortly." "But," still persists Towwouse, "this man hath been robbed of all he hath." "Well, then," answers she, "where 's his money to pay his reckoning?" The husband at last concludes not to contradict her. She compliments the wisdom of this last determination, by saying, "If the devil was to contradict me, I would make the house too hot to hold him."

However, Joseph is in the house, — Betty has managed to borrow some clothing of the hostler, — the surgeon speaks knowingly of the extreme danger of the unwelcome guest, — Mrs. Towwouse is apprehensive that she will have to bear the expense of a funeral, — and the parson, Mr. Barnabas, is called up to Joseph from the bar-room, to give him some ghostly consolation. He desires to know if he has any sins unrepented of; if he has, to make haste and repent of them as soon as he can, "that they may repeat over a few prayers together," — the hint in regard to haste in repentance being given because the company down stairs are about to prepare a bowl of punch, and no one is willing to squeeze the lemons until Barnabas comes. After being thus shrived, the sick man desires some tea; but Mrs. Towwouse answers that "she had just done drinking it, and could not be slopping all day," and orders a mug of beer to be carried to him instead. The appearance of Parson Adams now changes matters in favor of Joseph, and a few more diverting scenes, brimful of nature and character, conclude the first book. We know not anywhere else such fine ingenuity in exhibiting the selfish element in human nature, or such invincible good-humor in its representation.

A good portion of the rest of the novel is taken up with the adventures of Joseph and Parson Adams on their road homewards, and is full of humorous pictures of the English life of that period, high and low. Of Parson Adams, the most poetical character in any novel not written by Scott, — a man whose virtues had so endeared him to a bishop, that, at the age of fifty, he was presented with a handsome living of £23 a year, wherewith to support a wife and six children, — we shall hardly presume to speak. His vanity, simplicity, learning, benevolence, evangelical purity of mind, — his stout cudgel, pedestrian habits, and copy of Æschylus, — are as well known as anything in romance. The other characters are drawn with a fidelity which leaves nothing to wish. There is Fanny, simpler and purer than Pamela herself, a rose-bud with the morning dew upon it, just the true and innocent creature that we might expect in one who had followed the teachings of the good parson. There is Mrs. Slipslop, with her garrulous vulgarity, her town-bred airs, her impertinence to inferiors, her servility to superiors; mourning over the "frail sect," and always "confidious" that she is in the right; more eager to part with her virtue than others are to retain it, — the perfection of waiting-women, and worth all of Congreve's put together. There are Lady Booby, and Squire Booby, and Beau Didapper, vivid as life itself. Pamela, towards the close of the novel, is subjected to a process of caricature, whose merry maliciousness might well enrage Richardson. She is represented as seconding the entreaties of Squire Booby to make Joseph give up Fanny, as a match below the rank of her brother; and on being told that the girl is *her* equal at least, she answers, in a strain of the most exquisite imbecility, — "She *was* my equal; but I am no longer Pamela Andrews. I am now this gentleman's lady, and as such am above her. I hope I shall never behave with an unbecoming pride; but at the same time, I shall always endeavor to know myself, and question not the assistance of grace to that purpose."

The publication of Joseph Andrews gave the author increased reputation, but it made him bitter enemies among the friends of Richardson, and the paltriest means were taken to decry his talents and scandalize his reputation. Richardson himself was stung to the quick, and never forgave Fielding. His resentment took the form of contemptuous commiseration. Rancor ate into his heart, but he expressed it in the style of an offended saint, looking pityingly down on a low sinner who had attacked his unstained purity. He went so far as to deny invention to Fielding, and even after the latter's death pursued his memory with his deep, quiet, narrow, and unappeasable hatred. With regard to Joseph Andrews, he could not see any merit even in Parson Adams. Fielding, he said, took the character from Parson Young, "but made him more absurd than he is known to be." On an allusion of one of his correspondents to his own novel, he refers to it as the Pamela which Fielding "abused in his Shamela. Before his Joseph Andrews, (hints and names taken from that story with a lewd and ungenerous engraftment,) the poor man wrote without being read, except when his Pasquins, &c., roused party attention and the legislature at the same time." And to crown all, Richardson and his knot of admiring widows and spinsters comforted themselves with the faith that the author whom they made the target of their petty malice would be soon forgotten.

It is certain that Fielding would not, even to save himself from this prophesied oblivion, put out his reputation to nurse, and attempt to keep the bantling alive by milk diet and baby talk. He was in quest, not so much of praise or fame, as of a subsistence; and accordingly, soon after the publication of his novel, he brought out his comedy of The Wedding Day, at Drury Lane. It was acted but six nights, and the author received only £50. This comedy is not without humor, sprightliness, and character; but the stage was not Fielding's sphere. His careless scorn of the "patrons of the drama" came near producing the condemnation of this play on the first night of its representation. Garrick, who played Millamour, and who was then a young and skittish actor, entreated him to omit a particular passage, calculated to provoke the hisses of the audience, as such a repulse would so flurry his spirits as to disconcert him for the whole evening. "No!" replied Fielding, with an oath; "if the scene is not a good one, let them find *that* out." Garrick's fear proved to be correct; a storm of hisses and cat-calls greeted his utterance of the objectionable passage; and he retired, boiling over with rage and chagrin, to the green-room. He there found Fielding, in his most ecstatic mood, enveloped in tobacco-smoke, and glorious with champagne. "What 's the matter, Garrick?" said the dramatist, cocking his eye at the actor; "what are they hissing now?" "Why, the scene that I begged you to retrench; I knew it would not do; and they have so frightened me, that I shall not be able to collect myself the whole night." — "O," answered the author; "they HAVE found it out, have they?"

But while Fielding was thus bearing, cheerily enough, the miseries consequent upon his state of wretched dependence on his pen, dogged by creditors and racked by the gout, a new calamity, the most severe of his life, burst upon him. This was the death of his wife, a woman whom he tenderly and passionately loved, and who, in her devotion to his interests and happiness, and the smiling resignation with which she bore the consequences of his errors, deserved the bountiful admiration he afterwards lavished upon her in the character of Amelia. For once, at least, in his life, he was utterly broken down and disheartened. His affectionateness was as characteristic as his joyousness, and the rude shock which both received by this event almost drove him frantic. There is a curious story told about him, in this connection, which as it is in keeping with his character, we are inclined to believe, though it is not mentioned by Arthur Murphy, Scott, or Roscoe. Mrs. Fielding had a maid, who assisted her in taking care of the children. She was fondly attached to her mistress, and on the death of the latter, so piteously bewailed her loss, that she attracted the notice of Fielding in his affliction. As she seemed the only person who really echoed his own grief, he naturally enough was led into repeated conversations with her regarding the good qualities of his deceased wife. Thus mutually mourning the departed, they insensibly became mutually attached, and in the end they were married. She proved a faithful and affectionate wife; and though the houses of Denbigh and Hapsburg might not receive any additional splendor from the match, the girl was probably as virtuous and disinterested as any that their line could boast. There is something ludicrous in the dignity of Fielding's biographers, in avoiding this incident of his life. They should have recollected Mrs. Slipslop's righteous indignation at Mrs. Graveairs, for attempting to play the gentlewoman in a stage-coach: — "My betters! who is my betters, pray?"

Fielding, as soon as he recovered from the first shock of his wife's death, displayed no lack of industry in following his profession of authorship. Besides a volume of miscellanies published in 1743, in which was included "A Journey from this World to the Next," an unfinished work, marked by many of his peculiar excellences, but apparently aimless as to general design, — he produced "The History of the Life of the late Mr. Jonathan Wild the Great." This work smacks of the vulgarity of the localities to which its characters are principally confined;

but the general idea, that of showing how much of the greatness which passes in this world is identical in spirit with that of the highwayman, is enforced in a strain of irony which no other author then living could have approached. We can almost sympathize with Wild's detection of the analogies between his own actions and those of many vigorous characters who have exercised murder and rapine in a wider sphere of destruction. "For my own part," he says, "I confess I look on this death of hanging to be as proper for a hero as any other; and I solemnly declare, that, had Alexander the Great been hanged, it would not in the least have diminished my respect for his memory." The episode of Heartfree and his wife has many touches of genuine pathos, and the humanity of Fielding finely underlies the mocking praise he awards to their hard-hearted and selfish persecutor. The conversation between Wild and the Ordinary of Newgate is as deservedly celebrated as any passage in Joseph Andrews or Tom Jones. The sudden placability of the Ordinary, when Wild interrupts his holy invectives by offering to treat him to a bottle of wine, is exceeded only by his objection to that beverage. "Why wine? Let me tell you, Mr. Wild, there is nothing so deceitful as the spirits given us by wine. If you must drink, let us have a bowl of punch; a liquor I the rather prefer, as it is nowhere spoken against in the Scripture, and as it is more wholesome for the gravel, a distemper with which I am grievously afflicted." This work covers the whole philosophy of that system in accordance with which the strong prey upon the weak, and consider superior intelligence as given to men only to make them more ingenious wolves and more profound tigers.

In addition to these works, Fielding started, in 1745,

a paper in the whig interest, full of enthusiasm for the Hanoverian succession, entitled The True Patriot. This, with The Jacobite's Journal, commenced in 1748, expressed sufficient zeal for the cause of the ministry to entitle him to receive some of its favors; but his services were not appreciated, and meaner men bore off the rewards of loyalty. At last, in 1749, through the influence of his constant friend, Lyttelton, he received a small pension, with the office of Justice of Peace for Westminster and Middlesex. This was hardly a reputable position. The magistrates of Westminster were called trading justices, being paid for their services in fees, — "a mean and wretched system," says Scott, "which made it the interest of these functionaries to inflame every petty dispute which was brought before them, to trade, as it were, in guilt and misery, and wring their precarious subsistence out of thieves and pickpockets." Fielding was now brought into connection, as a justice, with the lowest and vilest classes of society, with rogues, vagabonds, and debauchees, and his own habits seem to have suffered from the character of his environments. To his honor, it must be admitted, he did not avail himself of the means his office afforded, of selling justice, or of wringing from the miserable their last pittance. He was too humane to make money by his position. His predecessor, with less business, had cleared £1000 a year; but Fielding says, in regard to himself, that by composing quarrels, "and refusing to take a shilling from a man who most undoubtedly would not have had another left, I had reduced an income of £500 a year, of the dirtiest money on earth, to little more than £300, a considerable portion of which remained with my clerk." He appears to have bent his powerful mind, while in this office, to an investigation of the causes and cure of the crimes which at that period were so common in England. His charge to the Grand Jury of Middlesex, and his Inquiry into the Increase of Thieves and Robbers, both full of just remarks and benevolent sentiments, were his chief productions on subjects relating to his magistracy.

His office, as we have seen, gave him but a slender income; but he could convince nobody of the fact. The Secretary of State told him, when he asked for an increase of his pension, that his office was not on all accounts a very desirable one, but that all the world knew it was lucrative. Fielding, therefore, was as poor as ever. Horace Walpole has left a picture of him at this time, at once laughable and mortifying. Rigby and Bathurst, two of Walpole's friends, carried a servant of the latter, on the charge of attempting to shoot his master, before Fielding. He sent word that he was at supper, and that they must call in the morning; but they pushed into the Justice's room, and found him banqueting with a blind man, a woman of doubtful character, and three Irishmen, "on some cold mutton and a bone of ham, both in one dish, and the dirtiest cloth. He never stirred, nor asked them to sit. Rigby, who had seen him come so often to beg a guinea of Sir C. Williams, and Bathurst, at whose father's he had lived for victuals, understood that dignity as little, and pulled themselves chairs, — on which he civilized." Rigby and Bathurst doubtless proved themselves insolent puppies by this conduct, and Horace Walpole an unfeeling one by his mode of narrating it; but there is little in this reflection to excuse the abject position in which the account places the magistrate.

It was amid the disgusting and ill-paid duties of this

office, and while under the influence of the habits it engendered, that Fielding composed Tom Jones, the great prose epic of English literature. He was indebted for the means of subsistence, while writing it, to Ralph Allen, Lyttelton, and the Duke of Bedford. The former has been immortalized, both in the character of Allworthy, and in the celebrated couplet of Pope: —

> "Let humble Allen, with an awkward shame,
> Do good by stealth, and blush to find it fame."

His kindness to Fielding was, we believe, wholly unsolicited. He once sent him two hundred pounds anonymously, or, at least, before he knew him in any other way than as a distressed man of letters.

Tom Jones was published by Andrew Millar, the Murray of that period. He was a shrewd, enterprising, and not illiberal bookseller, but celebrated, even in that generation of topers, for his devotion to the bottle. It is said that for years there was not a day in which he was not in that muddled state, which, in Bacchanalian phraseology, goes under the name of "boozy." In this condition he could always be found behind his counter, going through the business of his occupation with commendable gravity, and though hardly able to stand or speak, still contriving to avoid making mistakes in his dealings either with authors or customers. He bought Tom Jones for six hundred pounds, and, on its meeting with extraordinary success, generously presented the author an additional hundred, of his own free will.

In Tom Jones, Fielding has comprehended a larger variety of incidents and characters under a stricter unity of story than in Joseph Andrews; but he has given to the whole a tone of worldliness, which does not mar the delightful simplicity of the latter. As an expression of the power and breadth of his mind, however, it is altogether his greatest work, and in the union of distinct pictorial representation with profound knowledge of practical life, is unequalled by any novel in the language. We not only see all the personages as clearly as if they were brought bodily before our eyes, but so close and lifelike is the imitation, that the moment they converse, the page itself seems to speak, and, in our illusion, we hardly distinguish reading from listening. Characters and events are so softly and yet so indelibly impressed on the imagination, that we care not to discriminate between the memory of them and the memory of facts which have fallen within our own experience. It would almost seem to argue an unreasonable scepticism to doubt the existence of such a veritable personage as Square, lover of Plato and Molly Seagrim, with his brain full of transcendental morality, and his heart full of *descendental* appetites; of Thwackum, malignant orator of grace, and most graceless of boisterous malignants; of Ensign Northerton, the very pink of rakes, braggarts, and upstarts, with his profane disrespect of "Homo," his contempt of all learning associated in his mind with pedagogic flagellations, and his exultation at deceiving "the old put," his father, out of his intention of making him a parson; of Blifil, the most sublime of didactic coxcombs, with his deep and solemn shamming of virtue, so completely a hypocrite that he almost conceals himself, and seems more an appearance than a being; of Allworthy, in whose delineation the author's whole beneficence of heart overflows; and of Tom Jones himself, with his unguided heart glowing with all the impulses, disinterested and sensual, and allowing each to act of its own will, — sincere, generous, affectionate, and unprincipled. But above all, what shall we say of Squire Western, next to Falstaff the most universally popular of comic creations, and as genuine a lump of clay and passion as ever started into being under the magical touch of a humorist? His shrewdness, his avarice, his coarse kindness, his sense-defying Jacobitism, his irresistible unreasonableness; his brutal anger, making the page which chronicles it shake with oaths, interjections, and screaming interrogations; — loving his daughter as he loves his dogs and horses, and willing to use the whip and the spur the moment she does not obey him with due alacrity, as in the case of his other brutes, and loving himself with a depth of affection, with a disregard of everything else on and over the earth, which touches the pathetic in selfishness; — all these go to make up a character so natural, and yet so eccentric, as to disturb our faith in the dogma that reason is the separating line between man and the beast. Parson Supple, his spiritual adviser and boon companion, looking after the Squire's soul, and running on his errands, is a suitable appendage to this "good old English gentleman." Then there is Black George, the gamekeeper, oscillating between rascality and honesty, like a pendulum; the interesting and accomplished family of that gentleman; and Partridge, with his proverbs, and proverbial pedantry, the unfortunate scape-goat of the sins and vices of others. Sophia Western, whose rich, red lips almost peep through the page as we read; Mrs. Honor, her maid, a younger sister of Mrs. Slipslop, with the peculiarities of her blood tripping from her tongue in every impertinence she utters; Mrs. Waters and Lady Bellaston, admirably discriminated in their worthlessness; and Mrs. Western, and Mrs. Fitzpatrick, and Molly Seagrim, and Mrs. Miller, — all are indisputably genuine, though not altogether flattering delineations of female character.

We are, in fact, made acquainted through this book with England as it was in the middle of the eighteenth century. Every personage, from lord to chambermaid, — every incident, — every description of a custom, an amusement, a fashion of dress, — every form of colloquial speech, vulgar or delicate, — every allusion to the political parties which divided the country, is a mine of information; and the whole gives the lie direct to half the impressions we derive from history, and enables us to grasp the reality and substance of the national life. Squire Western is probably but a heightened representation of the country gentleman of that period, as he was found by Walpole or Newcastle, when the minister desired to push a measure through the House of Commons, and established commercial relations with its obstinate Jacobites and patriots "open to reason." Western would have imperfectly comprehended a question of national policy, but would be sure to have known the market price of votes. The political corruption of that period has been often laid to the different administrations of the government. But no reader of Fielding can fail to see how common it was, for a person holding a portion of the legislative power of the country, to consider it a piece of property, which should not be induced to utter a simple "aye" without an introduction to the secret-service money. There is a great difference between a prime minister who corrupts representatives, and a prime minister who has to deal with representatives who set themselves up for sale. In the latter case, that statesman would seem to be the best who contrives to purchase the largest number of votes with the smallest expenditure of the public money.

In addition to the wealth of character and incident in this novel, its fulness of spirit and humor, and its almost exhaustless capacity to amuse and to instruct, the story is distinguished from that of most works of fiction by its artistic unity and completeness. It contains nothing, if we except the episode of the Old Man of the Mill, which interferes with the main design. With a beautiful art, so felicitously concealed as to seem instinctive, incident grows out of incident, at once springing from and developing character; and the stream of events, growing broader with every accession, flows naturally forward to the catastrophe. The style also varies with the scenes, exhibiting a singular command of apt and pictorial language, and is especially delicious in the expression of irony and mock-heroic grandeur. The description of the battle between Molly Seagrim and half of the parish, in which she does such direful execution among the country nymphs and swains, is a masterpiece of triumphant parody. But no quotations or allusions would do any justice to the exquisite perfection of this novel, in respect either to its plot, its characters, or its style.

There has been much speculation on the question whether Tom Jones is an immoral work. Scott decides it somewhat after the manner in which Dr. Johnson decided a similar question regarding the morality of The Beggar's Opera. He says that the novel never added one libertine to the company of licentious debauchees; and he fears that the frankness and generosity of the hero have found as few imitators as his vice and indiscretion. This judgment, however, implies that all minds are healthy enough to escape contamination from immoral works of imagination, which is just the reverse of the fact.

The discussion of the question in respect to the novel under consideration may be considerably narrowed by attempting to define in what the immorality of a work consists. Some persons, without allowing for changes in national manners, pronounce coarse and direct expression, in plain, plump words, to be immoral; and in this sense Tom Jones shares the stigma with Shakspeare and Ben Jonson, with Dr. South and many a luminary of the Church. Others consider all representation of profligacy and falsehood, unaccompanied by resounding maxims declaring their naughtiness, to be immoral; and in this sense every delineator of life and character is bound to be immoral by the first principles of his art. Others, without the breadth of mind to take in the whole design and total effect of a work of imagination, condemn it as licentious by fastening their moral gripe on some particular scene, which should be viewed in its relations. A few, with a juster and more catholic judgment, confine the accusation to books *intended* to inflame the passions and unsettle the principles, coming from an incurably corrupt mind, which basely makes itself the pander to appetite and crime.

Certainly, in this last meaning, Tom Jones cannot be pronounced immoral. Fielding's object was, undoubtedly, that which he professed in his preface, — to recommend goodness and innocence; to show that no acquisitions of guilt can compensate for the loss of that solid inward comfort of mind which is the lot of the virtuous; to employ wit and humor in laughing men out of their favorite vices and follies; and to inculcate the truth, that virtue and innocence fall into the snares of deceit and villany chiefly through indiscretion. He also asserts that there is nothing in the book "inconsistent with the strictest rules of decency, or which can offend the chastest eye in its perusal,"—a statement which sounds ironical in this age, but which, we know, would not have seemed strange fifty years ago. There are persons living now who, in their boyhood, read Tom Jones aloud to their mothers and grandmothers, without any thought of impropriety on either side.

Not only must Fielding be acquitted of intentional immorality in his composition of the novel, but it must also be allowed that he has indicated the connection of vice and misery, indiscretion and discomfort, as closely as the logic of Chillingworth himself could rivet it. But the true question of literary morality lies back of all the considerations to which we have referred. The morality of a book is something unconsciously impressed upon it, and is independent of intention. It takes its tone from the character of the author, rather than from his opinions or his will. If sensuality or malice pervades his mind, it will find vent in his book, however cautiously he may abstain from directly expressing it, however affluent he may be in moral and religious commonplaces. Thus we see many a modern novel, professing the loftiest principles and sentiments, seemingly only too elevated to be practical, and yet as truly licentious as the amatory verses of Rochester, or the rakish comedies of Sedley; and many a treatise of theology, studded all over with Scripture quotations, and yet as malignant and irreligious in spirit as if it were inspired by the devil himself.

If we try Fielding by this test, we shall, it is true, find Tom Jones as moral as The Loves of the Angels, or The

Corsair, not to speak of Little's poems, Don Juan, and the prodigies of profligacy we import from France; but we shall not find it moral in the true sense of the term. Fielding suffered too much from his own vices and follies not to know what a miserable sham and deceit is that happiness which comes from a violation of moral laws, and he would have been the last man intentionally to recommend it to others; but his character was what his life had made it, and his sensations accordingly penetrate his verbal ethics, flash out in the turn of his sentences, and peep through the best-intentioned morsels of moral advice he is so ready to give. There were no malignant vices in his composition, nothing which urged him to defy heaven, or vilify and hate man; but he necessarily had too much toleration for what Gibbon, with characteristic indulgence to the sensual, calls the "amiable weaknesses of our nature;" and this prevents him from arranging his wonderfully vivid representations in relation to higher laws than those which inhere in the things themselves. He had, in short, if the term be admissible, a good deal of honest sensuality, — that is, he never elaborately disguised it in dainty sentiment and philanthropic metaphysics, according to the modern custom; and though the quality is a blot upon his works, and limits the upward movement of his mind, it is hardly so insidiously depraving as the Satanic sentimentality and sugared corruption which have succeeded it.

The brilliant success of Tom Jones, which lifted Fielding at once to an almost undisputed eminence among the great writers of his century, seems to have emboldened him to proceed in his new vocation. He accordingly commenced Amelia, and completed and published it in 1751, performing, at the same time, his duties as a magistrate, and occasionally throwing off a pamphlet on some subject which engaged public attention at the time. His proposal for making an effectual provision for the poor, proves that he had applied his mind with no inconsiderable force to social and political questions; and his short essay on the mysterious case of Elizabeth Canning, "in which," as Scott observes, "he adopted the cause of common sense against popular prejudice, and failed, in consequence, in the object of his publication," reflected credit on his sagacity and his benevolence.

Amelia is a novel not generally read, even by those who appreciate the other works of Fielding. It must be admitted that it indicates a decay of vigor, not in the delineation of character or in the vividness of particular scenes, but in that fusion of all the parts into a living whole, and that elastic and onward movement of the narrative, which are the charm of Tom Jones. It lingers and loiters at times around a character or an incident, not lovingly and in the spirit of enjoyment, as in Joseph Andrews, but seemingly from a lack of strength or invention to proceed. But of all his novels, it leaves the finest impression of quiet domestic delight, of the sweet home feeling, and the humanities connected with it. We have not the glad spring or the glowing summer of his genius, but its autumnal mellowness and mitigated sunshine, with something of the thoughtfulness befitting the season. Amelia herself, the wife and the mother, arrayed in all matronly graces, with her rosy children about her, is a picture of womanly gentleness and beauty, and unostentatious heroism, such as never leaves the imagination in which it has once found a place. This character Fielding is said to have drawn from the model of his first wife, while in Booth he intended, partly, at least, to represent the weaknesses, follies, and improvidence, which characterized himself. Nothing can be more beautiful than the fidelity with which Amelia adheres to her affectionate but unworthy husband, the refinement of love she displays in concealing from him her knowledge of his intrigue with Miss Matthews, and the full-hearted affection with which she greets him on his return from every adventure in which his imprudence has laid up a new store of sorrows for herself. Booth never thinks her unreasonable but on two occasions, when she insists on his breaking off his acquaintance with two friends, apparently from mere caprice. He afterwards discovers that they were pestering her with dishonorable proposals, and that she would not tell him the true reason of her dislike, from the apprehension that the result would be a duel.

Most of Fielding's pathos is unintentional and unconscious, and is commonly overlooked both by readers and critics; but there is one scene in this novel which goes directly to the heart. We refer to that where Amelia is represented alone at evening in her little room, expecting, after a weary day of anxiety and care, her husband to supper, and pleased at the idea that she has prepared a meal of which he is particularly fond. She waits hour after hour until midnight, but he does not come. It appears that he is at the gaming-table with Captain Trent, hazarding and losing guineas by the score, and laying up fresh troubles for himself and her. She, the same afternoon, had checked a desire to buy some little luxury for herself, because it would cost sixpence, a sum she thought she could not spare from their small hoard. We are inclined to forgive Captain Booth all his errors but this disappointment to Amelia. No reader ever mustered sufficient charity to cover that cruel thoughtlessness, although the wife pardoned it at once.

The characters of this novel are delineated in Fielding's most felicitous manner, and possess sufficient variety to have established a reputation for any other author. Dr. Harrison, a clergyman after the style of Parson Adams, but discriminated from him by his abruptness of tone, his greater knowledge of the world, and a cynicism assumed to veil a boundless beneficence, is a grand personation of practical Christianity. Sergeant Atkinson, with his deep, quiet, humble love, his devotion to Booth and Amelia, his self-sacrificing generosity, is one of those embodiments of goodness of heart which Fielding, to his honor, delighted to represent. The fair and frail and malicious Miss Matthews; the shrewd, knowing, learned, equivocal Mrs. Bennet; the vapid Mrs. James; Colonel Bath, with his high sense of honor, and perfect willingness to blow out the brains of his best friend on a punctilio; Colonel James, the polite town rake, complacent in his shallow baseness; the dogmatic young theological student, who violently disputes with Dr. Harrison, to the great chagrin of his politic father, who appreciates benefices better than logic; the little, round, fat Mrs. Ellison, the best-natured of pimps; and especially that wretched devotee of lust, and embodiment of all which is disgusting in sensuality, the lord who is her employer, — are characters which Fielding in his best days hardly excelled. The descriptions of town life, also, are so graphic, that we seem transported to the London of 1750. The masquerade at Ranelagh, and the scene at Vauxhall, where the two brainless town-bloods frighten Amelia and the children with their profanity and insolence, are daguerreotypes of manners. The author evidently intended that the novel should have a moral effect upon his readers, and the fact that many scenes would now be accounted coarse or licentious only proves that manners have changed. The Beaux Stratagem, or Love and a Bottle, would now be considered strange productions to find in the hands of a lady; yet the virtuous and tender Amelia, who reads Barrow's sermons with so much profit, and whom Dr. Harrison considers the saint of his church, is represented as solacing a weary hour of impatient watching in perusing "the admirable comedies" of Farquhar.

The comparative failure of Amelia threw Richardson and his admirers into ecstacies. Mrs. Donallan asks him if he is going to leave them to Captain Booth and Betty Thoughtless for their examples. "As for poor Amelia, she is so great a fool, we pity her, but cannot be humble enough to desire to imitate her." Richardson, in reply, assures her that Captain Booth has done his own business; that the piece is as dead as if it had been published forty years ago, as to sale; and that Mr. Fielding "seems in his last journal ashamed of it himself, and promises to write no more." He compliments his correspondent on her "admirable" remark, that, by several strokes in the novel, Fielding "designed to be good, but lost his genius, low humor, and spirit, in the attempt." Again, he chuckles over the assumed fact, that Fielding had been beaten by his own imitators, and that since the time "his spurious brat, Tom Jones," met with its "unaccountable success," the public have discovered what "stuff" they have been admiring. But his happiest expression of petty rancor is contained in that letter, written in 1752, in which he affects to pity Fielding; describes how he insulted the sisters of the latter, by his depreciation of their brother; and narrates the whole in a strain of moral coxcombry unexcelled in the annals of Pharisaic criticism. "I *could not help* telling his sisters that I am equally surprised at, and concerned for, his continual lowness. Had your brother, said I, been born in a stable, or been a runner at a sponging-house, one should have thought him a genius, and wished he had had the advantage of a liberal education, and of being admitted into good company." He goes on to say, that it is beyond his conception, that a man of family, having "some learning, and who really is a writer, should descend so excessively low in his pieces. Who can care for any of his people?" But the most ludicrous outbreak of conceit, both of respectability and wit, follows this precious specimen of Christian commiseration. "A person of honor," he says, "asked me, the other day, what he could mean by saying in his Covent Garden Journal that he had followed Homer and Virgil in his Amelia. I answered, that he was justified in saying so, because he must mean Cotton's Virgil Travestied, where the women are drabs and the men scoundrels." Keats represents himself as once being in a very genteel circle of wit-snappers, who, in speaking of Kean, the actor, affected to regret that he kept such low company. Keats remarks, that he wished at the time he was one of that company. No one can read Richardson's correspondence, and be bored by the insipidity of his female toadies and persons of honor, without being perfectly willing to exchange their refinement for Fielding's "excessive lowness."

Fielding was superior to the small malice and miserable vanity which would prompt such a mode of attack as that adopted by Richardson. To his large and tolerant mind, it would have appeared ridiculous to wreak a personal spite against an author by depreciating his works. Pope and Swift had both referred to him in early life, with a contemptuous fleer at his talents; but it never entered his brain to refuse to quote and praise them because they disliked him. In the fifth number of the Jacobite Journal, published at a time when he knew that Richardson was exulting over his supposed failures, and making his genius the butt of his insolent pity, he speaks in terms of high eulogy of Clarissa Harlowe. He knew human nature too well not to divine the meanness to which the delineator of Clarissa and Clementina would descend, when his sensitive vanity was stung by ridicule; but it was a part of his philosophy to view such things with good-natured indulgence, and not hesitate to acknowledge the good qualities which might exist in connection with vices so paltry and so malignant.

Millar, Fielding's publisher, paid a thousand pounds for Amelia, thinking it would meet with the success of Tom Jones; but while it was in press, he obtained a hint that it was an inferior work, and might turn out a bad speculation. His stratagem to save himself from loss indicated the ingenuity of a master-mind in "the trade." At a general sale to the booksellers, he told them, with his accustomed tipsy gravity, that he should sell his other publications at the usual terms, but that there was such a demand for Amelia he should be compelled to decline all offers for that except at a reduced discount. The booksellers, cunning as they were, were all deceived by his manner, greedily swallowed the bait, and the whole edition was ordered before it was published.

After the publication of his last novel, Fielding

returned to his former occupation of newspaper essayist, and commenced, in 1752, The Covent Garden Journal. In this paper he published some of his most agreeable essays. His style in these has the cosiness and abandonment of an after-dinner chat, and is peculiarly felicitous in gossiping comments on literature and manners. In this journal he was drawn into a verbal quarrel with Smollett, who had established a fame, by Roderick Random and Peregrine Pickle, second only to his own. The Journal was discontinued on account of Fielding's health, which now suffered from a complication of diseases, of which the principal were asthma, dropsy, and jaundice. The physicians recommended a milder climate as the only means of preserving his life, and Lisbon was fixed upon for his residence. Before he went, however, he undertook, at the request of the Duke of Newcastle, and for a fee of six hundred pounds, to extirpate some gangs of robbers and murderers who infested the metropolis. After performing this duty with great sagacity and complete success, he prepared for his voyage. On the 26th of June, 1754, he took that melancholy leave of his children which he has described with such affectionate pathos in his Voyage to Lisbon. This, his latest work, cut short by death, indicates that his mind was bright and his spirits joyous to the very verge of the tomb. He died at Lisbon, in the beginning of October, 1754, in the forty-eighth year of his age. His family, consisting of a wife and four children, were left penniless, but were preserved from want by the kindness of Sir John Fielding, and the ever-active charity of Ralph Allen.

It would seem that the most rigid moralist, in reviewing the events of a life illustrated by virtues so imperfectly rewarded, and by vices so severely expiated, as that of Fielding, would be inclined rather to regret his misfortunes than harshly to condemn his faults. His whole existence, from the age of twenty, was one long struggle with fortune, in which he bore humiliations and experienced distresses which would have crushed a more sensitive spirit at the outset. His life, judged by its external events, without taking into account the character of the man, appears as wretched as any chronicled in the calamities of genius. But it was the peculiar constitution of his nature, that those qualities which whirled him into excesses blunted the edge of the miseries into which his excesses plunged him. In his lowest state, he rarely desponded, rarely lost the vigor of his intellect and the gladness of his disposition. Lady Montague, writing soon after she heard of his death, says that "his happy constitution (even when he had with great pains half demolished it) made him forget every evil, when he was before a venison pasty or over a flask of champagne; and I am persuaded," she adds, "he knew more happy moments than any prince upon earth. His natural spirits gave him rapture with a cook-maid, and cheerfulness when he was starving in a garret." As a consequence of this felicity of disposition, he never whined about his misfortunes, never scolded the public for neglecting him, never represented his sensualities and weaknesses as the result of his ardent genius. From all nauseous cant of this kind, which so commonly infects authors and their biographers, Fielding's sense of humor would have preserved him, even if he had not been saved from it by his sense of the pleasurable. And that much abused noun of multitude, the World, against whose injustice poets have ever stormily inveighed, may find two consolations, at least, for its comparative neglect of Fielding;—in the thought that it could not possibly have lavished upon him an amount of wealth which his improvidence would not instantly have wasted; and in the reflection that, but for his poverty, he never would have produced those exquisite creations of humor and imagination, with their large knowledge of human nature and their large toleration of human infirmity, which have made his name immortal.

DANA'S POEMS AND PROSE WRITINGS.*

THIS collection of the writings of one of our deepest and most suggestive thinkers ought to have been made before, although, from the preface, we should judge that the author had undertaken a somewhat unwilling duty in making it even now. It contains all of Mr. Dana's poems and prose writings formerly published, together with a large addition, in the shape of reviews and essays originally contributed to various periodicals, and now for the first time collected. The matter in the second volume will be new to most readers who are familiar with The Buccaneer and The Idle Man, it being wholly composed of articles reprinted from the North American Review, the Spirit of the Pilgrims, and a few other sources. The volumes will undoubtedly take a prominent place in American literature, among the best mental productions of the country; and our object in the present article is, to give a hasty view of the qualities of mind and disposition they display, and the peculiar individuality pervading the whole. We would not do Mr. Dana the injustice to judge his writings by any less exacting principles than those which apply to the higher class of minds.

* Poems and Prose Writings. By Richard Henry Dana. New York: Baker and Scribner. 1850. 2 vols. 12mo. pp. 443, 440. — *Christian Examiner, March*, 1850.

In Mr. Dana's nature there is evidently no divorce between literature and life, and he belongs to a class of authors widely different from those who follow letters as a profession, as a trade, as a means of amusing others or displaying themselves. His writings carry with them the evidence of being the genuine products of his own thinking and living, and are full of those magical signs which indicate patient meditation and a nature rooted in the realities of things. From his prevailing seriousness, everything, too, has a meaning and purpose, and bears directly on the conduct of life; and there are passages of a certain still and deep intensity which seem forced from a mind eloquent from restrained agony, and expressive at the expense of impairing its vitality. The objects of thought seem to press so closely upon his heart and brain, that he cannot remove them to that safe distance which admits of their being cheerily contemplated; and he therefore has little of that free swing and felicitous audacity of manner, natural to thinkers in whom subject and object are in genial companionship. The general impression which his works leave on the mind is the combination of earnestness and conscientiousness in the spirit of the author, — an earnestness which, in spite of his clear-seeing and quick-shaping imagination, is apt to become didactic when it might be representative, and a conscientiousness which has a nervous and morbid, as well as a muscular and healthy movement.

There is, indeed, in Mr. Dana's nature a singular disagreement between faculty and disposition. His intellect has an instinctive tendency to objects; is clear, sure, and bright, in its vision; endowed with the discerning power of the observer and the divining power of the poet, and, in its natural action, equally capable in the region of facts and in the region of principles. His sensibility, also, is strong and direct, quick to feel the flush and stir of great passions, and impatient of obstacles which obstruct the expression of its wealth of emotion. As far as regards intellect and passion, he appears the most objective and sympathetic of our poets; but the moment we pass into the more subtile sources of character, curious to scan the qualities which lie nearer the heart of his being, we discover widely different elements at work in the region of his sentiments. As shy and sensitive as they are deep and delicate, these sentiments exact more of society and mankind than either can give; and the result is a peculiar development of mental disgust, compounded of self-distrust and dissatisfaction with the world, which reäcts both upon his intellect and his sensibility, introduces a subjective element into his clearest representations, and sometimes hurries his mind from objects into ideal reveries suggested by objects. His finer affections, the saint-like purity of his moral feelings, the sentiments of awe, wonder, reverence, and beauty, incorporated with his religious faith, though fine and rare elements of his soul, are hardly elements of power, for they have not been harmoniously blended with the other qualities of his character. Had these, which are most assuredly the deepest things in his nature, flowed in a healthy current through his intellect, the creative power of his mind would have been increased, a more joyous and elastic spirit would bound through his productions, and his large nature would have had a grander impetus in its lyric expression, and a sunnier energy in its representations of external life. As it is, we have in these volumes the records of a great mind, but of one which appears to have been placed in circumstances not conducive to its genial development, — a mind in whom noble virtues and refined sentiments have acted as restraints rather than inspirations; — humility being separated from force; modesty producing a slightly morbid self-consciousness, generating self-distrust, and impairing the will's vital energies; exquisite sensibility to the beautiful expended more in contemplating than in creating beauty; moral sentiment divorced from moral audacity; — and all these subtile inward workings and cross movements of elusive emotions going on in a really broad and high mind, resolute in its grasp of the realities of things, with instincts for the great in thought and the daring in action, and, at times, tearing its way into expression with a fierce rending apart of the fine web of feelings in which its activity is entangled. In many of his writings he seems a kind of Puritan-Cavalier, with the Puritan's depth of religious experience without his self-will, with the Cavalier's tastes and accomplishments without his self-abandonment; and he accordingly has neither the strength of fanaticism nor the impetus of sensibility.

This inward shrinking from the exercise of undoubted power, this moral fastidiousness of a strong moral nature, this mental disgust "sickling o'er" the energies of a great mind, though doubtless to be referred, in some degree, to inward constitution, must be accounted for principally by the fact that Mr. Dana's life has been one of antagonism to the tastes and opinions of the community in which he was placed. As a poet, as a critic, as a speculator on government and social phenomena, he has shown the force, grasp, and comprehensiveness, of his intellect; but he has always been in opposition to current schools and systems. If this had been owing to a natural combativeness of disposition, it would have brought with it its own "exceeding great reward;" for, on the ground of mere self-satisfaction, few persons are more to be envied than pugnacious disputants: but Mr. Dana's nature is as averse to controversy as it is solicitous for the truth, and he found himself in opposition because he had positive principles in art and philosophy as distinguished from conventional rules and empirical generalizations. At present his views would, generally, excite nothing more than respect and admiration for the thinker; but at the time they were first announced they fell upon a politely unsympathizing audience, disposed to consider them as the freaks of spiritual caprice, and perfectly masters of that subtile superciliousness which eats into the very heart of a man who is at once modest and earnest. His critical principles were radically those of Lessing and Schlegel, of Wordsworth and Coleridge, principles which are an accurate philosophical statement of the processes of all creative minds; but he did not possess the peculiar egotism which enabled Wordsworth, and the peculiar dogmatism which enabled Coleridge, to bear with dogged contempt, or voluble and passionate replication, the common smiling indifference and the occasional sharp attacks of his opponents. This lack of recognition when there is really nothing in the mode of presentation to excite silent or stormy opposition, — this struggle of one man against ten thousand, to substitute positive principles for empirical rules, — is especially saddening to a nature as sympathetic as it is strong, and as shy as it is earnest. Mr. Dana persisted, in spite of unpopularity, it is true, and wrote in verse and prose according to his own ideas; but his persistence lacked geniality. A notion appears to have risen in his mind of a natural antithesis between popularity and excellence, — a sure sign, perhaps, that popularity was necessary to the healthy action of his nature; that he required echoes of his mind from without to assure him that there was really power within. Cheerfulness, and the joyous exercise of creative energy, are so characteristic of assured genius, that we doubt if such an antithesis ever arose in a thoroughly live and sunny nature. If Mr. Dana had been as popular as he deserved, if the richness and depth of his mind had been gladly recognized, the present volumes would hardly have been a tithe of his contributions to literature, and we should have had now a different class of personal qualities to emphasize as characteristics. There are, in authorship, professors of the impudent and supercilious, who require a sharp resistance on the part of the public to tame their wilful and aggressive egotism; but Mr. Dana belongs to a class who arrive at the fact of their excellence rather by an induction from the results they produce on the public mind than by self-esteem; and to such, a lack of recognition is hurtful.

The compositions of Mr. Dana, produced under the circumstances we have indicated, evince sufficient intensity both of sensibility and intellect; but it is that kind of intensity which declares rather than disputes with power, — which is strong on positive grounds, but unavailable in attack. Accordingly, in many of the articles published in the second volume, we discern, in the side references to opposite opinions, no hearty invective, no bold strokes of satire; but the fine superciliousness of the mechanical school of critics is met, on his own part, with a scorn as fine. Mr. Dana is not a good hater, because his mind needs sympathy more than it dislikes antagonism, and because austere principles are connected in his mind with gentle feelings, not with aggressive passions; and his impatience at error, therefore, rather frets than foams into expression.

Though there is hardly a page in Mr. Dana's writings which does not declare him a poet, his poems are comparatively few. These are now generally well known, though their rare merit has not yet been heartily recognized. Mr. Dana is properly of no particular "school" of poetry, but in the direction given to his poetic faculty we perceive the influence and inspiration of Wordsworth and Coleridge. In his preface to The Idle Man, he speaks of his friend Bryant as having lived, when quite young, where few works of poetry were to be had, "at a period, too, when Pope was still the great idol in the Temple of Art;" and that, upon his opening Wordsworth's Ballads, "a thousand springs seemed to gush up at once in his heart, and the face of nature, of a sudden, to change into a strange freshness and life." Something of this effect Wordsworth appears to have exerted upon Mr. Dana; an effect, however, which never was manifested in a conscious or unconscious imitation of his author, and which tended to develop rather than submerge his individuality. Though he looks at nature somewhat in Wordsworth's spirit, he never looks with Wordsworth's eyes, but always with his own. The leading characteristics of his poems are the calm, clear intensity of his vision of objects, and his power of penetrating them, through and through, with life and spiritual significance. His imagination has a Chaucerian certainty in representing a natural object in its exact form, color and dimensions, the image before his intellect being as real as if it were before his eyes; and if he fail at all as an objective poet, he fails in interpreting its true life and meaning. Nature to him is ever symbolical of spirit; but, instead of evolving hers, he will often superadd his own. In both processes there is life as well as form, but in one case we have the life of nature, in the other the life of the poet. There are grand examples of pure objective imagination in Mr. Dana's poems, in which what is peculiar in the author's spirit does not penetrate the description, and the whole scene has the delicious remoteness of artistical creation; but commonly a subtile tinge of individual sentiment is diffused over the picture he so distinctly presents, and the impression which it leaves tells us that the life communicated to our hearts is not the life of nature, but of one individual's experience. Were Mr. Dana a purely subjective poet, his imagination playing whatever freaks with objects the caprices of his individuality might dictate, the difficulty of describing the action of his mind would be greatly lessened; but the elusive quality in his genius, which analysis is continually toiling after in vain, comes from the conflict in his nature between the objective tendency of his intellect and the subjective tendency of his disposition. We will give a few extracts illustrative of the varying operation of his imagination, according as it works impersonally or with his peculiar moods. The following, for instance, is pure picture: —

"And inland rests the green, warm dell;
The brook comes tinkling down its side;
From out the trees the Sabbath bell
Rings cheerful, far and wide,
Mingling its sound with bleatings of the flocks,
That feed about the vale among the rocks."

Here we have complete self-forgetfulness, the mind gazing at the scene it has conjured up, and representing it as a distinct reality. In the following there is a faint intrusion of the individual in the picture: —

"'T was twilight then; and Dian hung her bow
Low down the west; and there a star
Kindly on thee and me, from far,
Looked out, and blessed us through the passing glow."

In the following exquisite poem, the imagery is so clear, that we are at first hardly aware that the whole takes from the sadness of the mood in which it is contemplated a dreamy melancholy, delicious but slightly morbid.

"THE LITTLE BEACH-BIRD.

"Thou little bird, thou dweller by the sea,
Why takest thou its melancholy voice,
And with that boding cry
Along the breakers fly?
O, rather, Bird, with me
Through the fair land rejoice!

"Thy flitting form comes ghostly dim and pale,
As driven by a beating storm at sea;
Thy cry is weak and scared,
As if thy mates had shared
The doom of us: Thy wail, —
What doth it bring to me?

"Thou call'st along the sand, and haunt'st the surge,
Restless and sad: as if, in strange accord
With the motion and the roar
Of waves that drive to shore,
One spirit did ye urge, —
The Mystery, — the Word.

"Of thousands, thou, both sepulchre and pall,
Old Ocean! A requiem o'er the dead,
From out thy gloomy cells,
A tale of mourning tells, —

Tells of man's woe and fall,
  His sinless glory fled.

"Then turn thee, little bird, and take thy flight
    Where the complaining sea shall sadness bring
      Thy spirit never more;
      Come, quit with me the shore,
  And on the meadows light,
    Where birds for gladness sing!"

Vol. I., pp. 129, 130.

We might extract from Factitious Life, Thoughts on the Soul, The Dying Raven, and Daybreak, numerous passages where this melancholy deepens into gloom, if not despair, and while the poet's hold upon the form of natural objects is as sure as ever, the spirit is thoroughly individual. These poems could only have come from a deep experience of life, and there is a breadth of solemnity to them which is not without its charm; but the fatal objection to them is, that they do not communicate life. Their tendency is rather to awaken a conviction of wickedness than to inspire the energy of virtue. As lessons in psychology, however, they have great value.

One of the best of Mr. Dana's minor poems is that on Chantrey's Washington. We extract it, as one of the very few tributes to Washington worthy the grandeur of the subject.

" Father and Chief, how calm thou stand'st once more
Upon thine own free land, thou wonn'st with toil!
Seest thou upon thy country's robe a soil,
As she comes down to greet thee on the shore?

" For thought in that fine brow is living still, —
Such thought as, looking far off into time,
Casting by fear, stood up in strength sublime,
When odds in war shook vale and shore and hill; —

"Such thought as then possessed thee, when was laid
Our deep foundation, — when the fabric shook
With the wrathful surge which high against it broke, —
When at thy voice the blind, wild sea was stayed.

"Hast heard our strivings, that thou look'st away
Into the future, pondering still our fate
With thoughtful mind? Thou readest, sure, the date
To strifes, — thou seest a glorious coming day.

"For round those lips dwells sweetness, breathing good
To sad men's souls, and bidding them take heart,
Nor live the shame of those who bore their part
When round their towering chief they banded stood.

"No swelling pride in that firm, ample chest!
The full, rich robe falls round thee, fold on fold,
With easy grace, in thy scarce conscious hold:
How simple in thy grandeur, — strong in rest!

"'T is like thee: such repose thy living form
Wrapped round. Though some chained passion, breaking forth,
At times swept o'er thee like the fierce, dread north,
Yet calmer, nobler, cam'st thou from the storm.

"O mystery past thought! — that the cold stone
Should live to us, take shape, and to us speak, —
That he, in mind, in grandeur, like the Greek,
And he, our pride, stand here, the two in one!

"There 's awe in thy still form. Come hither, then,
Ye that o'erthrong the land, and ye shall know
What greatness is, nor please ye in its show, —
Come, look on him, would ye indeed be men!"

Vol. I., pp. 127, 128.

The Buccaneer is the most celebrated of Mr. Dana's poems, and though the plan of the story is open to objections, and it fails to reach that mystical element of the mind which it addresses, the characterization and scenery evince great closeness and force of imagination. With some obvious faults, it appears to us to exhibit more of the depth, strength, and daring of genius, than any other American poem. Everything is realized with such intensity that it could not have been written without tears and shudderings, and there are portions of it so vividly real and lifelike that the reader almost reproduces the author's mental agony in reproducing his conceptions. The stern condensation of the diction corresponds admirably with the concentrated strength with which the author grasps the central idea and every minor detail of the poem. The fierce passions raging through the whole are relieved by numerous passages replete with the sunniest beauty and repose. Throughout the whole, nothing is described, everything is represented; and we can hardly recollect a stanza in which the attention is drawn away from objects to note the words which present them.

But in this poem, and in all of Mr. Dana's poems, we notice two defects which must always interfere with his popularity as a poet. He has great distinctness of mental vision, but little visionary charm; a shaping imagination, but no poetic atmosphere encircling the forms he creates. He realizes with great power, but the ideal is almost lost in the realization. This is the more remarkable, as it is in atmosphere more than form that the great poets of the present century, and especially his own favorites among them, excel all others. The other defect of his Muse is a lack of melody. This, we think, is not a natural, but a somewhat wilful defect, — a mode of showing his contempt for the smooth conventional versification which he has so much decried as a critic. As a prose-writer he is often exquisitely melodious. Let the reader compare the essay on Domestic Life, or that entitled Musings, with any poem in the present collection, and he cannot but be struck with the musical flow of the one, as contrasted with the comparatively rugged tramp of the other.

As a prose-writer Mr. Dana is principally known by his essays and stories published in The Idle Man. The second volume of the present collection of his works contains, in the shape of fugitive articles originally contributed to periodicals, as strong evidences as are furnished by his more elaborate production that his rank as a writer, in respect to mere excellence of style, is second to no other author in the country. The prominent figure in The Idle Man is Paul Felton, certainly a creation which no reader could have dreamed would glare out upon him from the pages of a book bearing such a title. In respect to mere power over the sensibilities, the story of Paul and Esther is the greatest of Mr. Dana's works, and it exhibits a mingled firmness and vividness of vision, in gazing into the blackest gulfs of Satanic passion, which cannot but awaken at times the reader's admiring wonder. But the impression it leaves upon the mind is one of unrelieved horror; and we suppose that the author, on his own principles of taste, would declare that such an impression was altogether removed from the purpose of art. Should an actor imitate nature so perfectly, that, when he is stabbed on the stage, he conveyed to our minds the same feelings we should experience in witnessing a murder committed in the streets, he would be called a bad actor. The line separating the sympathies awakened by ideal and actual distress cannot be mistaken, and the novelist who aims to call out the latter succeeds only in producing the horrible, not the beautiful or sublime. The power displayed in Paul Felton, therefore, is not communicated to the reader, but leaves him both weak and miserable. In the story of Tom Thornton, we have almost equal power, with more relief. Edward and Mary is a simple story, in which the author throws himself confidingly upon the finer sentiments in their primitive action, and the result is true romance. The article on Kean's Acting is probably the finest piece of critical writing which any English performer ever called forth. In a far different style are the essays entitled Domestic Life, and Musings. The serene and beautiful wisdom so melodiously conveyed in these has a still, searching power, which penetrates into the very substance of the soul, and both purifies and tranquillizes.

As a critic, Mr. Dana manifests the same hold upon the solidities and realities of life, and the same dislike for the superficial in intellect and the conventional in manners, which characterize the whole strain of his meditations. His sensibility to poetic excellence has a depth and acuteness which no mere critic could reach, and his statements are often better and truer than the most labored analysis of a less sympathetic and imaginative mind. The articles in the present collection, on Allston's Sylphs of the Seasons, Hazlitt's Lectures on the English Poets, Pollok's Course of Time, The Sketch Book, and Edgeworth's Readings on Poetry, are generally of the highest order of critical merit. The author deals always with concrete principles, not with abstract propositions, and his articles are therefore full of original power and beauty, and ever contributions to the subjects he discusses. They contain sentences of clear sweetness, of vivid description, of penetrating remark, which leave a lingering sense of delight in the mind long after it has passed on to the topic which succeeds. The observations with which Mr. Dana commences the review of Allston's poem are more poetical than any extracts he makes from it. "His mind," he says, "seems to have in it the glad but gentle brightness of a star, as you look up to it, sending pure influences into your heart, and making it kind and cheerful. . . . . . He has not only an eye for nature, but a heart too; and his imagination gives them a common language, *and they talk together*. . . . . He views his scenes with a curious and exquisite eye, instilling some delicate beauty into the most common thing that springs up in them, imparting to it a gay and fairy spirit, and throwing over the whole a *pure, floating glow*." Allston's satire, he says, "appears so bright and playful, that the fairest prospects look gladder in it, and we see it flickering along the more gloomy, like a stream of moonlight, stretching a glittering and silvery line over the steely blackness of the waters, as they lie sleeping under the brown, solemn hills."

The following extract, relating generally to the poet, is exceedingly beautiful, and illustrates that union of power and repose which constitutes so much of the charm of Mr. Dana's prose style: —

"Little, indeed, do such men see, that the out-of-door industry, which leads to wealth and importance, owes much to the poet for its thriving existence; that the poetry of a people elevates their character, and makes them proud of themselves; quickens the growth of the nicer feelings, and tones the higher virtues; that it causes blessings to shoot up round our homes; smooths down the petty roughness of domestic life, and softens and lays open the heart to the better affections; that it calls the mind off from the pursuits of the tainted and wearing pleasures of the world, and teaches it to find its amusements in the exercise of its highest and purest powers; that it makes the intellect vivacious, and gives an interest and stir to the society of the wise; shames us from our follies and crimes, turns us to the love and study of what is good, gives health to the moral system, and brings about what must always go along with the virtue of society, the beauty of order and security. Little, too, do they know of the poet's incessant toil. His eyes and thoughts are ever busy amidst the forms of things. He looks into the intricate machinery of the heart and mind of man, and sees its workings, and tells us to what end it moves. He goes forth with the sun over the earth, and looks upon its vastness and sublimity with him, and searches out with him every lesser thing. His studies end not with the day; but when the splendor of the west has died away, and a sleepy and dusky twilight throws a shadowy veil over all things, and he feels that the spirit which lifted him up and expanded his frame, as he looked forward on the bright glories of the setting sun, has sunk slowly and silently down with them, and that the contemplative light about him has entered into his heart, and the gladness of the day left him, he turns and watches the lighting up of the religious stars, by which he studies in soberer and more intent thought the things that God has made."

The essays in the second volume on Old Times, The Past and Present, and Law as suited to Man, are among the best evidences which Mr. Dana has given of the philosophical capacity of his mind. They are good illustrations of the difference between principles and propositions, the author's imagination and sentiment, as well as his understanding, being active throughout. They are characterized by the intensest spirit of meditation, and a calm, strong grasp, and close application, of principles. The introspective and retrospective elements of his nature, however, appear in these essays in their most refined operation. The past is subtly identified with its ideals, the present is criticized in the light of those ideals, and tested by their most exacting requirements. The result is a kind of despair for the present, and a lack of hopefulness in surveying the future. Democracy, especially, has little justice done to it. But still, the most besetting sins and dangers of the country are exhibited in an original and forcible manner, without any appeal to the controversial passions, and the essays leave a profound impression of the author's depth of nature.

From the exceedingly complex character of Mr. Dana's genius, we have been able, in these hasty observations, to give but an imperfect exhibition of that peculiar combination of mental and moral qualities which constitutes the life of his writings. The best criticism on the present volumes is that which most strongly directs the public attention to them, for they cannot be read without mental and spiritual improvement; and we trust that their circulation will be large enough to give a flattering idea of the estimate placed in the United States upon great and rare powers devoted to high purposes.

APPENDIX.

THOMAS HOOD.*

THE name of Thomas Hood is known wherever language is put upon the rack. Every civilized Englishman who uses words is acquainted with the great word-twister. He is the acknowledged monarch of Pun-land. All other luminaries "pale their ineffectual fire" before the quick sparkle of his multitudinous quibbles. He has made punning a kind of genius. He has redeemed it from the detractions of the dull and pedantic. Any man may now play upon words, without having his friend point significantly to the gallows, and murmur that "he who makes a pun would pick a pocket." What King James, and Bacon, and Shakspeare, and Donne, and Cowley, could not do, — what Canning and the whole Anti-Jacobin club could not effect, — has been done by Thomas Hood. The analogies of sound seem now as much prized as those of thought. The fact that the greatest men in all ages have displayed a love for this kind of wit, must be admitted as a strong argument in its favor. The "verbal Unitarians," as Hood calls his opponents, have been compelled to abate the insolence of their censures, and relax the grimness of feature with which they once frowned defiance on double-meanings. The great family of Words, which might be supposed most interested in the issue of the struggle, have willingly given up their frames to the torture, and suffer martyrdom daily. The priests in the Inquisition of Verbiage, with their racks, wheels, scourges, and hot-irons, are

* "Whims and Oddities," and "Prose and Verse."

doing what is called a "fair business;" and every shriek drawn from the agonies of a tortured word is registered as a pun.

Hood, then, has so far influenced the legislation of letters as to turn quibbling from a crime into a fashion ; but his own popularity as a humorist is not owing altogether to his word-twistings. He has one of the most singular minds ever deposited in a human brain. Whims and oddities come from him, because he is himself a whim and oddity. He seems of different natures mixed. He has the fancy, if not the imagination, of a poet, and some touches of pathos almost equal to the most brilliant scintillations of his wit. Behind his most grotesque nonsense, there is generally some moral, satirical, or poetic meaning. He often blends feeling, fancy, wit, and thoughtfulness, in one queer rhyme, or quaint quibble. The very extravagance of his ideas and expression; the appearance of strain and effort in his puns; the portentous jumbling together of the most dissimilar notions by some merry craft of fancy; and the erratic, dare-devil invasion of the inmost sanctuaries of conventionalism, have, in his writings, a peculiar charm, which we seek for in vain among his imitators, or among the tribe of extravagant wits generally. We do not believe he would be so fine a humorist, if he were not so much of a poet. There is a vein of gènial kindliness in his nature, which modifies the mocking and fleering tendencies of his wit.

Hood was no humorist in the sense in which the word is sometimes employed. He was no mere provoker of barren laughter, but a man whose mirth had its roots deep in sentiment and humanity. He saw the serious side of life as clearly as the ludicrous. He knew what thin partitions separate in this world tears from laughter; that the deepest feeling often expresses itself in the quaint oddities of caricature; that wisdom sometimes condescends to pun, and grief to wreathe its face in smiles. Indeed, there is occasionally a little misanthropy in him. A close observer of his writings will often see a bitter personal experience of the author embodied in the most farcical and bewildering freaks of his fun. Hood makes us sympathize more quickly with the troubles of his life, from not thrusting them in our faces, with the usual parade of sorrow and lamentation. We laugh *with* him, and feel *for* him. Few writers have ever succeeded in blending so much thought and sentiment, so much true humor and no less true pathos, with the most extravagant drollery and fanciful exaggeration.

Two of the most ludicrous of Hood's punning poems are the lachrymose ballads of "Sally Brown and Ben the Carpenter," and "Faithless Nelly Gray." The mockery, in these exquisite *morceaux*, of the plaintive style of the modern ballad, glistens with wit and humor. They are so well known that to extract from them would be an impertinence. "The Wee Man" is another queer specimen of his drollery. In the poem called "Jack Hall," (Jackal) the resurrectionist, he commences with wailing the custom of disinterring bodies, and remarks, with much logical feeling: —

"'T is hard one cannot lie amid
The mould beneath a coffin lid,
But thus the Faculty will bid
Their rogues break through it!
If they don't want us there, why did
They send us to it?"

The situation of the lover, who comes to sentimentalize over his mistress's grave, is thus vividly portrayed: —

"The tender lover comes to rear
The mournful urn, and shed his tear —
Her glorious dust, he cries, is here!
Alack! alack!
The while his Sacharissa dear
Is in a sack!"

Here is a grave, grim, and dismal pun: —

"Death saw two players playing at cards,
But the game was not worth a dump,
For he quickly laid them flat with a spade,
To wait for the final trump!"

Hood's wit plays about the tomb somewhat daringly, but still he can hardly be said to disturb its sanctities. In the ballad of "Mary's Ghost" he makes the poor spirit lament the distribution of her former body among the physicians. She cries: —

"O William dear! O William dear!
My rest eternal ceases;
Alas! my everlasting peace
Is broken into pieces.

"The body-snatchers, they have come,
And made a snatch at me;
It 's very hard them kind of men
Won't let a body be."

After much agonizing description, respecting the disposition of the several parts of her once compact frame, she concludes: —

"The cock it crows — I must be gone!
My William, we must part!
But I 'll be yours in death, although
Sir Astley has my heart.

"Don't go to weep upon my grave,
And think that there I be;
They have n't left an atom there
Of my anatomie."

One of the finest things in "Prose and Verse" is the piece called "The Great Conflagration." It refers to the burning of the Houses of Parliament, in 1834, and consists chiefly of letters written by Sir Jacob Jubb, M. P., and various members of his household, descriptive of the event. Sir Jacob was severely burnt, "by taking his seat in the House, on a bench that was burning under him. The danger of his situation was several times pointed out to him, but he replied that his seat had cost him ten thousand pounds, and he could n't quit. He was at length removed by force." The richest epistolary gem is the letter of Ann Gale, housemaid. Her speculations on the fire are very deep. She understands that "The Lords and Commons was connected with a grate menny historicle associashuns, *wich of coarse will hav to make good all dammage.*" Her feelings are strongly enlisted in favor of the members. "Ware the poor burnt-out creturs will go noboddy nose. Sum say Exetur Hall, sum say the Refudge for the Destitut, and sum say the King will lend them his Bensh to set upon." She tells her correspondent that the fear of fire leaves her no peace. "I don't dare to take my close off to go to bed, and I practise clambering up and down by a rop in case, and I giv Police Man 25 a shillin now and than to keep a specious eye to number fore, and be reddy to ketch anny one in his harms. * * * * O! Mary, how happy is them as livs lick you, as the song says, 'Fur from the buzzy aunts of men.' Don't neglect to rake out evvery nite, see that evvery sole in the hows is turned down xtinguished, and allways blo youreself out befoure you go to youre piller."

"The Bridge of Sighs," "The Lady's Dream," and the "Song of the Shirt," all having relation to the claims of poverty and wretchedness, are included in this collection. The long prose paper, entitled "Copyright and Copywrong," originally contributed to the London Athenæum, represents Hood pleading for his own craft, in his own peculiar way. The question never was discussed with more liveliness, if with more cogency. In alluding to American republications, he disclaims hostility to the United States in very characteristic expression. "The stars and stripes," he says, "do not affect me like a blight in the eye, nor does Yankee Doodle give me the ear-ache. I have no wish to repeal the Union of the United States; nor to alter the phrase in the Testament into 'republicans and sinners.' In reality, I have rather a Davidish feeling toward Jonathan, remembering whence he comes, and what language he speaks; and holding it better in such cases to have the wit that traces resemblances, than the judgment which detects differences, — and perhaps foments them." Toward the close of one portion of his quaint pleadings for the rights of authors, Hood bursts out in an eloquent acknowledgment of his obligations to literature, and to men of genius. "They were," he says, "my interpreters in the House Beautiful of God, and my Guides among the Delectable Mountains of Nature. They reformed my prejudices, chastened my passions, tempered my heart, purified my tastes, elevated my mind, directed my aspirations. I was lost in a chaos of undigested problems, false theories, crude fancies, obscure impulses, and bewildering doubts, — when these bright intelligences called my mental world out of darkness like a new creation, and gave it 'two great lights,' Hope and Memory, — the past for a moon, and the future for a sun."

This touches the real point in every discussion respecting the rights of authors. We owe them a debt of gratitude, which we should take pleasure in repaying. Instead of doing this, we avail ourselves of every subterfuge of quibbling, to justify the most selfish and heartless conduct towards them. The book that comes to us as a benefactor, — which opens to our view boundless domains of beauty and grandeur, — which makes itself "felt in the blood, and felt along the heart;" is it consistent that we should be so careful to reckon its exact value in the current coin of the land? Is it not ridiculous for us to play a huckstering trade with the man who is to pour into our minds the infinite riches of his genius? While our hearts are overflowing with kindliness for him who has peopled our solitude with beings of unearthly sweetness and majesty, — who has thrown celestial light around the bed of sickness and pain, — who has spoken a word of cheer to us in many a period of sorrow and abasement, — whose great heart has beaten close to ours in many a moment of passionate exaltation; — who, by the sweat of his brow and the sweat of his brain, has passed long years of labor in order that our lives might be made more beautiful and happy, — shall we grudge him the just rewards of his labor, — shall we compliment ourselves on our shrewdness in being able to steal from him the means of subsistence? What an antithesis is here, — what wonderful exaltation of thought and feeling, — what consummate littleness and meanness of action! We treat our greatest friend and benefactor, for whom our love and gratitude should be boundless, not only worse than we would treat a common acquaintance, but worse than we would treat our butcher or tailor. We would have our imaginations exalted, our hearts kindled, our minds stored; and then pride ourselves principally on our cunning in evading all payment for such a priceless good. We fear that our shrewdness here overleaps itself. It may be questioned whether or not the serene and beautiful face of literature can be seen in its loveliness, or felt in its power, while it is in such close approximation to the all-absorbing Dollar.

LEIGH HUNT'S POEMS.

There are some authors whose writings and conduct we do not applaud or condemn by any fixed "laws" of taste or propriety. They are free of the "Principles of Rhetoric." They are allowed to sing and sin, of their own sweet will, without regard to Doctors Blair and Whately. At first they are ridiculed and denounced; but, after the time-honored tortures of criticism have been rigorously applied to discover whether their peculiarities are ingrained or merely affectations, they are allowed to practise whatever verbal gymnastics and pyrotechnics they please. Critics gradually grow weary of stretching them on the rack. Readers, after a few petulant remonstrances, silently assent to the claims of their individuality. Conservatism nods its sullen acquiescence. And thus literary radicals, whose first sallies brought down upon their heads the most scorching satire, are soon seen side by side with the legislators and scrupulous Pharisees of letters, and their praise is echoed from lips which once curled in polite disgust at their outrages. It is discovered that there is originality, perhaps genius, in their singularities of thought and diction, and that a man may write agreeable works without taking the "best models" for his pattern.

Leigh Hunt must be considered, on the whole, to belong to this class. In spite of his faults, there is something quite bewitching in his character and poems. We hardly judge him by the same laws we apply to other poets; we are willing to take him as he is. The same errors and fooleries which would be insufferable in another, alter their aspect, if not their nature, as observed in the easy impudence of his chirping egotism. No man has been more severely attacked, no man is more open to censure; yet we feel that none can bear it with a more careless philosophy. The true object of punishment is to reclaim, and Hunt was past reclaiming before critics began to punish. All severity is lost upon him. He is what he is by virtue of his nature. The jauntiness, the daintiness, the vanity, the flippancy, the accommodating morality, which look upon us from his life and writings, and which, in their rare combination in one peculiar mind, made Byron call him an honest charlatan who believed in his own impostures, would be disgusting if less in harmony with the character of the individual; but, considered as part and parcel of Leigh Hunt, and of him alone, they are often pleasing.

Hunt has had bitter enemies and warm friends; but, from his position as a liberal, his enemies have possessed the advantage of arraying against him the prejudices of party, as well as skilfully availing themselves of the weak points in his transparent nature. For many years he was pursued with the fiercest animosity of political and personal hatred. His name has been used by a clique of unscrupulous writers as a synonyme of everything base, stupid, brainless, and impudent. His poems have been analyzed, parodied, misrepresented, covered with every epithet of contempt, pierced by every shaft of malice. Men like Gifford and Wilson have sacked the vocabulary of satire and ridicule, have heaped together all phrases and images of contumely, to destroy his reputation, and render him an object of universal scorn. It must be confessed that the faults of his mind and manner, the faults of his taste and conduct, the presumption with which he spoke of his eminent cotemporaries, the flippancy with which he passed judgments on laws and government, laid him open to animadversion, and were, in some instances, apologies for the malice and severity of his adversaries. For a number of years he was so pertinaciously attacked in Blackwood's Magazine, in connection with his friends, Keats and Hazlitt, that it almost seemed as if the prominent object of that flashing journal was to crush one poor poet and his associates. He was stigmatized as the founder and exponent of the "Cockney school of poetry." His poems were held up as a strange compound of vulgarity and childishness—as a sort of neutral ground between St. Giles and the nursery. His style was represented as a union of all in expression which is coarse and affected, with all that is feeble and babyish. Byron, who pretended at one time to be his friend, says, in a letter to Moore—"He believes his trash of vulgar phrases, tortured into compound barbarisms, to be *old* English;" and adds, of the "Foliage," that "of all the ineffable centaurs that were ever begotten by self-love upon a nightmare, I think this monstrous Sagittary the most prodigious."

That this cruelty, and, in numerous cases, elaborate dishonesty of criticism, has produced no apparent change in his disposition, has never led him to correct or alter any of the besetting sins of his style, and has not diminished his popularity, is a singular fact, and one calculated to illustrate how small can be the influence of malignant criticism, both upon the mind of the object and the taste of readers. The friends of Hunt have borne patiently all the attacks which their association with him has provoked, and those who have suffered most by the connection have been the most uncompromising of his advocates. There must be much frankness and genial kindness in his nature, there must be much in him to love, or he could not have numbered among his friends men so opposite in taste and opinion as Shelley, Talfourd, Lamb and Proctor. Shelley, at one time, gave him £1400 to extricate him from pecuniary difficulties.

The character of Hunt is so closely connected with all he has written, that it is difficult to consider them apart. "Rimini" is the most popular of his poems, and it contains qualities which will long sustain its reputation. Its excellences and its faults are both individual and peculiar, and we hardly know of a poem more open to criticism. The subject itself is not pleasant to contemplate, and it requires the nicest tact and most cunning sophistry to reconcile it to the moral sense of the reader. We are required to confound misfortune with crime, and express pity instead of indignation at unnatural wrong. The morality, separated from the poetry, is pernicious. There may be solitary instances where the greatest injury that can be inflicted on a husband may be performed by a brother, and the crime spring from circumstances which seem to mitigate its enormity, but it is dangerous to tamper with such instances, and attempt to reconcile them with the usual impulses of affection. If such a deviation from nature and rectitude be made the subject of an elaborate poem; if it be accompanied by a luxury of description which lulls the conscience, and creates an unconscious sympathy with the offenders; if the parties be represented as superior beings, worthy of our esteem and love; if they are decked in all the trappings of fancy and sentiment, and the steps from weakness to crime be taken over a velvet path, which gives no echo and leaves no footprint; and if the author, all the while, is himself fooled by his own casuistry, and warmly sympathizes with his creations, we do not see how the effect of such an assault upon the conscience, through the affections and sense of beauty, can be otherwise than injurious. The poet who deals with such a subject should have an exact perception of moral distinctions, and no loose notions about the intercourse between the sexes; but Hunt is not such a person. His are the "self-improved morals of elegant souls." We believe that he might have taken the plot of Hamlet, and converted the crime of Gertrude and the King into a dainty weakness, ending tragically, but with such sadness and pathos that his readers would have justified him in burying the lovers in "one grave, beneath a tree," and not have wondered that

> ———"on fine nights in May,
> Young hearts betrothed used to go there to play."

We are in the custom of congratulating ourselves on the purity of English literature in this age, as contrasted with the coarseness of the elder time. This purity, in many cases, is only in expression. A person of delicacy may be offended with many words in Shakspeare, may be disgusted with the hardy licentiousness of Rochester and Sedley, but may be corrupted with the smooth decency of verbiage which covers so much immorality of principle in much contemporary poetry and romance.

We perhaps err in treating Hunt as if he were amenable to the usual laws of morality and taste, after having exempted him from their dominion; but still no reader of healthy mind can fail at times to be provoked by his lack of manliness, his effeminacy in morals, his foppery in sentiment. There is a want of depth, seriousness and intensity, in him, which often justify petulance, if not anger, in the reader. His sense of physical beauty is exceedingly keen and nice, but it rarely rises to spiritual beauty. He may almost be described as a man with a fine fancy and fine senses. Outward objects awake his feeling of luxury, fill him with delicious sensations, and that is all. But judged by himself alone, thinking of him as Leigh Hunt, we cannot fail to find much in him to admire. His perception of the poetry of things is exquisitely subtle, and his fancy has a warm flush, a delicacy, an affluence, which are almost inimitable. He is full of phrases and images of exceeding beauty, which convey not only his thoughts and emotions, but also the subtlest shades and minutest threads of his fancies and feelings. To effect this, he does not always observe the proprieties of expression. He often produces verbal combinations which would make a lexicographer scowl, if not curse, and his daintiness and effeminacy sometimes produce prettinesses and "little smallnesses," which are not in the best taste. He is full of such epithets and phrases as "balmy briskness," "firming foot," "feel of June," "sudden-ceasing sound of wateriness," "scattery light." He manufactures words without any fear of the legislators of language. He links serious ideas to expressions which convey ludicrous associations to other minds. But with all abatements, it cannot be denied that his style, in its easy flow, its singing sweetness, and the numberless fancies with which it sparkles, is often of rare merit. Many phrases and lines of exquisite delicacy and richness might be caught at random in carelessly reading one of his poems. "Low-talking leaves," "dim eyes *sliding* into rest," "heaped with strength," "the word *smote* crushingly," are examples. The following is fine:—

> ——"Far away
> Appeared the streaky fingers of the dawn;"

and this line:—

> "The peevish winds ran cutting o'er the sea;"

and this:—

> "The least noise smote her like a sudden wound."

The following lines convey an image of a different kind:—

> "A ghastly castle, that eternally
> *Holds its blind visage out to the lone sea.*"

Here is a condensed and splendid description:—

> "Giovanni pressed, and pushed, and shifted aim,
> And played his weapon like a tongue of flame."

In the "Feast of the Poets" the most delightful, fanciful, witty and impudent, of Hunt's poems, there are numerous passages worthy of being garnered in the memory. The judgments of Hunt's Apollo are not always correct, but they have the advantage in sprightliness over most criticisms. At times we are reminded, in the style, of the "polished want of polish" of Sir John Suckling. The following description of Phœbus has a mingled richness and raciness to which none can be insensible:—

> "Imagine, however, if shape there must be,
> A figure sublimed above mortal degree,
> His limbs the perfection of elegant strength—
> A fine flowing roundness inclining to length—
> A back dropping in—an expansion of chest,
> (For the god, you'll observe, like his statues was drest,)

His throat like a pillar for smoothness and grace,
His curls in a cluster — and then such a face,
As marked him at once the true offspring of Jove,
The brow all of wisdom, the lips all of love;
For though he was blooming, and oval of cheek,
And youth down his shoulders went smoothing and sleek,
Yet his look with the reach of past ages was wise,
And the soul of eternity thought through his eyes."

The satire in this "Feast," on some of the poets and dramatists of the period, is often very felicitous. After mentioning a number of scribblers, who called upon Apollo, he fleers at two of them in a couplet of much point: —

"And mighty dull Cobb, lumbering just like a bear up,
And sweet Billy Dimond, a patting his hair up."

He accounts for the absence of Colman and Sheridan, by remarking that "one was in prison, and both were in liquor." The following is a good fling at Gifford: —

"A hem was then heard consequential and snapping,
And a sour little gentleman walked with a rap in."

Dr. Wolcott has a hard rap given to him in a very characteristic couplet: —

"And old Peter Pindar turned pale, and suppressed,
With a death-bed sensation, a blasphemous jest."

The following lines contain a magnificent description of the god of the lyre, in all the glory of his divinity: —

"He said; and the place all seemed swelling with light,
While his locks and his visage grew awfully bright;
And clouds, burning inward, rolled round on each side,
To encircle his state, as he stood in his pride;
Till at last the full deity put on his rays,
And burst on the sight in the pomp of his blaze!
Then a glory beamed round, as of fiery rods,
With the sound of deep organs and chorister gods;
And the faces of bards, glowing fresh from their skies,
Came thronging about with intentness of eyes —
And the Nine were all heard, as the harmony swelled —
And the spheres, pealing in, the long rapture upheld —
And all things above, and beneath, and around,
Seemed a world of bright vision, set floating in sound."

These passages must be allowed to display wit, fancy and sentiment, even by the haters of Hunt. Indeed, there is a charm in his grace of expression, and often in his light impertinence and flippant egotism, which no criticism can destroy. There is every reason to suppose that his poems will long survive the life of their author, and the reputation of the majority of his assailants.

THOMAS CARLYLE AS A POLITICIAN.

It would doubtless be unjust to deny Carlyle's claim to be considered a thinker on practical subjects; but he is an intense rather than a calm and comprehensive one. A comprehensive thinker looks at everything, not singly, but in its relations; an intense thinker seizes hold of some particular thing, exaggerates it out of its proper place in the economy of the world, and looks at everything in its relation to his own hobby. In reasoning on the evils of society and government, there is nothing so unphilosophical as to growl or snarl. If a man cannot look an evil in the face without rushing into rage at its prevalence, and considering that evil as the root of all others, he will do little for reform. Indeed, Carlyle appears to us to find delight in getting the world into a corner. Nothing pleases him more than to shoot a sarcasm at statesmen and philanthropists who are grappling practically with some abuse; in this way warning everybody to avoid particular medicines, and come to him for a universal panacea. Thus his works on social evils are substantially little more than savage jests at the depravity of mankind, and contemptuous fleers at those who are attempting to mitigate it. It is needless to remark that he is not always consistent; but this is the general character of his political writings. He criticizes human life as he would a play or a novel, and looks to his own taste alone in passing his judgments.

In "Past and Present," and "Chartism," Carlyle states his views regarding the source and character of the evils afflicting the British nation, and the means by which they may be mitigated and removed. "Past and Present" is the most splendidly written and carefully meditated of the two. It contains many sentences of remarkable force and beauty, with numerous touches of that sly, savage humor peculiar to the author. The tone of the work, however, is one of perfect discontent. The style bristles with Carlyle's usual extravagance about society and government, declaring both to be shams and unveracities, and sneering at all plans for improvement which the ingenuity or benevolence of others has framed. If we understand Carlyle aright, he considers that the constitutional government of England is a humbug; that William the Conqueror and Oliver Cromwell were the best governors that England has ever had; that since Cromwell's time the country has been governed by Sir Jabesh Windbag, strong in no faith but that "paragraphs and plausibilities will bring votes;" and that everybody is a fool or a flunkey except Thomas Carlyle. He hates every form of government which it is *possible* to establish in this world — democracy among the rest. If his work may be said to have any practical bearing on politics, it is this — that a governor is wanted with force enough to assume arbitrary power, and exercise it according to the dreams of mystics and sentimentalists. His system is a compound of anarchy and despotism. His ideal governor is a man blessed with an incapacity or indisposition to explain himself, who rises up some day and cries — "The government of this country is a lie, the people cannot make it a reality, but I can and will." His notion of the wretched condition of society is disheartening enough. Man, he tells us, has lost all the soul out of him. "This is verily the plague-spot — centre of the universal social gangrene, threatening all modern things with frightful death. You touch the focal centre of all our disease, of our frightful nosology of diseases, when you lay your hand on this. There is no religion; there is no God; man has lost his soul, and vainly seeks antiseptic salt. Vainly; in killing kings, in passing Reform Bills, in French Revolutions, Manchester Insurrections, is found no remedy. The foul elephantine leprosy reäppears in new force and desperateness next hour." Sad condition of poor depraved humanity! A whole generation, except one man, without souls, and that one exception without his senses! It is curious to notice the illusions of an understanding so powerful, when governed by a sensibility so tempestuous. It would be unjust, however, to question the depth of many detached thoughts, and truth of some of the speculations, in this volume.

* * * * *

It would be useless to deny that Carlyle's work on Cromwell is one of great merit; that it places many equivocal acts of Cromwell in a truer light than that in which they have formerly been viewed, — that there is an attempt to represent the subject dramatically from the heart of the man — and that the whole representation blazes with that stern, rough, intense, and fiery eloquence, which flames through the other writings of the author; — but still no reader, with a grain of moral sense, or common sense, can fail to see that Carlyle's zeal for Cromwell has completely blinded him to all the bad qualities of his character; and that, in the remarks on the Irish war, at least, he has compromised every principle of morals, and every instinct of humanity, in his eagerness to make out a case for his hero. In his contempt for what he is pleased to call the "rose-colored" sentimentality of those who love peace, and shrink with horror from rapine and murder, he hardly seems aware that, under the influence of a morbid sentimentality of another kind, he himself has come forward to whitewash Oliver Cromwell. We may judge of his love for his subject, by his willingness to sacrifice justice, mercy and truth to it. In his justification of Cromwell's wholesale massacres in Ireland — in echoing the bigoted or crafty religious phrases under which Cromwell himself veiled their enormity — in that perversion of sympathy by which he would try to make us honor, not the heroic men who fought for their cause against hope, but their cold-blooded murderer — and, finally, for attempting to give the sanction of religion to the whole — Carlyle appears as a sort of compound historian, made up of Machiavelli, Sir Harry Vane, Jack Ketch and Mr. Squeers. It would be just as easy to defend the master of "Dotheboys Hall," and make him out a philanthropist, as to give any character of religion or mercy to Cromwell's cruelties in Ireland. Besides, the great Protector needs none of this puffing. His fame, stained as it is with some crimes, is as clear as that of many other great men of action. But the mode pursued by Carlyle would make history and biography more immoral and detestable than the most licentious fictions. It would canonize all guilt which has been accompanied by energy; it would hold up bigotry, tyranny, hypocrisy, murder, as things noble and great; it would make Hampden and Washington give way to Danton and Mirabeau. Besides, it destroys all discrimination in judging character, and daubs vices with the same eulogy it occasionally vouchsafes to virtues. The thing would appear ridiculous in any other mode of representation than that adopted by Carlyle, but he possesses a singular power in corrupting the moral sense through appeals to the senses and the imagination, and in making the reader ashamed of the axioms of morals and religion, by stigmatizing those who abide by them as superficial, incapable, and deficient in *insight*.

The English Revolution of 1640 began in a defence of legal privileges, and ended in a military despotism. It commenced in withstanding attacks on civil and religious rights, and ended in the dominion of a sect. The point, therefore, where the lover of freedom should cease to sympathize with it is plain. It is useless for the republican to say that every revolution of the kind must necessarily take a similar course, for that is not an argument for Cromwell's usurpation, but an argument against the expediency of opposing a king's assaults on the rights and privileges of the people. The truth is that the English Revolution was at first a popular movement, having a clear majority of the property, intelligence, and numbers, of the nation on its side. The king, in breaking the fundamental laws of the kingdom, made war on the community, and was to be resisted just as much as though he had been king of France or Spain, and had invaded the country. It is easy to trace the progress of this resistance, until, by the action of religious bigotry and other inflaming passions, the powers of the opposition became concentrated in the hands of a body of military fanatics, commanded by an imperious soldier, and representing a small minority even of the Puritans. The king, weak and vacillating, made an attempt to establish arbitrary power, was resisted, and after years of civil war, ended his days on the scaffold. Cromwell, without any of those palliations which charity might urge in extenuation of the king on the ground of the prejudices of his station, took advantage of the weakness of the country, after it had been torn by civil war, usurped supreme power, and became the most arbitrary monarch England had seen since William the Conqueror. No one doubts his genius, and it seems strange that any one should doubt his despotic character. This, however, is growing into fashion, even among sturdy democrats and republicans.

The truth is, that Cromwell's natural character, even on the hypothesis of his sincerity, was arbitrary, and the very opposite of the character of a champion of freedom. It seems to us supremely ridiculous to talk of such a man as being capable of having his conduct determined by a parliament or a council. He pretended to look to God, not to human laws or fallible men, for the direction of his actions. In the name of the Deity he charged at the head of his Ironsides. In the name of the Deity he massacred the Irish garrisons. In the name of the Deity he sent dragoons to overturn parliaments. He believed neither in the sovereignty of the people nor the sovereignty of the laws; and it made little difference whether his opponent was Charles I. or Sir Harry Vane, provided he were an opponent. In regard to the inmost essence of tyranny, that of exalting the individual will over everything else, and of meeting opposition and obstacles by pure force, Charles I. was a weakling in comparison with Cromwell. Now, if, in respect to human governments, democracy and republicanism consist in allowing any great and strong man to assume the supreme power, on his simple assertion that he has a commission from Heaven so to do, — if constitutional liberty is a government of will instead of a government of laws, — then the partisans of Cromwell are justified in their eulogies. It appears to us that the only ground on which the Protector's tyranny can be considered more endurable than the king's, consists in the fact that from its nature it could not be permanent, and could not establish itself into the dignity of a precedent. It was a power depending neither on the assent of the people, nor on laws and institutions, but simply on the character of one man. As far as it went, it did no good in any way to the cause of freedom; for to Cromwell's government, and to the fanaticism which preceded it, we owe the reäction of Charles the Second's reign, when licentiousness in manners, and servility in politics, succeeded in making virtue and freedom synonymous with hypocrisy and cant.

In regard to Cromwell's massacres in Ireland, he simply acted as Cortés did in Mexico, and Pizarro in Peru, and deserves no more charity. If he performed his barbarities from policy, as Carlyle intimates, he must be considered a disciple of Machiavelli and the Devil; if he performed them from religious bigotry, he may rank with St. Dominic and Charles the Ninth. We are sick of hearing brutality and wickedness, either in Puritan or Catholic, extenuated on the ground of bigotry. The bigotry which prompts inhuman deeds is not an excuse for sin, but the greatest of spiritual sins. It indicates a condition of mind in which the individual deifies his malignant passions.

The style of the book on Cromwell is occasionally a trial even to the lovers of Carlyle's picturesque and shaggy diction, and few men can pronounce some of the sentences aloud without running the risk of being throttled. To follow the course of his thought through the sudden turns and down the abrupt declivities of his style, exposes one at times to the danger of having his eyes put out of joint. Carlyle is said to have copied his style from Jean Paul; but we should think he had copied it rather from Swiss scenery. Of all English styles, it reminds us most of the terrible alexandrines of old George Chapman's Homer, whose words we are sometimes compelled to dodge, as though they were missiles hurled at us by the gigantic combatants they so graphically describe. Carlyle, indeed, sometimes speaks as Ajax spoke, who, when enraged, according to Chapman, "throated his threats." His style is a faithful symbol of his powerful but perverse nature, in all the inconsistency of its formal contempt of formulas and canting hatred of cant.

NOVELS OF THE SEASON.*

THERE was a time when the appearance of a clever novel would justify its separate examination in a review, and a nice discussion of the claims of its Mr. Herbert or Lady Jane to be enrolled among men and women. But in this age of ready writers, romances must be reviewed in battalions, or allowed to pass unchallenged. Every week beholds a new irruption of emigrants into the sunny land of fiction, sadly disturbing the old balance of power, and introducing a fearful confusion of names and habits. Within a few years, all the proprieties of the domain have been violated by the intrusion of hordes of ruffians, pickpockets, and vagabonds. Sir Charles Grandison finds himself face to face with Jack Shep-

* Jane Eyre, Wuthering Heights, The Tenant of Wildfell Hall, Hawkstone Bachelor of the Albany, Harold, Grantley Manor, Vanity Fair.

pard, and no scorn sparkling in the eyes of Di Vernon can abash the impudence of Mr. Richard Turpin. The swagger of vulgar villany, the lisp of genteel imbecility, and the free and easy manner of Wapping, are now quite the rage in the Elysian fields of romance. Another evil is the comparative absence of individualities, amid all the increase of population. Opinions have nearly supplanted characters. We look for men, and discern propositions; for women, and are favored with woman's rights. Theologians, metaphysicians, politicians, reformers, philanthropists, prophets of the general overturn and the good time coming, the march-of-intellect boys in a solid phalanx, have nearly pushed the novelist aside. The dear old nonsense which has delighted the heart for so many centuries is so mixed up with nonsense of another kind, that it cannot be recognized either in drawing-room or kitchen. The sacred flame, it is true, still burns in some sixpenny or ninepenny novelettes, the horror of the polite and the last hope of the sentimental; but it burns in a battered copper lamp, and it burns among ruins.

Accordingly, in the novels whose titles grace the head of the present article, our readers must not expect to find, in its full perfection, that peculiar aspect of human weakness of which the novelist is the legitimate exponent. They must be content with a repast of matters and things in general, among which may be named some good philosophy, several dishes of controversial theology, much spicy satire, a little passable morality, a little impertinent immorality, and a good deal of the philosophy of history and the science of the affections.

The first three novels on our list are those which have proceeded from the firm of Bell & Co. Not many months ago, the New England States were visited by a distressing mental epidemic, passing under the name of the "Jane Eyre fever," which defied all the usual nostrums of the established doctors of criticism. Its effects varied with different constitutions, — in some producing a soft ethical sentimentality, which relaxed all the fibres of conscience, and in others exciting a general fever of moral and religious indignation. It was to no purpose that the public were solemnly assured, through the intelligent press, that the malady was not likely to have any permanent effect either on the intellectual or moral constitution. The book which caused the distemper would probably have been inoffensive, had not some sly manufacturer of mischief hinted that it was a volume which no respectable man should bring into his family circle. Of course, every family soon had a copy of it, and one edition after another found eager purchasers. The hero, Mr. Rochester, (not the same person who comes to so edifying an end in the pages of Dr. Gilbert Burnet,) became a great favorite in the boarding-schools, and in the worshipful society of governesses. That portion of Young America known as ladies' men began to swagger and swear in the presence of the gentler sex, and to allude darkly to events in their lives which excused impudence and profanity. Accordingly, while one portion of the community was clamoring for the reäppearance of the principles of the Pilgrim Fathers, another was vociferating impotent Byronics against conventional morality.

While fathers and mothers were in a state of inconceivable agony at this strange conduct of their innocents, and with a pardonable despair were looking for the dissolution of all the bonds of society, the publishers of Jane Eyre announced Wuthering Heights, by the same author. When it came, it was purchased and read with universal eagerness; but, alas! it created disappointment almost as universal. It was a panacea for all the sufferers under the epidemic. Society returned to its old condition; parents were blessed in hearing once more their children talk common sense, and rakes and battered profligates of high and low degree fell instantly to their proper level. Thus ended the last desperate attempt to corrupt the virtue of the sturdy descendants of the Puritans.

The novel of Jane Eyre, which caused this great excitement, purports to be edited by Currer Bell, and the said Currer divides the authorship, if we are not misinformed, with a brother and sister. The work bears the marks of more than one mind and one sex, and has more variety than either of the novels which acknowledge the paternity of Acton Bell. The family mind is strikingly peculiar, giving a strong impression of unity; but it is still male and female. From the masculine tone of Jane Eyre, it might pass altogether as the composition of a man, were it not for some unconscious feminine peculiarities, which the strongest-minded woman that ever aspired after manhood cannot suppress. These peculiarities refer not only to elaborate descriptions of dress, and the minutiæ of the sick-chamber, but to various superficial refinements of feeling in regard to the external relations of the sex. It is true that the noblest and best representations of female character have been produced by men, but there are niceties of thought and emotion in a woman's mind which no man can delineate, and which only escape unawares from a female writer. There are numerous examples of these in Jane Eyre. The leading characteristic of the novel, however, and the secret of its charm, is the clear, distinct, decisive style of its representation of character, manners, and scenery; and this continually suggests a male mind. In the earlier chapters there is little, perhaps, to break the impression that we are reading the autobiography of a bold, powerful and peculiar female intellect; but when the admirable Mr. Rochester appears, and the profanity, brutality, and slang of the misanthropic profligate give their torpedo shocks to the nervous system, — and especially when we are favored with more than one scene given to the exhibition of mere animal appetite, and to courtship after the manner of kangaroos and the heroes of Dryden's plays, — we are gallant enough to detect the hand of a gentleman in the composition. There are also some scenes of passion, so hot, emphatic, and condensed in expression, and so sternly masculine in feeling, that we are almost sure we observe the mind of the author of Wuthering Heights at work in the text.

The popularity of Jane Eyre was doubtless due to the freshness, raciness, and vigor of mind, it evinced; but it was obtained not so much by these qualities as by its frequent dealings in moral paradox, and the hardihood of its assaults upon the prejudices of proper people. Nothing causes more delight, to at least one third of every community, than a successful attempt to wound the delicacy of their scrupulous neighbors, and a daring peep into regions which acknowledge the authority of no conventional rules. The authors of Jane Eyre have not accomplished this end without an occasional violation of probability, and considerable confusion of plot and character; and they have made the capital mistake of supposing that an artistic representation of character and manners is a literal imitation of individual life. The consequence is, that in dealing with vicious personages they confound vulgarity with truth, and awaken too often a feeling of disgust. The writer who colors too warmly the scenes through which his immaculate hero passes is rightly held as an equivocal teacher of purity; and it is not by the bold expression of blasphemy and ribaldry that a great novelist conveys the most truthful idea of the misanthropic and the dissolute. The truth is, that the whole firm of Bell & Co. seem to have a sense of the depravity of human nature peculiarly their own. It is the yahoo, not the demon, that they select for representation; their Pandemonium is of mud rather than fire.

This is especially the case with Acton Bell, the author of Wuthering Heights, The Tenant of Wildfell Hall, and, if we mistake not, of certain offensive but powerful portions of Jane Eyre. Acton, when left altogether to his own imaginations, seems to take a morose satisfaction in developing a full and complete science of human brutality. In Wuthering Heights he has succeeded in reaching the summit of this laudable ambition. He appears to think that spiritual wickedness is a combination of animal ferocities, and has accordingly made a compendium of the most striking qualities of tiger, wolf, cur, and wild-cat, in the hope of framing out of such elements a suitable brute-demon to serve as the hero of his novel. Compared with Heathcote, Squeers is considerate and Quilp humane. He is a deformed monster, whom the Mephistopheles of Goethe would disdain to acknowledge, whom the Satan of Milton would consider as an object of simple disgust, and to whom Dante would hesitate in awarding the honor of a place among those whom he has consigned to the burning pitch. This epitome of brutality, disavowed by man and devil, Mr. Acton Bell attempts in two whole volumes to delineate; and certainly he is to be congratulated on his success. As he is a man of uncommon talents, it is needless to say that it is to his subject and his dogged manner of handling it, that we are to refer the shriek of dislike with which the novel was received. His mode of delineating a bad character is to narrate every offensive act and repeat every vile expression which are characteristic. Hence, in Wuthering Heights, he details all the ingenuities of animal malignity, and exhausts the whole rhetoric of stupid blasphemy, in order that there may be no mistake as to the kind of person he intends to hold up to the popular gaze. Like all spendthrifts of malice and profanity, however, he overdoes the business. Though he scatters oaths as plentifully as sentimental writers do interjections, the comparative parsimony of great novelists in this respect is productive of infinitely more effect. It must be confessed that this coarseness, though the prominent, is not the only characteristic of the writer. His attempt at originality does not stop with the conception of Heathcote, but he aims further to exhibit the action of the sentiment of love on the nature of the equivocal being whom his morbid imagination has created. This is by far the ablest and most subtile portion of his labors, and indicates that strong hold upon the elements of character, and that decision of touch in the delineation of the most evanescent qualities of emotion, which distinguish the mind of the whole family. For all practical purposes, however, the power evinced in Wuthering Heights is power thrown away. Nightmares, and dreams through which devils dance and wolves howl, make bad novels.

The Tenant of Wildfell Hall is altogether a less unpleasing story than its immediate predecessor, though it resembles it in the excessive clumsiness with which the story is arranged, and the prominence given to the brutal element of human nature. The work seems a convincing proof that there is nothing kindly or genial in the author's powerful mind, and that, if he continues to write novels, he will introduce into the land of romance a larger number of hateful men and women than any other writer of the day. Gilbert, the hero, seems to be a favorite with the author, and to be intended as a specimen of manly character; but he would serve as the ruffian of any other novelist. His nature is fierce, proud, moody, jealous, revengeful, and sometimes brutal. We can see nothing good in him except a certain rude honesty, and that quality is chiefly seen in his bursts of hatred, and his insults to women. Helen, the heroine, is doubtless a strong-minded woman, and passes bravely through a great deal of suffering; but if there be any lovable or feminine virtues in her composition, the author has managed to conceal them. She marries a profligate, thinking to reform him; but the gentleman, with a full knowledge of her purpose, declines reformation, goes deeper and deeper into vice, and becomes at last as fiendlike as a very limited stock of brains will allow. This is a reversal of the process carried on in Jane Eyre; but it must be admitted that the profligate in The Tenant of Wildfell Hall is no Rochester. He is never virtuously inclined, except in those periods of illness and feebleness which his debaucheries have occasioned, thus illustrating the old proverb, —

"When the devil was sick, the devil a monk would be;
When the devil was well, the devil a monk was he."

He has almost constantly by him a choice coterie of boon companions, ranging from the elegant libertine to the ferocious sensualist, and the reader is favored with exact accounts of their drunken orgies, and with numerous scraps of their profane conversation. All the characters are drawn with great power and precision of outline, and the scenes are as vivid as life itself. Everywhere is seen the tendency of the author to degrade passion into appetite, and to give prominence to the selfish and malignant elements of human nature; but while he succeeds in making profligacy disgusting, he fails in making virtue pleasing. His depravity is total depravity, and his hard and impudent debauchees seem to belong to that class of reprobates whom Dr. South considers "as not so much born as damned into the world." The reader of Acton Bell gains no enlarged view of mankind, giving a healthy action to his sympathies, but is confined to a narrow space of life, and held down, as it were, by main force, to witness the wolfish side of his nature literally and logically set forth. But the criminal courts are not the places in which to take a comprehensive view of humanity, and the novelist who confines his observation to them is not likely to produce any lasting impression except of horror and disgust.

The next work on our list is Hawkstone. This is a theological novel, the hero of which is a knight-errant of the Church of England. Though the book contains many powerful and some pathetic scenes, and is written with considerable force and beauty, events are made so subsidiary to doctrines, that it can hardly claim the dubious honor of being called a novel. Its authorship is ascribed to Professor Sewall, of Oxford, a learned gentleman, who took a prominent part in the disgraceful scene at that university on the occasion of presenting President Everett with an honorary degree. From his connection with that paltry outburst of religious and political bigotry, the character of his opinions may be inferred. He looks upon the world through a pair of theological spectacles, and instead of seeing things as they are, he views them altogether in relation to his creed. Were he a fanatic, we might excuse his illiberality, for passion is some extenuation of dogmatism; but the bigotry of our author is of that cool, smooth, contemptuous, self-satisfied kind, which irritates without stimulating. Assuming to speak by the authority of the Church, he quietly makes his own perceptions the limits of human intelligence, and from his pinnacle of self-content judges mankind. His whole wisdom consists in opposing the world as it is, and taking the exact opposite view of every question from that taken by liberal men. He is not content with stigmatizing Chartists, Radicals, and Whigs, but takes every opportunity to inform his readers what poor creatures are Sir Robert Peel and the Duke of Wellington. It is difficult to say whether he most dislikes Papists or Dissenters, but we should judge there was more rancor in his representations of the former than the latter. To be sure, the sects he despises may have the consolation of knowing that he has represented his own church in the person of a young clergyman whom every reader must consider an impertinent puppy; but he has done it with a beautiful unconsciousness of the fact.

We hardly know of a book which shows a greater ignorance of the world, or more intolerance and dogmatism based on so small a foundation of common sense. If the writer confined himself to theology, and contented his egotism with connecting all dissent from his own dogmas with folly or sin, he might be allowed to pass with a herd of other self-constituted popes, of whom Ranke makes no mention; but when he invades every department of moral, social, and political science, and views with a certain pitying contempt the labors of great and good men, convicting them of ignorance, presumption, or wickedness, because they do not hold the same extreme notion of the functions and offices of the Church of England which he is pleased to entertain, it is difficult to treat his absurd intolerance with common courtesy. In his speculations on political economy, especially, he revels in all the impertinence of ignorance, and wantons in helpless and hopeless fatuity. He has discovered that it is a sin to take interest on money, and has made a masterly assault on the law of supply and demand. In his next work he will probably take ground against the attraction of gravitation. The only allusion he makes to the United States is quite in character; he speaks pityingly of "that unhappy country." He did not probably think, at the time, that the country was happy in possessing persons who would call for five editions of his book, and that our tolerant novel-readers would vouchsafe to it the same attention they give to Harrison Ainsworth and George Sand.

Hawkstone is interesting in one respect, as it exhibits the degree of dogmatism of which every true Englishman is capable, and in which he is only equalled by the Russian serf. Education seems to work but little change in him, as far as regards the solidity of his self-esteem, though it may mitigate the blindness and ferocity of its expression. Here is a man having all the characteristics of a scholar and a gentleman, whose mind from early youth has been trained in what are called liberal studies, and yet he has acquired no power of learning from other minds, no toleration for what he considers error, no comprehension either of heart or head. It is true that this bigotry is one cause of England's colossal power. It makes every man self-sufficient, places him in a surly antagonism to other nations, and by teaching him to despise foreigners, stimulates the courage by which he is enabled to violate their rights. The moment the mind of the nation rose from its local ethics to general principles of reason or morality, its manners and institutions, and with these its material supremacy, would pass away.

Very different from Hawkstone, both in style and opinion, are the sparkling and pungent Bachelor of the Albany, and The Falcon Family. Both are not so much novels as dashing essays on life and manners cast in a narrative form; but they are replete with brilliant common-sense, and the interest they lack in regard to events and characters is supplied by the unflagging vigor and elastic spring of the style, and the perpetual sparkle of satire and epigram. The author's mind preserves that due balance between sharpness and good-nature which is the condition of pleasantry, and touches in a light and graceful, but decisive manner, on a hundred topics, without exhausting one. His style is strewn with verbal felicities, and there are passages exhibiting one continuous glitter of the glancing lights of fancy and wit. Occasionally a string of sentences goes off in epigrams, one sentence after another, like a series of percussion-caps.

The author is a sensible but superficial English whig, and like all his class, whether brilliant or stupid, he has a contempt for extremes, without understanding the internal causes which lead men into extremes. The most exhilarating portions of his novels are those in which he subjects the pedantic absurdities of the "earnest" men of the day to a process of merry caricature, or with a few probing witticisms emancipates the air shut up in a political bubble. He takes life himself in evident good humor, and is troubled very little with the mysteries of his nature or his mission to the human race. He does not appear to think that the eyes of the world are upon him, or that his utterance of an axiom is to make an era in the history of humanity. But it must be admitted that in avoiding bathos he also avoids depth, and purchases his persiflage at the expense of all serious thought. Life with him is composed of two portions, a portion to be enjoyed and a portion to be laughed at, and with this comprehensive philosophy it cannot be expected that he should succeed in the exhibition of character or passion. Most of his personages are embodied epigrams, or rather jokes elevated to the dignity of persons. There is a great difference between being jocose and being a jest.

In Harold, the Last of the Saxon Kings, Sir Bulwer Lytton has attempted an historical romance, and has certainly displayed scholarship, research, and remarkable talent, in the undertaking. But we fear that the work derives little help from the subject. The author is master of a style which is singularly attractive, and contrives to give a degree of interest to everything his pen touches, whether he treats it well or ill. No one can read Harold without feeling the force of this charm, but we think it is less felt in this novel than in many of his less ambitious productions. Neither in Harold, nor in The Last of the Barons, does he evince the power of a great historical novelist. The great defect of Harold, especially, is its heterogeneousness. Fact and fiction are either placed side by side or huddled together, instead of being fused into one consistent narrative. Harold, the Saxon king of history, and Harold, the hero of Sir Bulwer Lytton's romance, so modify each other, that the result somewhat resembles Mrs. Malaprop's Cerberus, — he is "two gentlemen at once." Indeed, though it cannot be said that the author is devoid of imagination, he does not possess the faculty for any available purpose of history or romance. As he unconsciously blends his own morbid feelings with his representations, he cannot vividly reproduce the persons and events of a past age in their original life and coloring, as the historian Thierry has done in his Norman Conquest; and therefore, though his imagination, considered separately, may be larger than that of many graphic and picturesque historians, he has not in any degree their power of historical imagination. We think that this will be evident to any clear-headed person who will take Harold and Duke William as they appear in the charming pages of Thierry, and compare them with the same princes as conceived by Sir Bulwer Lytton. If this defect in regard to historical personages was balanced by a power of combining the elements of human nature into new forms of character, through the creative processes of the imagination, he might still be a great novelist; but in this respect, also, Bulwer is deficient. Though in romance and the drama the power of creating or delineating character supposes a healthy mind, gifted with a sure vision of external objects, and capable of a quick sympathy with opposite natures, this power is still often possessed in a limited degree by men who can create original characters, but are incapable of reproducing real persons. In Godwin's Life of Chaucer, and in his historical productions generally, his kings, dukes, barons, and rebels, are as dead as those of Mr. Hallam; and yet the power of vital conception cannot be denied to the author of Caleb Williams and St. Leon. Though a creative imagination is thus sometimes possessed by persons deficient in its inferior form of historical resurrection, all ample minds will be found to possess both. An intellect thoroughly alive cannot be content with names of persons or with aggregates of abstract qualities, in contemplating either actual or possible life, but by its very nature conceives living beings.

Now, we must profess our inability to discover any capacity in Sir Bulwer Lytton to conceive character at all. With considerable respect for his talents and accomplishments, we think that he always fails in every attempt demanding creative energy or clear representation. As an historical novelist, he stands half-way between Scott and James, between truth and truism. He is often faithful to the external fact, but never penetrates to its internal meaning. The readers of his novels are made acquainted with life and character in the past or present, not as they are in themselves, but as his own ingenious and brilliant, but morbid and discoloring mind, has conceived them. He is an illustration of Kant's theory, that the qualities of objects are not perceived by the mind, but projected from it; and accordingly all his novels, whether the hero be Pelham or Warwick, Devereux or Harold, leave a similar impression. A character goes into his head as Duke William or Lafranc, but it ever comes out Sir Edward Bulwer Lytton, Bart.

This absence of objective perception, this confinement of the mind within itself, is not only fatal to Bulwer's claims to dramatic delineation, but it explains the sombre and unsatisfying tone of his productions. There is a singular lack of cheerfulness in his novels, and they are accordingly read without any refreshment to the intellect. Compare him with Fielding, or Goldsmith, or Scott, or Dickens, novelists widely differing from each other, and it will be readily seen how different is his feverish excitement and hectic flush from their healthy and bracing tone. After reading one of Bulwer's novels, we have a feeling that mankind is composed of scoundrels and sentimentalists, and that the world is effete. The atmosphere is that of a hot-house, not the exhilarating breeze of the moors. The vices of the novelist have that character of sickly licentiousness which we might expect from the rhetorical character of his virtues. He is not a free-spoken fellow like Fielding, and in his whole writings there is not one burst of honest and hearty sensuality, such as we often meet in the author of Tom Jones; but instead of this we have plentiful quantities of the "self-improved morals of elegant souls," in which adultery and seduction are gracefully adorned in alluring sentiments, and saunter, with a mincing gait, to the pit that is bottomless.

In Harold, to be sure, there is a marked improvement in our author's literary morals. As Thomas Moore wrote pretty little hymns to offset his pen's early peccadilloes, so Bulwer ventures in the present novel on Platonic love to compensate for the peculiar kind of passion he has inculcated in other novels. It must be delightful news to many good people, that the author of Pelham and Paul Clifford has sown his wild oats, and now ranks "in the first file of the virtuous;" and as he formerly seemed to object to marriage because it interfered with the natural rights of passion, he now has no other quarrel with it than that it is needless to the pure love of the soul. The lady whom history pronounces to be Harold's mistress Bulwer converts into the object of Harold's spirit love, while he follows history in giving Harold a wife, but one whom he marries as a matter of state convenience and policy.

This is a notable reconciliation of the conflicting claims of earth and heaven, which will doubtless much edify the saints.

There are two besetting peculiarities of Bulwer's mind which are more prominent, perhaps, in Harold than in any other of his novels. These are an affectation of philosophy, and an affectation of noble sentiments. By the former we do not mean that pervading air of thoughtful ennui which is not always an unpleasing characteristic of his diction, but his assiduous personification of abstract terms, his emphatic mode of uttering commonplaces, and his way of reaching climaxes in dissertation by fiercely printing axiomatic phrases in capital letters. These are cheap substitutes for depth of thought, but to us they are more endurable than his substitutes for depth of feeling. His fine sentiments and delicate emotions can hardly impose on any mind which has arrived at the consciousness of sentiment and emotion, or understands the difference between elegance and genuineness. They are the cheap manufactures of mere rhetoric, contrived with malice aforethought to awaken the reader's admiration. The heart never speaks its own language in Bulwer's writings. No outbreak of genuine passion seizing and shaping its own expression, no touch of humanity falling from the pen with a beautiful unconsciousness, ever surprise and delight us in his pages. There is one infallible test of a man's sincerity which Bulwer's expression of sensibility cannot stand for a moment. Natural emotion compels the mind to lose itself for the time in the objects which stir and arouse it. Now, Bulwer, instead of celebrating the beauty and grandeur of what he feels, is continually celebrating the beauty and grandeur of his feelings. This is the exact difference between real and rhetorical passion, and it is a difference of some moment.

Indeed, allowing to Bulwer the merit of wit, fancy, learning, an ingenious mechanical apparatus of understanding, and considerable power of appropriation, he is still, in all that relates to the living movements of the heart and brain, the most superficial writer that ever acquired the reputation of a great novelist. As his capacity, such as it is, is under the control of a morbid egotism and a still more morbid vanity, his productions appear more like the consequences of intellectual disease than like intellectual nutriment. This disease is as regularly taken by persons at a certain age of the mind, as the measles are at a certain age of the body,

If Bulwerism, however, saves any intellect from Byronism, it doubtless has its uses. The varioloid is bad in itself, but it is better than the small-pox. There is, strictly speaking, no food for the mind in Bulwer, bad or good — nothing which the intellect can assimilate. With Byron it is different; the great English poet's vitality may be the vitality of poison, but it is still life.

We cannot pass from Bulwer to Lady Georgiana Fullerton without taking a perilous leap. Grantley Manor is a novel having the rose-color of Young England and the purple light of Puseyism on its pages, and doubtless presents a very one-sided view of many important matters with which it deals; but it evinces talent of a very high order, and is one of the most pleasing novels of the season. The author is perhaps too elaborate in her diction, and is stirred too often by an ambition for the superfine, to catch that flowing felicity of style which should be the aim of the novelist — a style in which sentences should only represent thought or fact, and never dazzle away attention from the matter they convey. But with some faults of manner and some blunders in plot, the novel evinces considerable dramatic power, and has a number of striking characters. The interest is well sustained, though rapidity of movement in the story is ever subsidiary to completeness of delineation in the characters. Perhaps the chief element in the plot, and the source of all the agony which torments the principal personages, is too provokingly slight to be strictly probable; but it serves its purpose of developing the piety of Ginevra and the selfishness of Neville. No one can criticize the novel with any justice to the writer, without keeping constantly in mind that her object is not so much a consistent, or even probable story, as a forcible and subtile representation of character, as influenced by events best calculated to bring out all its hidden virtues or vices. Thus, Neville, who is about as abject a combination of arrogance, selfishness, and littleness of spirit, as ever was chosen for a hero, would probably pass in ordinary life for a free, hearty, independent, and high-toned gentleman. One event converts him into a compendium of small vices such as Sir Forcible Feeble himself might hoot at. Besides, his degradation was necessary to bring out all the resources of Ginevra's nature, and it is but common gallantry to admit the right of a lady writer to abase the hero rather than the heroine, when it is necessary to degrade either.

Ginevra is an original and beautiful delineation, the foundation of whose character is imagination, intensified by passion and purified by religion. So fine a union of sensibility and fortitude, of impulse and will, is a rare appearance in a popular novel. Margaret, her half-sister, a sweet, good-natured creature, with a magnanimous superficiality of feeling, is well conceived and sustained, though the writer ventures on some perilous edges of experiment in her case, and barely saves her, in two or three instances, from being a failure. Walter is genuine and manly in general, with an occasional touch of sickliness and feebleness. Though far from being a lady's man, he is unmistakably a man delineated by a lady. Colonel Leslie is a bore and a blunder. Perhaps, to those who appreciate results from the difficulties in the way of their production, the delineation of the amiable but commonplace old people of the novel will be considered a great proof of the writer's skill in character. It evinces much of the shrewdness and nicety of Miss Austen — qualities which we should hardly expect to see in connection with so strong an idealizing tendency, and with so much passionateness.

Vanity Fair, by W. M. Thackeray, one of the most brilliant of English magazine writers, is an attempt, somewhat after the manner of Fielding, to represent the world as it is, especially the selfish, heartless, and cunning portion of it. The author has Fielding's cosy manner of talking to his readers in the pauses of his narrative, and, like Fielding, takes his personages mostly from ordinary life. The novel, though it touches often upon topics which have been worn threadbare, and reproduces many commonplace types of character, is still, on the whole, a fresh and vigorous transcript of English life, and has numerous profound touches of humanity and humor. Sir Pitt Crawley, coarse, uneducated, sordid, quarrelsome, his sharp, narrow mind an epitome of vulgar shrewdness, is a sort of combination of Sir John Brute, Sir Tunbelly Clumsey, and Squire Western; but though exceedingly ludicrous, is hardly natural. George Osborne, Dobbin, and Amelia, are characters almost literally true, and are developed with most consummate skill and fidelity. Mr. Osborne, we fear, is too fair a representative of the English man of business of the middle class, — selfish, arrogant, purse-proud, cringing to superiors and ferocious to inferiors, rejoicing in a most profound ignorance of his own meanness and cruelty, and ever disposed to rise on the ruin of his neighbors. That disposition in English society, of every class, to trample on the one immediately beneath it, and to fawn on the one immediately above it, Thackeray felicitously represents in this and other characters of his novel. Nothing can be more edifying than Mr. Osborne's conversations with his son George on his intimacy with men of rank who fleece him at cards, and on his duty to break off a match with Amelia, after her father has become bankrupt. But the finest character in the whole novel is Miss Rebecca Sharp, an original personage, worthy to be called the author's own, and as true to life as hypocrisy, ability, and cunning, can make her. She is altogether the most important person in the work, being the very impersonation of talent, tact, and worldliness, and working her way with a graceful and executive impudence unparalleled among managing women. She indicates the extreme point of worldly success to which these qualities will carry a person, and also the impossibility of their providing against all contingencies in life. Becky steadily rises in the world, reaches a certain height, makes one inevitable mistake, and then as steadily falls, while many of her simple companions, whom she despised as weaklings, succeed from the very simplicity with which they follow the instinctive sagacity of pure and honest feeling. Colonel Rawdon Crawley, a brainless sensualist, whom Becky marries, and in some degree reforms, but who, by having an occasional twinkle of genuine sentiment in his heart, always was her superior, is drawn with a breadth and a nicety of touch which are rare in such delineations. The exact amount of humanity which coëxists with his rascality and stupidity, is given with perfect accuracy. Old Mr. Sedley is a most truthful representation of a broken-down merchant, conceived in the spirit of that humane humor which blends the ludicrous and the pathetic in one. Joe Sedley, the East Indian, slightly suggests Major Bagstock. He has the Major's physical circumference, apoplectic turn, and swell of manner, with the addition of Cockney vulgarity and cowardice. His retreat from Brussels, just before the battle of Waterloo, is described with the art of a comic Xenophon.

Of all the novels on our list, Vanity Fair is the only one in which the author is content to represent actual life. His page swarms with personages whom we recognize at once as genuine. It is also noticeable, that Thackeray alone preserves himself from the illusions of misanthropy and sentimentality; and though dealing with a host of selfish and malicious characters, his book leaves no impression that the world is past praying for, or that the profligate have it. His novel, as a representation of life, is altogether more comprehensive and satisfying than either of the others. Each may excel him in some particular department of character and passion, but each is confined to a narrow space, and discolors or shuts out the other portions of existence. Thackeray looks at the world from no exclusive position, and his view accordingly includes a superficial if not a substantial whole; and it is creditable to the healthiness of his mind, that he could make so wide a survey without contracting either of the opposite diseases of misanthropy or worldliness.

THE END.

www.ingramcontent.com/pod-product-compliance
Lightning Source LLC
LaVergne TN
LVHW020104110826
845151LV00001B/55

* 9 7 8 1 4 2 5 5 4 4 2 5 6 *